European Misunderstanding

By the same author:

Histoire économique et sociale de la Cinquième République, Paris, La Découverte/Maspéro, 1983-1988.

Capitalisme et mode de vie, Paris Le Cerf, 1972

La Bourgeoisie financière au pouvoir, Paris, Maspéro, 1977

with Bernard Billaudot and Yves Barou
Croissance et crise : vers une nouvelle croissance, Paris, La Découverte, 1985.

Le Remparts de l'argent, Paris, Odile Jacob, 1991

with Philippe Frémeaux, Dominique Sicot
Changer d'économie, Paris, Syros, 1992

Chômage, demande, traitement de choc, Paris, Editions Balland, 1994.

Aux politiques qui prétendent réduire le chômage : lettre ouverte, Paris, Balland, 1995.

European Misunderstanding

André Gauron

Translated by Keith Torjoc

Algora Publishing

Originally published as *Le malentendu européen*, © Éditions Hachette Littéra-tures, 1998.

Library of Congress Cataloging-in-Publication Data 99-052299

Gauron, André.
    [Malentendu européen. English]
    European misunderstanding / André Gauron;
    translated by Keith Torjoc.
        p. cm.
    Includes bibliographical references.
    ISBN 1-892941-07-4 (alk. paper)
    1. European Union. 2. Europe — Economic integration. I. Title
HC240.G63313 1999
337.1'42—dc21   99-052299

Front cover: from Mark Tansey, *Derrida Queries De Man*

New York
www.algora.com

Table of Contents

The European Question

Since its origin, the integration of Europe has been based on a mis-understanding. A misunderstanding named "Fear." Not fear of Communism, which had been such an easy pretext for so long, but fear of Germany. It has been haunting Europe since the end of the Second World War and has determined the politics of France. Thus was born the condominium that France and Germany believed they could impose on their partners. Chancellors and Presidents — Adenauer and de Gaulle, Schmidt and Giscard d'Estaing, Kohl and Mitterand — embodied this plan. But can France and Germany still lead the construction of Europe? The question is not often asked, out of fear of causing a seismic political event not only on both sides of the Rhine, but throughout Europe. How could it be otherwise, since the Franco–German relationship is founded on "the will to preserve peace on the continent," of which it considers itself the guarantor — as if peace were not the business of all the European people. However, the question must be raised.

Progressive enlargement of Europe, quite as much as the fall of the Berlin Wall, deeply transformed the initial conditions of European construction. France and Germany have just over a third of the population and a little less than half of the total Gross Domestic Product of the Europe of 15 members; they have lost the legitimacy they jointly derived from their demographic and economic weight. In addition, the collapse of Communism, which allowed German reunification and the reunion of the two halves of the continent, has changed the terms of German security. Under these conditions, one should not be surprised if the show of voluntarism manages neither to overcome the differences nor to clarify the misunderstandings, which are recognized on both sides as "sufficiently profound and recurring as to be troubling."[1]

The hour is particularly propitious for reconsidering the construction of Europe. A page of history was turning as President Mitterand and Chancellor Kohl retired from the political scene — the last statesmen whose European leadership bore the imprimatur of the Second World War. Everywhere in Europe, a new generation of political leaders gradually is coming to power. In addition, while xenophobia and racism are on the rise, the Christian Democrats who had dominated European thought for a half-century are giving way to liberal conservatism. Social democracy, for its part, has survived, but not without a profound *aggiornamento*. Still, the page will be turned once and for all only on the day when the European misunderstanding is resolved. For that, we must face the debate raised by the German question.

"The German question is, par excellence, the European question."[2] Pronounced in 1966, General de Gaulle's proposition strikes to the heart of the debate. It is European (he explained) for historical, geographical, intellectual reasons that could apply to any other state in Europe. But, he added, "It is European because forever, Germany has felt anguish, even fury, fed by her own uncertainty as to her borders, her unity, her political regime, her international role; and the more unsettled her destiny has been, the more unsettling it seems to the rest of the continent." On the other side of the Rhine, Chancellor Kurt Kiesinger echoed this by referring to the prospect of German unity. Germany, unified Germany, is at a critical size: too big not to play a role in the balance of forces, too small to be able to keep the forces around her in equilibrium.[3]

The fall of the Berlin Wall reopened the debate on Germany. Margaret Thatcher said, with her usual brutality: "Germany, which has always oscillated unpredictably between aggression and self-doubt . . . [is] by her very nature more a factor of destabilization than of stabilization in Europe."[4] The Germans would respond a few years later by again invoking their country's special involvement in the events of the past. We must avoid seeing Germany, says a CSU-CDU document, "stuck again in the uncomfortable position of being in the middle. In the past, this position between the East and the West prevented Germany from establishing an unambiguous framework for its domestic affairs and kept it from achieving a stable and durable equilibrium in its external relations. Her attempts to overcome this situation by the conquest of hegemony, at the center of every European conflict, have failed."[5]

During the Liberation, the Allies thought they had the answer to the debate and the doubts. They would take Germany's affairs directly in hand. Neither reparations nor indemnities would be levied, but they would define Germany's borders themselves, as well as the unity of the country, the political regime, and the international role, without consulting the people or the new German leadership. That would be the "punishment" of Potsdam, where Germany's post-war fate was decided. Once more, history decided somewhat differently.

With the Cold War, which tossed part of Germany into the Soviet camp, the Allies were forced to thoroughly re-examine their attitude with respect to Germany. They had imagined it remaining unified; Stalin imposed the partition into two States. They had wanted it stripped of its mining and coal resources; France had to resolve itself to restoring the Saar. They had started to dismantle the factories and to demilitarize the country, in the face of the "Soviet threat;" the Americans pushed for a prompt rebuilding of its economic power and its army. Only the decentralized democratic system escaped this revision, with considerable autonomy of the regional government that was set up by the allied military authority. Under these conditions, how could the past be exorcised? The allies were divided on this question: by integrating Germany into a multitude of institutions — NATO, OSCE (later to become OECD), the Council of Europe, the Western European Union — answered the Americans and the British; by integrating it into a European ensemble, suggested the French. Sovereignty was recovered, but constrained for some, shared for the others. The two steps were taken concurrently; they always are.

The German question is also a French question *par excellence*. Since Great Britain withdrew, concentrating on Empire rather than on Europe, France alone had to take the initiative. Finding itself isolated in not wanting a German renaissance, France had to invent the means by which to render it impotent. And that was Europe. To dilute German power: such would be, and such is, the objective of France's policy in Europe. The ECSC Treaty, the Euratom Treaty, the Treaty of Rome, the Elysée Treaty, the Treaty of Maastricht, whether we are talking about coal and steel, nuclear power, the customs union, defense or currency, the goal is the same every time. Under the cover of Europe,

France hopes to use Germany's power to benefit its own economy. For, right from the start, everyone understands that Germany can only re-emerge as "powerful."

Germany was not fooled by the French machinations. But it found them to be in its own interests, temporarily. Chancellor Adenauer's priority was to attain sovereignty with equal rights; his successors' is gradually to affirm the legitimacy of "German national interests." But they have a common goal, reunification. Born of the Franco-German question, Europe is being built according to the rate of Franco-German co-operation. The Benelux countries and Italy, like the United States, expected this to help secure a lasting peace and to fix Germany into the "Western camp" vis-à-vis the Soviet threat; they supported this *pas de deux*. New members were brought into the union throughout the '70s and '80s, but none of them questioned this assumption.

But the Europe that is being built this way is anything but European — that is, free from the Nation States. After the Liberation, France had no more intention than Great Britain of disappearing into a European ensemble. Neither one planned to give up its place on the world stage. No one wanted to see his national identity dissolving into a "European identity" that was carefully not defined. National interests determine the conduct of European affairs, and only the elected leaders can address them. As soon as the first divergences come up in day-to-day management, the federalist approach that underlies the ECSC[6] institutions, disappear and the intergovernmental structures gain ground. Once national interests come into play, the High Authority of the ECSC does not have legitimate authority to resolve questions that concern the States. In Messina, where the Treaty of Rome was being negotiated, the governments adjusted their focus and set their watches to the hour of the nations. The power would go to the Council of Ministers of the States, not to the Commission (which was to be the forerunner of a future federal government). The latter preserves only the power to make proposals, even thought it secured a "monopoly" on that.

Thus was born the "Community" method: European proposals, international (called "intergovernmental") decisions. The possibility of decision-making by majority tempered this retreat from the federal option. The crisis unleashed by General de Gaulle in July 1965, which led six months later to the "Luxembourg Compromise,"[7] closed the door again on the federal way for quite some time. The States safeguarded their sovereignty, but they were obliged to learn the art of compromise. The intergovernmental co-operation retrieved all these rights. In Europe, compromise is anything but an innovation; rather, an old acquaintance. For centuries, at least since the 1648 Treaty of Westphalia,[8] it has governed the relationship between European states. And we know what happened: It made Europe a battlefield.

The Treaty of Maastricht would appear over time as the ultimate attempt to preserve the illusion that France entertains — of dominating Germany by enclosing it in a European ensemble. Today, still, for President Chirac, the Franco-German axis remains the means of building an "autonomous Europe under the leadership of an independent France, in competition with the United States."[9] We only think of Germany, be it divided or unified, as a captive of Europe, dissolved within Europe. However, the collapse of Communism has released it. How could the dream of a Germany that would be synonymous with Europe, that would dominate Europe and direct its every step to suit Germany's interests and ambitions, and that would make a weapon of its recovered sovereignty — fail to reappear? It is natural that reunification was accompanied by a wake-up call to German national feeling. It is understandable that it inspires fears and questions, even in Germany. But let us not make Germany the scapegoat of European problems. Are its national pride, its will to make its leadership prevail, and its need to bolster its identity, any less legitimate and less European than France's? What other prospect do we offer to Germany? The post-war period is over. It is time to substitute the European question for the German question.

But how can we imagine creating Europe without the citizens as the driving force, without political passion as the heart? Looking back, people will be astonished that for nearly a half-century Europe could have been a political project from which politics was excluded. Any debate on the goals pursued and the ways to achieve them is banned; any interpellation on the design of Europe is prohibited. Admittedly, the defenders of Maastricht acknowledge that the Treaty is not perfect. They recognize that the citizens were not consulted. Still, they do not acknowledge that one may criticize the options chosen after long and difficult negotiations. To question is already to be against. Isn't it urgent to move ahead, to make progress with the construction that is presumably threatened by the retrograde proponents of Nation States? Later, we are told, when European construction is complete, there will always be time to correct and amend, if it still seems necessary. The Council of Amsterdam's failure to re-found Europe on its citizens shows that this hour will never come to be.

The reasons for refusing political debate are numerous. The illusion that political union must "naturally" follow from economic and monetary integration combines with the will to retain political power at the national level. The Franco-German tête-à-tête rests on the conviction that the ancestral quarrel will be overcome only if it is discussed as a series of "technical" questions by animated leaders with an unshakeable will to compromise. It prohibits any other approach. In Luxembourg and Brussels, Jean Monnet and his successors always considered Europe to be too serious a matter to be left to public passions. In Paris, Bonn, Rome, and other capitals, the governments were convinced very early on that it was too important to be addressed by any democratic authority other than them. Thus every party concerned deferred the hour when it would be necessary to consider transferring sovereignty, i.e. abandoning their power. Instead of European construction becoming a European affair *par excellence*, some have depoliticized it, while others have reduced it to a matter of domestic politics.

Rather than a "return of the States,"[10] the conditions of European construction have allowed the permanence of the States. Behind the appeals for greater federalism, the dance of the relations of powers makes sure of that. Introducing committees of national civil servants into the execution of the decisions, and introducing subsidiarity into the definition of the division of competences, have proven to be instruments for renationalizing significant domains that had been presented or promised to the Community. The Single Act and the Treaty of Maastricht were unanimously presented as accelerating European integration. However, Laurent Cohen-Tanugi hit the nail on the head when he wrote, "It's all coming out as though the States wanted to exploit the lack of consensus to take their revenge on a process that was starting to get away from them."[11] The more the leaders announce fresh "progress" in the construction of a European Union, the more, actually, it recedes. The fear of a "German Europe" is used as bogeyman to justify perpetuating a Europe built of separate nations.

Any European public space, where the ways and the means could be democratically discussed without mediation by the national governments, was carefully isolated. National interests lead the way. At the

UN as in the international economic and monetary meetings, the European nations, members of the Security Council or G7, deny Europe any representation. Since the passions tend to become nationalist, they are played down in order to avoid building up dark clouds over Europe. The world of sports is emblematic. Sports organizers remain "nationalist." The number of European competitions has increased, but they remain international. The European Court of Justice imposed a single market for soccer. But there are no European teams[12] to participate in the great world events — the Olympic Games, soccer's World Cup, world championships for track and field or figure skating, etc.. Everywhere in the construction of Europe, national entities rule the day.

Do we really want Europe? For anyone who has considered himself to be "building Europe" for the last 50 years, the answer is beyond doubt. But look closer, and it is not so clear. European citizenship, introduced with the Treaty of Maastricht,[13] is founded on States, not on humans right and fundamental freedoms; national economic policies are maintained simultaneously with the realization of the single market and the march toward the single currency; European defense and expansion in the East are carried out through NATO and only American intervention restored a hint of peace in Yugoslavia [Bosnia]; institutional reform consolidates intergovernmental power and places it further beyond the reach of democracy. Europe has the European flag, it looks like Europe, and it is called Europe; but it is not Europe in the true sense.

The intergovernmental conference that opened in Turin in 1996 was concluded in Amsterdam without bringing answers to the questions left outstanding at Maastricht in December 1991 when, to mask their lack of vision for the future, the heads of state and of government set the goals and the date for the IGC. The IGC would have to do what they were unable to do: to revise the Treaty that they were on the point of signing and of which the policy portion remained hopelessly empty. But in six years, no real progress was made, except for the change of government in Great Britain that unblocked the decision-making processes. As at Maastricht, institutional reform was deferred to a later date, this time after the year 2000. Contrary to the commitments made, the citizen, once again, was kept out of the debates. No government is asking him for his opinion by referendum; the sanction would probably be severe. Neither does any of the governments seem to be in a hurry to open up again the question of institutional reform.

As a new generation of politicians takes up the reins of government, almost simultaneously in the majority of European countries, a
page is turned in the construction of Europe. These men may be Europeans, but their motives are very different. The passionate striving to
ensure peace, born of the smoking ruins left by two global conflicts, is
no longer the animating force that drives European construction.
Europe is now a "practical necessity," as the new German chancellor
says, the obligatory point of passage to achieving each one's "national
interests." For Paris, Berlin, Rome, Madrid or London, there is no alternative to Europe. This makes it less urgent to do away with the nation-
states, an objective that very much preoccupied the founders of this
European construction. To found the sense of a European identity on
human rights while reaffirming the sovereignty of the states — that is
the new dialectic that Lionel Jospin and Gerhard Schroeder have taken
on, and that Tony Blair (supported by some of the conservatives) seeks
to share with the British.

Europe needs a new ambition; it needs that "European spirit" that
Paul Valery called upon shortly after "the Great War."[14] It needs a vision collectively assumed by the people. Reinforcing Franco-German
friendship is essential to ensure peace on the continent — and the
Franco-British *Entente Cordiale*, too. But the Franco-German pair has
exhausted its historical role and can no longer claim to lead Europe.
While the misunderstandings between France and Germany have not
completely prevented European construction from progressing, every
day it becomes more obvious that they are a significant deterrent. But
this is neither a French question, nor a German question. The misunderstanding is a European question. It must find a European answer;
and it can only be political.

Notes

1. *France-Allemagne: comment aller de l'avant?* Joint document by the French and German Ministries for Foreign Affairs, Paris-Bonn, photocopied, December 20, 1996.
2. February 4, 1966, quoted by Pierre Guillen, *La Question allemande de 1945 à nos jours*, Paris, Imprimerie nationale, 1996, p. 7.
3. Jacques-Pierre Crougeon, *Où va l'Allemagne*, Paris, Flammarion, 1997, p. 205.
4. Margaret Thatcher, *10, Downing street, Memoires*, Paris, Albin Michel, 1993, p. 657.
5. CSU-CDU Parliamentary groups, *Réflexions sur la politique européenne*, Bonn, photocopied, September 1994.
6. European Coal and Steel Community.
7. See below, the Search for the Holy Grail.
8. The Treaty of Westphalia, which put an end to the Thirty Year War, established the princes' religious freedom and parcelled out Germany. Moreover, it weakened Austria by forcing it to forward all the levied money and men to the Diets of the Empire. Many historians consider that it made Germany into the battlefield of Europe.
9. Cited by Jean Daniel, *Le Nouvel Observateur*, January 9, 1997.
10. Laurent Cohen-Tanugi, *Le Choix de l'Europe*, Paris, Fayard, 1995, p. 64.
11. *Ibid.*, p. 65.
12. The constitution of European sporting teams appeared in the mandate given in 1984 by the council of Fontainebleau to the ad hoc *committee* for "the Citizens' Europe."
13. Item N2 of the Treaty on the European Union.
14. Paul Valéry, "La Crise de l'esprit," *Variété*, in *Œuvres*, t. 1, Paris, Gallimard, coll. "La Pléiade."

THE ORIGIN OF EUROPEAN UNIFICATION

Chapter 1

Historical Roots

Paris — La Défense. The *Grande-Arche* subway station. An escalator brings the visitor to the heart of a trade center. At the end of the hall is a sign indicating the "Sources of Europe" on a blue background, the color of the European Community. Hardly has the visitor perceived a corner of the sky, beyond the concrete walls between which he advances, when he goes down again and enters between frosted glass and steel. What a strange symbol this is, that seems to come from the depths of the earth, leading to a temple of consumerism; relations of power and the market, the modernity of the "Great Arch" and the impetuosity of Europe. Are these vivacious people bustling in every direction supposed to evoke the image of a gushing wellspring of Europe and its effervescent plans? The symbolism is strong, but it is misleading.

The place where the visitor comes looking for Europe is more like a crypt hidden under the flagstones of a cathedral than a bubbling spring. There is no opening that would restore Europe to life, that would allow a little light and air to enter. There is nothing that recalls a wellspring. The reception hall, a large concrete room weighed down by an immense, underutilized counter of shiny wood, invariably deserted, seems a good setting for meditation. The Bookshop-Cafeteria to the left does nothing to contradict this impression. One would like to hear voices there, to eavesdrop on passionate debates about European unification. But alas, only silence reigns! At the other end, a light shines but there is no sound that might attract you. A receptionist, motionless as wax, watches silently over the bulletin boards and information folders, since the occasions to respond to questions are rare.

Or maybe she is guarding the media library, the cathedral of information on the European Union, where nothing can be removed without permission. An electronic gate guards this underground repository. Similar security prevails in the photocopy section. "Library" is the wrong term, as there are very few books. "Sources" would be a fitting description of the documents placed at the public's disposal: an extension service (only since this Center was opened) of the European Commission, the European Council and the European Parliament. A meeting room and a reading room hold the new Europe's archives, still very young. For here, the thousand year history of the continent, its peoples and its nations, begins with the Treaty of Rome on a certain March 25, 1957.

Brussels — Midday. With a little luck, the 9.04am TGV coming from Paris will enter the station. But its timing is not guaranteed. If it reaches Lille in an hour, it is delayed because of construction on the Belgian line. Europe is late. It is still under construction. The railway, the station and the buildings of the Community, everywhere you look things are moving. Berlaymont, Charlemagne — the buildings that initially sheltered the Commission and the Council services — were just sufficient for a small Europe of six or even nine members. At twelve, the buildings were already too tight. And they certainly were not in scale with the ambitions for the construction of a Europe that it seems nothing must interrupt or stop. And the Parliament will not measure up, either. Nor Brussels, which seems ready to raze its own past in order to supplant Strasbourg. No cost is too high. And the real estate agents aren't complaining.

Whether you take the subway or a taxi to reach the Commission or the Parliament, whether you arrive by foot or by car, you have to take Belliard Street and plunge into the underpass that takes you to this long street between the walls of two heartless grey buildings. Dive in, and risk the dizzying depths. Europe begins just two steps from this black hole, foul with the noise and the polluting gases of an endless fleet of vehicles. Europe, here, is Corbusier revisited. There is no room for glass and steel, nor lightness and transparency. Europe is still a construction zone but already needs to inspire a sense of power. For the moment, if you want to avoid this underpass, there is still one passage that connects the two Parliament buildings. But you'd have to take a muddy back street to get to it. This is how Europe is being built. . .

Can Europe ignore Europe? Can it cut its roots without weakening the whole structure? Leave off going to the sources, much less going back to the beginning; stop delving in the realm of shadows. It
would be more worthwhile to exhume the past. Europe does not start
with Rome, neither the Rome of Romulus nor that of the Treaty, even if
it did claim to be founding a new Europe. No one even knows where
Europe's name comes from. A recent history of Europe[1] says that five
centuries before the Christian era, the Greek historian Herodotus acknowledged his uncertainty — which persists to this day. But if
Europe is lost in legend, one certainty remains. Europe cannot wipe
away the past, its own past. It cannot forget that every attempt at
unity has led to division, that the State based on Law was countered
by the will for power, and finally, that trade has always fought with
culture to break barriers and cross frontiers.

Unity or division? "Europe," writes sociologist Edgar Morin, "is a
Complex (*complexus*: something that is woven together) whose purpose
is to combine, without blending, the greatest diversities and to associ-
ate opposites in such a way as to make them inseparable."[2] Ever since
civilization spread across the European continent, antagonisms have
shaped its history and carved it into pieces. Athens against Rome, the
Roman Empire against the German and Celtic peoples, Christians of
the West against Christians of the East. Charles V, Napoleon, Hit-
ler — anyone who tried to unify Europe by force only succeeded in
uniting the other kingdoms and States against him, and ended in failure. For centuries, the making and breaking of coalitions has motivated armies of diplomats. Neither their intelligence nor their skill, nor
their cunning and cynicism, could get them through the obstacles that
stand in the road to unity — and in some cases, they were themselves
the cause of the obstacles. Any success was transitory.

Charlemagne was an exception. A great warrior to be sure, he
fought on every frontier of Europe to conquer some challengers and to
repulse others. But since he was crowned, in the year 800, he was more
preoccupied with consolidating his empire and with building institutions than with taking up arms. He was, according to historians, both
"king *and* emperor; he reigned over Francia *and* the Western empire; he
was all-powerful *and* respected the rights of others, an active, effective
force *and* a mediator. More than any other in his times, he connected

the local and the particular to the universal."[3] Claimed as much by France as by Germany, he personifies the original unity of Europe.

But the image is contestable. Charlemagne's Europe was a "little Europe" that leaves out Spain, England, Scotland, Scandinavia, southern Italy and Sicily. Caesar, who carried Roman *imperium* further, would have a better claim to the title of Europe's mythical founder. And furthermore, Charlemagne's empire did not survive the death of his son, Louis the Pious, who divided it into three kingdoms. Three princes is at least one too many. It would not take them long to cast Europe into a series of wars lasting for several centuries.

A very Christian emperor, Charlemagne was canonized in 1165 by Frederick I Barbarossa, who made him the first emperor of the Holy Roman Empire. But, let's not forget that Charlemagne's consecration in Rome caused the first rifts within the Roman Church, and that it was the starting point of political and religious battles that tore Europe apart for several centuries. The legend of Charlemagne persists in vain. In a Europe searching for a mythical figure to identify with, the emperor is only the symbol of a fundamental misinterpretation.

Furthermore, the Western empire paved the way to the great schism between Christians, which cut Europe in two and whose echo is still present today. From the conquest of Constantinople during the fourth crusade, followed by its fall at the hands of the Turks two and a half centuries later, was born an enduring hatred between Catholic, Orthodox and Moslem communities. More recent conflicts between Serbs, Croats, Bosnians and Albanians are its remote but still vivid reflection. And this schism opened the way to further divisions. Never again would faith manage to unify Europe. The Church would attack the empire. After Charlemagne, it sought to seize the emperor's "golden scepter," emblem of his command; the States would subvert the power of the Church. Thus, in the 13th century, the religious, social, cultural unity of Latin Christendom was "close to realization;" but "this moment, so ephemeral, was (also a period) when the power of the States was being strengthened."[4]

These divisions had many positive effects. They are part of the "weaving" referred to by Edgar Morin. This compartmentalization which took shape at the verge of a unified Christian Europe, as Jean-Baptiste Duroselle says, brought about "a fundamental benefit, invaluable for future freedoms. Europe thus escaped the confusion of lay and religious powers that is certainly one of the sources of totalitarianism and fanaticism."[5] Still, upon closer examination, laicization was not accomplished in the same way throughout all of Europe. France, a lay Republic, seems to be something of an exception. Religion did not leave the State and recede to become a private belief in every case.

The European Union encompasses an extreme diversity of situations.[6] Its religious geography has been more or less in place since the 17th century. Then Great Britain definitively broke with the Pope to create the Anglican Church, headed by the monarch. Germany left the matter for its princes to decide and remained divided between Catholics and Protestants from then on. In the countries that remained Catholic, Italy, Spain, Portugal, and Ireland, the Church held sway over the social, cultural, and political life for a long time. Now it is losing ground everywhere apart from Ireland (but that is largely due to the struggle against English occupation there). As for Greece, it testifies to Orthodox Christendom. In the east, between Poland, the Czech Republic, Slovakia, Hungary, and the Baltic States, the differences are equally numerous. So many characteristics influence the politics, education, culture and social life of our countries. Nobody thinks of erasing them, it would be a futile enterprise; but such and such action by the Community can, one day, bump up against them and revive ancestral quarrels that are never completely extinct.

Ideas are often put to the service of weapons, but sometimes they are used against them. But only to come up against something worse than war — fanaticism. In Europe, where (almost) every spring has seen soldiers on the march, people are always calling for a way "to alleviate the conflicts with a benevolent mutual understanding." Stefan Zweig, an Austrian writer from the first half of this century, used this formula in reference to Erasmus, a citizen of Rotterdam from the late 15th century. This humanist, to whom Zweig devoted an admirable work, belonged, he says, "to no party." Like him "he always felt that fanaticism, that disastrous genius of human nature, would destroy his peaceful world and his own life."[7] But his will for universal harmony ran into the intolerance of a young Augustine monk, Martin Luther, who smashed what remained of Christian unity.

A century later, a similar attempt at reconciling Christians on the initiative of the German mathematician and philosopher Leibniz would fail due to the same intolerance, this time in the person of French Catholic bishop Monseigneur Bossuet, tutor of the Dauphin and intransigent defender of the absolutism of Louis XIV. In his work on *La*

Crise de la conscience européenne (*The European crisis of conscience*), Paul Hazard gave an account that echoes that of Zweig. Like Erasmus, Leibniz knew that to realize his ideas of harmony would require an abolition of war. But the one exhorted the young Emperor Charles V to take this tack "at a time when everyone was suing for peace, all the people and all the nations of Europe,"[8] while the other "proposed to exile the disputes"[9] by directing the warlike furies of the people and their princes toward remote conquests (which is what Jules Ferry did two centuries later with the conquest of Tonkin, distracting the French from the notion of revenge against Germany).

"To make peace permanent," a certain Abbot de Saint-Pierre proposed to Leibniz to work out a pact "which would bind the sovereigns and their successors, by which they would each engage not to support more troops than their neighbors and than necessary; and if despite everything some conflict comes to be created, the Union will arbitrate, and if need be, it will make war upon any prince who refuses to obey a regulation established by it." Organizing the meticulous details of this dream, with the precision of utopians, he became infatuated with a word that seemed to embody all his hopes: the word "European." European court, European force, European republic. If anyone would listen to him, Paul Hazard observes with irony, "instead of remaining a battle field, Europe would have become a society." Leibniz responded "with melancholy, that all that keeps men from being delivered of an infinity of evils, is will."[10] The German philosopher Emmanuel Kant took up the same idea, with no more success. A little more than a half-century later, Victor Hugo would chair the 1850 Peace Congress in Paris. However, it took until the 20th century for the idea to become a reality. But neither the League of Nations, created after the First World War, nor the UN which succeeded it after the Second, took the place of men's will, always so dubious. The European Union itself did not end the political-religious war in Northern Ireland nor prevent another one from setting ex-Yugoslavia ablaze.

Another powerful time for forging European unity was the Republic of Letters. Conceived by the French Huguenot Pierre Bayle (who left the comté of Foix to settle in Rotterdam, from which he fought the Catholic intolerance of "the Great Century") it was not just a dream. Within this literary Europe, ideas circulated more quickly than people. An ideal republic as dreamed by the philosophers and wise men of the 17th century, this was a Europe without borders and states. "Upon entering it," noted the Polish historian Krzysztof Pomian, "one left behind his denominational affiliation as well as any fidelity with regard to country, people, even family, each of which is comparable to the accidental, to the specific and the particularity, to what is not constitutive of the human being as such, and which is contrary to reason — which, alone, represents the universal, the necessary and the global."[11] The Republic of Letters did not put an end to the crumbling of States and their subdivisions. But, from this second European unification, to use Pomian's expression, was born the freedom of individual conscience.

After the separation of the spiritual and temporal powers, the time had come for the individual to be emancipated from all powers. In a few decades, at the three extremes of Europe, Copernicus, the Pole, Galileo, the Italian, and Newton, the Englishman, gave the Earth[12] a new position in the universe and wrecked the geocentrism of the Church doctrines. Empiricism, deism, natural law, social morality, happiness on earth, science and progress, "such are the ideas and the wills which, before the end of the 17th century, became aware of each other and were linked to constitute the doctrines of relativity and the human. "Everything is ready;" concludes Paul Hazard; "Enter, Voltaire."[13] These ideas, this new model of humanity born out of the European crisis of conscience, are still with us today. They are the bases for the construction of the European entity. They are not the only ones.

State of Law or will for power? Anyone who goes back to the sources of Europe comes upon an astonishing event: the advent of the State of Law. In the second half of the 17th century which, in France, Louis XIV sat on the throne and absolute monarchy was triumphant. But between England and Holland, three philosophers were laying the foundations of freedom: Thomas Hobbes, Baruch Spinoza and John Locke. The first freed the individual from servitude by proclaiming the *right to security*, i.e. the right to preserve his life, because man can have no greater desire. The second added *freedom of conscience*, because without the freedom of his own judgment and belief, no one is secure. Locke, finally, took the right that any individual has to the possession of his life, his body and his conscience, and extended it to the fruits "of the work of his body and the work of his hands." For, as Locke said, work "fixed my right of ownership by withdrawing the objects from the common state where they were."[14] Thus is individual ownership established. It is the foundation of human rights (but also the basis for capitalist accumulation), for the law and the State to guarantee. The latter have, adds Locke, "no other purpose than to preserve them." Frenchman Jean Bodin's reflection, a century earlier, on the bases of the nature of sovereignty, was now complete. Political power was definitively separated from property. "The relation between sovereign and subject is no longer exerted by control (by force) but by law." Now the course of history in Europe could veer in new directions.

The first swing occurred in England with the Bill of Rights (1689), promulgated by William of Orange. John Locke, who left Holland (where he had had to exile himself) with William, inspired it. It was the first time that a text outlining the relationship of the public powers would assert that "the power of the laws are superior to that of the king." The sovereign no longer owned the power, he had to submit himself from now on to the law. In today's Europe, which hardly loves the English since they throw a wet blanket on the passion for unification and European construction, the lesson of the English Revolution of 1688 deserves to be retained. In just one shot, it gave Europe parliamentary democracy (submitting public expenditure to vote by elected officials), Habeas Corpus (the guarantee of individual rights) and the first central bank, the Bank of England (the separation of national debt from the royal purse). The individual was protected, in one fell swoop, against the triple jeopardy of taxation, the police force and bankruptcy (or devaluation). The security of his person, business and patrimony was guaranteed. London thereby gained an irresistible attractive force and very quickly dethroned Amsterdam. The birth of English capitalism drained the continent of capital and ensured Great Britain two centuries of prosperity. [15]

On the other hand, on the continent these ideas met with profound incomprehension. In contrast to England, the debate going on in France on the eve of the Revolution was less about protecting individual rights than about changing the relationship between the State and the citizens; the freedom of conscience was less important than the proclamation of political rights. The Declaration of the Rights of Man and of the Citizen, approved by the Constituent Assembly on August 26, 1789, is "civil and voluntary" in inspiration. It is not merely "limited to the rights of *Man*, because the society to which it applies does not exist in a natural state," writes Blandine Kriegel. It is also a declaration of the rights of the *Citizen* and "would form a preamble to the Constitu-

tion (of which) it would establish the founding principles."[16] This shift
presaged others that would, at the end of 19th century, be carried to the
breaking point by what has come to be called "legal positivism," which
reverses the relationship between Law and State. The State is no
longer the guarantor of freedoms which are rooted within the individual; it is the subject and the source of the Law. Whereas the Bill of
Rights limits the power of the State, legal positivism restores it and
opens the way to all forms of totalitarianism. For, it is too often forgotten, Nazism as well as Communism also claim to be legal orders, only
where the State is everything and the individual nothing.

The doctrines of humans right are founded on reason. "Political
romanticism," of which the German philosopher Johann Fichte is the
leading theorist, sets greater store by instinct. As Blandine Kriegel
says, "It substitutes the fatherland for the State, faith for the law, and
soon, war for peace." Standing against the Napoleonic occupation
which caused the collapse of the Holy Roman Empire, Fichte preached
a new education that "should destroy free will completely and educate
the will in the direction of rigorous subservience to what is necessary."[17] The celebrated *Addresses to the German Nation*, which he delivered
in Berlin in 1807-1808, buried human rights — including the foremost,
the right to life. They opened the door to the worst adventures of nationalism, which would lead from exaltation of the nation to the fatal
convulsions of the Third Reich. Human rights on one side, political
romanticism and legal positivism on the other, this doctrinal conflict
made "Europe both the cradle and the tomb of the State of Law."[18]
European construction shows its heritage, when it claims to be based
on law.

Can we then "think Europe" without thinking the history in
which it is steeped? Let's take another look at Edgar Morin. "If Europe
is the Law, it is also force; if it is democracy, it is also oppression; if it
is spirituality, it is also materiality; if it is measure, it is also dispropor-
tion; if it is reason it is also myth — including that within the idea of
reason."[19] And let's listen to Paul Hazard evoking the years 1670-1715.
"At that time, no one had yet invented the theory of the superiority of
one race over another. The substance of the word "fatherland" had not
yet been analyzed. No one had even gotten a clear notion of what a nation could be. To the feelings evoked in man's heart by the call of the
soil and the bell-tower, no one had added the intellectual work which
explains them and justifies them. But they experienced those feelings;

and in the face of national characters, universal and equalizing reason lost its rights."[20] Let us reconsider our century that has just come to a close. It invented neither wars not genocide, nor racism, totalitarianism or imperialism. But it carried them to a hitherto unknown degree, reducing to nothing the concepts of human rights, tolerance and respect for the other, not to mention reason and progress. Humanity according to Godot.

In the aftermath of the Second World War, the desire for unity in Europe was motivated by a revulsion to the horrors of war, violence and fanaticism. For the first time, the initiative came not from the world of letters but from politicians themselves. Starting in 1948, Winston Churchill presided over a Congress of Europe, at the Hague, with Leon Blum and Robert Schuman, Konrad Adenauer, Paul-Henri Spaak, and Alcide de Gasperi, leading to the creation of the Council of Europe. Once more, the enterprise almost died at birth, and Leibniz's response to the Abbot de Saint-Pierre was validated once again. But fear of Germany as much as that of Communism impelled Europeans to join together. Jean Monnet applied his intelligence, his energy and his international relations in service of this cause. However, he required as a precondition to any negotiation that the future institutions would be granted a supranational status. Great Britain balked. (It still imagined itself as the center of a vast global empire). On the verge of uniting, Europe was split.

Winston Churchill, as a disciple of Locke, left politics; Monnet preferred economics and went on to provide the foundation of the progressive construction of a European market. Does business need competition from politics? The need to foster business by unifying the markets and currencies is, indeed, an old concern in Europe. Fernand Braudel's commentary, in his masterly fresco *Civilisation matérielle, économie et capitalisme XVe-XVIIIe siècle* (*Civilization and Capitalism: 15th-18th Century*) is unequalled. The formation of the national markets was an important moment in Europe's economic development. Not that trade volumes depend on it — they follow the flows of capital. Neither trade barriers (domestic or foreign) nor the exchange of currencies can stop tradesmen. They have always carried on their business. The economic climate, however, is decisive. "If it does not favor business," having a national market will make no difference; "for when the economic situation is favorable, the economy accommodates everything, and overcomes every obstacle."[21] National markets, the historian observes, accelerate circulation and drive up demand, without which the Industrial Revolution would never have taken place. But they did not come along spontaneously. "The national market was a system imposed both by the political will (which is not always effective in such matters), and by the capitalist tensions of commerce, in particular foreign and long distance trade."[22]

If there are parallels between the formation of the market nationals and that of the European single market, there is also a difference. Let us follow Braudel's observations to the end: "Thus one establishes the acquired economic coherence of a given political space, this space *being of a certain size*, above all what we call the territorial State and which one would more readily call the *national State*. Within this framework, political maturity precedes economic maturity."[23] Can today's European unification reverse these terms and allow economic maturity to precede political maturity, with the single market and single currency preceding the formation of a European State? Will Jean Monnet be proven right, on every point, against the old British lion?

This question lies at the heart of the current debates over the single currency and, broadly speaking, over the result of the plan to use the economy to build European unity. The object of this book is to attempt to answer it.

Let us pause a moment on this choice. Why the economy? Can Europe, as a sovereign entity, be built on the economy? Can the market succeed where faith, ideas and weapons have each failed in turn? "If it were to be remade, we would have to start with culture." These words, so often ascribed to Monnet, were never uttered by him — nor written, nor most likely thought, as the idea is contrary to his liberal conviction. As a follower of Adam Smith, the founder of the liberal economy, he thought that only trade brings people closer and supports peace and prosperity, while culture has seemed to many leaders to be inseparable from assertions of specific identities that carry within them the seeds of hatred and fanaticism.

Commerce or culture? Never in Europe's history was the unity of the continent founded on trade. On the contrary, the fantastic dynamism of capitalism was a result of Europe's division. Several authors have defended this thesis. "The expansion of capitalism draws its origins and its *raison d'être* from political anarchy," wrote the sociologist Jean

Baechler.[24] The European continent's political fragmentation was its
great fortune. Rival ambitions forced the princes to seek ways to increase their kingdoms' wealth in order to finance wars. They thus
granted broad freedom to commerce and to the cities, which supported
the growth of the economy. It is characteristic of Europe that, "for
more than a thousand years, (it) never managed to build so much as the
beginning of a political order, (that would cover) European initially,
then the globe." The historian Immanuel Wallerstein[25] defends the
same thesis, comparing China to Europe. "The empire is responsible
for managing and defending a vast territory and a sizable population
which absorbs all its attention, its energy and its revenue." The com-
parison could be extended to the colonial empires, which contributed
nothing significant to capitalist expansion (apart from the settling of
new territories, which ensured its geographical extension). These empires took up considerable financial and human resources which im-
peded British and French economic growth immediately after the Second World War. The same is true of the Soviet Union, whose central
monopoly on power over all activity led to its impotence. But by contrast, the gradual unification of the United States was a fantastic
stimulus to the development of North American capitalism.

No one knows why or when Jean Monnet was credited with this
idea of rethinking European construction from the basis of culture. In
the end, it doesn't really matter. The popularity of the saying does,
however, point up the growing disillusionment among those who had
hoped that the economy would be just the thing to overcome national
resistances. The development of trade between European countries
was supposed to gradually create a feeling of belonging to that same
unit, was supposed to launch a culture which, being material and commercial, and thus a bit vulgar, would be common to all Europeans. The
liberals (in the economic sense of the term) discovered with horror that
it made no difference that Frenchmen, Englishmen, Germans, Italians
and the others could buy the same cars, furnish their homes with the
same household appliances and sound systems, eat the same cereals for
breakfast, drink the same beer and the same wine. It did not make their
lifestyle uniform and national sentiments were not reduced to those
folk festivals, of which the tourists — those modern consumers — are
so fond.

In this regret for not having started with culture, there is also a
dream that *culture* (that aspect which deserves the name because it is

embodied in art) was European even before Europe was being built. Shakespeare and Oscar Wilde are English, Cervantès, El Gréco, and Goya are Spanish, Rabelais, Molière, Voltaire, Delacroix, Hugo, Cézanne — French, Goethe, Wagner, Nietzsche — German; Kafka is Czech, Mozart and Beethoven Austrians, Dante, Michelangelo, Raphaël, Verdi — Italian, and so on. But they are equally European. The majority traveled throughout Europe, going from court to court wherever they were called and fleeing exile or persecution as well. Their work constitutes a patrimony shared by every one of us. They are read, admired, listened to without any question of nationality. They express a time that belonged to all of Europe. Of course, each one shows traces of a national heredity, characteristic features of the various peoples which still come through to us today. But they were able to give a universal scope to the ideas, the feelings and the emotions they expressed, which make them recognizable as ours: the aspiration for freedom.

This homage to culture also acknowledges the fact that the origins of Europe are not to be found in the creation of the Common Market, and the rediscovery that there does indeed exist, deeply rooted in our history, a patrimony, a set of values, a culture by any definition, shared by all the peoples of Europe. A culture that is identified with the humanistic tradition, bearing the values of freedom, human rights, tolerance, universality. But bearing in mind that European culture rejects the harmony that haunts the European imagination (but which is only a chimera); that it embodies the everlasting tension between the individual and society, the aspiration for freedom against the conservatism which defends the established order; that it attains the universal only because it is identified with this conflict. Thus originates the misunderstanding expressed by sociologist Dominique Wolton, when he speaks of "a Copernican change compared to the European tradition that had been dominant since the Enlightenment," supposed to have taken place in European culture. "When everything opens its boundaries and is homogenized — under the pressure of the market," he says, "culture can no longer symbolize openness; it becomes, rather, an essential factor of identity and isolation." [26]

Did Monnet and his contemporaries get their timing wrong? Were they, unwittingly, following in the footsteps of the diplomats who, at the Congress of Vienna in 1815, thought they were making something new by recreating the Europe of monarchies? They saw culture as a distinction, a social position, like something dead that has been passed down to us and should be preserved. They did not see it as a life force, a vital force creating new freedoms. They were afraid it would carry along values from the old world that they wanted to revitalize by organizing it better. After the Napoleonic wars, there was a need to repel the ideas of the Enlightenment promoted by the Revolution; following the Second World War, Monnet and his friends sought to contain the evolution of a new culture that came from America with the landing of the "Navy," which would soon submerge Europe. They stopped where culture met the market, where it was refashioned by the market. By forgetting culture, they missed seeing America's modernity, missed understanding its universality, missed speculating about the new social positioning which the market conferred in the quest for personal freedom, missed the transition from critical reason to commercial reason.

Setting the economy apart from culture means failing to understand the crisis of culture which, to use Hannah Arendt's expression, is only "the wear and tear of tradition." But Europe stuck with tradition. Cinema became "art and essay," when its American homologue aimed to be an industry, as capable as the Europeans of producing masterpieces. Music was no different. Europe cultivated its orchestras and its operas and invented the festival for the cultivated public, where to be seen is as important as to listen. On the other side of the Atlantic, rock'n'roll was born, which expressed in its own way all of youth's aspiration to freedom and peace. Music for the masses, it was the forerunner of a trend destined for a great future when electronic technology would meet the consumer market. It expressed both a new relationship with oneself, sexual liberation, and a new collective consciousness, through huge gatherings of which Woodstock remains the standard. And "culture becomes showbiz," wrote MacLuhan in 1970, noting that "rock'n'roll is an electro-acoustic event, connecting the planet magnetically."[27] Globalization was on the march.

Originally from Germany, where she studied philosophy, Hannah Arendt emigrated to the United States after being driven out by Nazism. Early on, she perceived that the emergence of a mass culture implied the mutation of culture into leisure, or entertainment.[28] Even the term "mass culture" seemed wrong, to her. "It doesn't mean that culture is spreading among the masses, but that culture is destroyed to make room for leisure," she wrote. The problem lie not in the masses but in the fact that "this society is primarily a society of consumers, where leisure time is no longer used for improvement or to achieve a better social position, but to consume more and more, and to have more and more fun." Leisure pastimes "are consumer goods intended to be used until they are used up, just like any other consumer goods. . . . And since consumption makes its goods disappear, it must constantly provide new articles. Taking into account the 'gargantuan appetites' of the leisure industry, producers for the mass media are plundering the whole field of culture past and present in the hope of finding suitable material. And this material cannot be displayed just as it is; it has to be adapted so that it becomes leisure, it has to be prepared so that it is easy to consume."[29] We see examples everywhere we look, but nothing expresses this metamorphosis better that Walt Disney's theme parks, entirely nourished by a European culture which is blenderized and presented as pablum for the Americans!

The market is not entirely to blame; it is only the vector by which "the culture" of leisure is disseminated. The crisis of culture is anchored in the secularization of society which gives "now" precedence over the long haul. Works of art used to express a kind of immortality of society; they exalted values which transcended mankind's always fleeting action. And they still speak to us "beyond the centuries." By contrast human action, said Kant, has "a sad contingency. We don't know where it starts, we don't know what consequences it may have; so one might ask, does action have any value?"[30] However, for work to be supplanted by action required the technological support which makes each person's "now" accessible to everyone, which abolishes time as well as space. It required a veritable revolution, the discovery of electricity and its properties, so that the voice, sound and image could be transported at the speed of light. The world, which until the middle of the 19th century had existed in the continuum of eternity, has ever since chased after instantaneity. The Internet is the latest, and surely not the last, demonstration. Culture could not withstand such an upheaval.

This refusal to face the future has locked Europe into an impossible contradiction: it opened its economies to the market as never before, but its culture has dug in its heels to resist the same market. Of course, this resistance has not stopped anything. The dazzling development of electronic media, from radio to digital, television to multimedia, and the continuous expansion of mass consumption could only amplify the crisis of culture. Many artists and intellectuals have demonstrated anti-Americanism (they did not, however, refuse the pecuniary advantages offered by an expanding market), and this has meant that France failed to build a leisure industry that could compete with the American one. This resulted in a demand for protection, symbolized by the television broadcasting quotas. However, the artists and producers were not so much trying to protect themselves from the market as trying to get a foothold in it. Culture did not benefit from this; quite to the contrary. Its universality, which makes it a weapon in any fight for freedom, is pitted against its role in defining group identities, which become an "isolating factor." To build Europe on culture would require opening it up to the future.

The founders of the new Europe started with activities that had made it wealthy in the past: coal, steel, agriculture. These are all sectors where the institutions of the European Community would soon have to manage declining employment. They did not open a new page in history; they balanced the accounts of three Franco-German wars, two of which had set ablaze the whole continent of Europe and spread across the entire planet. In twice calling upon the United States to put an end to the conflict, the Europeans acknowledged their inability to perpetuate their world domination. While reorganizing itself, Europe sought to stem its decline. Germany, vanquished, had to give up its power. Great Britain and France still hoped to escape that fate, putting off for a few decades an identity crisis of which the construction of Europe would become the "Gordian knot." Thus, Europe was born from a negative plan, which the fall of the Berlin Wall reduced to naught.

Notes

1. *Histoire de l'Europe*, under the direction of Jean Carpentier and François Lebrun, Paris, Le Seuil, Points-Histoire, 1990.
2. Edgar Morin, *Penser l'Europe*, Paris, Gallimard, 1987, p. 25.
3. Robert Morrissey, *Charlemagne figure de l'Europe*, Notes from the Saint-Simon Foundation, June 1997.
4. Jean-Baptiste Duroselle, *L'Europe, histoire de ses peuples*, Paris, Perrin, 1990, p. 140.
5. *Ibid.*
6. See Henri Mendras, *L'Europe des Européens*, Paris, Gallimard, Folio-Essais, 1997.
7. Stefan Zweig, *Erasme*, Paris, Grasset, Les Cahiers rouges, 1988, p. 16 and 17.
8. *Ibid.*, p. 111.
9. Paul Hazard, *La Crise de la conscience européenne 1680-1715*, Paris, Fayard, Le Livre de poche, p. 411.
10. *Ibid.*, p. 412.
11. Krzysztof Pomian, *L'Europe et ses nations*, Paris, Gallimard, 1990, p. 93.
12. Nicolaus Copernicus (1473-1543) discovered that the Earth turns around the sun, Galileo (1564-1642) that it is round and Isaac Newton (1642-1727) that it exerts a force of gravity on objects.
13. Paul Hazard, *op. cit.*, p. 314.
14. John Locke, *Deuxième traité de gouvernement civil*, Paris, Vrin, 1977, p. 92.
15. It was not, however, until the middle of the 19th century that a real parliamentary system would be established, with responsibility for the cabinet before Parliament; and universal voting rights were established gradually only after 1867.
16. Blandine Kriegel, *Les Droits de l'homme et le Droit naturel*, Paris, PUF, 1989, p. 36.
17. J.G. Fichte, *Discours à la nation allemande*, Deuxième discours, Paris, Aubier Montaigne, 1975, p. 78.
18. Blandine Kriegel, *Cours de philosophie politique*, Paris, Le Livre de poche, 1996, p. 94.
19. Edgar Morin, *op. cit.*, p. 33.
20. Paul Hazard, *op. cit.*, p. 371.
21. Fernand Braudel, *Civilisation matérielle, économie et capitalisme XVe-XVIIIe siècle*, Paris, A. Colin, 1975, t. 3, p. 247.
22. *Ibid.*, p. 237.
23. *Ibid.*, p. 235.
24. Jean Baechler, *Les Origines du capitalisme*, Paris, Gallimard, coll. "Idées," 1971, pp. 122-126.
25. Immanuel Wallerstein, *Capitalisme et économie-monde*, Paris, Flammarion, 1980, pp. 58-59.
26. Dominique Wolton, *La Dernière Utopie*, Paris, Flammarion, 1993, p. 296.
27. *Rolling Stone*, November 12, 1970, cited in David Buxton, *Le Rock*, Paris, La Pensée sauvage, 1985, p. 122.
28. Hannah Arendt, *La Crise de la culture*, Paris, Gallimard, coll. "Folio-Essais," 1971, pp. 258-271.
29. *Ibid.*, p. 270.
30. Cited by Hannah Arendt, *op. cit.*, p. 112.

Chapter 2

The Shadow Cast by the War

On November 9, 1989, night had long since fallen on Berlin when radios the world over announced that "the Wall" had just half-opened, and that thousands of East Berliners had swarmed Check-Point Charlie to get into West Berlin. Already, Berliners on both sides were busy, pick axes in hand, two days before bulldozers came to tear down the intolerable symbol of the division of their country. Rostropovich, the famous violoncellist, greeted the incredible event in his own manner: by playing to freedom. What an extraordinary image this diminutive man presented. installed with his instrument at the foot of a wall destined for imminent destruction. In the year when France celebrated the bicentennial of its Revolution, a universal revolution if there ever was one, revolution was on the march once more.

For months, East German youth had been forcing open the doors of freedom. All summer, driving at breakneck speeds in their old Trabants[1] (destined to disappear a few months later, along with the wall), they were heading for Hungary. But that year, the young Germans were not going on their traditional summer holidays; they pushed forward to the Austrian border, a few miles from Vienna. On September 11, the Hungarian government gave in. Then, the West German embassy in Prague was taken by storm, and some 6,000 East German refugees moved in. In Leipzig, every Monday, for months, thousands of people gathered on Karl-Marx Platz following events at the St. Nicolas Church. But after October 9, their number kept growing. Two days earlier, at the conclusion of the military parade in honor of the forty years of the Communist regime of the GDR, the Secretary General of the Communist Party of the USSR, Mikhaïl Gorbachev, had said in a press statement: "Those who arrive too late are punished by the forces of life." The Communists arrived too late — in Berlin as in Warsaw, Prague and Budapest. And even in Moscow.

One by one, Communist regimes were swept away, less by popular pressure that by Gorbachev's decision that Soviet troops could not be used to maintain order. That was the sea change that made it possible for history to accelerate. For ten years the Poles had fought for that day, for ten months the Hungarians had been on the march. In ten weeks, Honecker's regime disappeared. Ten days would be enough for the Czechs to sweep away Husak, the executioner of the Prague Spring. No one realized, at the time, that Chancellor Kohl had not been idle meanwhile. For months, he had stepped up contacts with the Soviet leadership to obtain their neutrality in the developments in Central Europe in exchange for massive financial aid, without which the Soviet regime could not survive.[2] History was shaken again. Gorbachev would not be able to stop it this time, and was himself swept off by a last attempt to turn back, in 1991.

In Paris, London, Washington . . . the leaders were late. It would be unjust to claim that they didn't see it coming or that they had not wished for this to happen. In his New Year's Day wishes in 1982, François Mitterrand had pleaded for the end of the Europe of Yalta. In *On Germany, On France*,[3] he recalls having launched the topic again during that same year with Helmut Schmidt, linking the unification of Germany (already "written in history") to the weakening of the Soviet Empire. In 1984, during a conversation with Margaret Thatcher, who greeted the suggestion with skepticism, he had set the date for before the end of the century. But Mitterand, like everyone else, had failed to foresee the collapse of Communism — its peaceful denouement, of course — or, more important, its consequences for Europe. In London, Thatcher was quite simply hostile toward any development in the heart of Europe, considering, as she writes in her memoirs, that "by its very nature, Germany is more a factor of destabilization than of stabilization in Europe." But she was supported neither in Paris nor in Washington, where she found herself, with the arrival of George Bush in the White House, "face to face with a government which considered Germany its principal European partner . . . with the impression that she could no longer count on American cooperation as before."[4]

How could one visualize the post-Yalta period, when the key to change in Europe resided in Moscow, suspended by the reforms Gorbachev launched with *perestroïka*? The future of the USSR depended on their success. Who could imagine that their failure would open the way for freedom to return to Central Europe? Gorbachev was racing against the clock. But since he linked his policy to the Deutsche mark that Chancellor Kohl offered to him liberally in exchange for his non-intervention in Central Europe, a principle accepted since 1987, the fate of Communism in those countries was sealed and the unification of Germany was within reach. Kohl had never given it up and he had placed it on the agenda during the Christian Democrats' congress that was held in Bremen on September 11, 1989, when the Austrian-Hungarian border was opened. But the leaders held back. They feared that it would give Gorbachev problems with his military forces, and compromise reforms under way in the USSR and democratization in Central Europe. In fact, the Secretary-General of the CPSU played upon this with consummate art to obtain ever more financial aid from the "Westerners."

"A major event," said Mitterrand in his speech on the German unification. Major events in themselves, the prospect of German unification and the fall of Communism had even greater ramifications with regard to the building of Europe. Europe, in the wake of the Second World War, was born from the double threat to peace that Germany and the USSR represented at that time. Every European problem is rooted there. Some wanted to integrate; some refused integration in favor of a Europe made up of separate States. The improbable notion of constructing an integrated European defense would require political union first. That was why economic integration was the route chosen from the start. The division of Germany had been a consequence of the extension of the Communist regimes in Central Europe; it could be undone only with their disappearance. For years, that was considered unlikely.

Since the revolution of October 1917, Communism had challenged capitalism. In *Le Grand Schisme*, published in 1948, Raymond Aron defined the stakes of the war that the West was preparing to wage. No territorial conquest was required. "Today, everything is up in the air, the economic regime, the political system, spiritual convictions, the survival or disappearance of a leading class." The nature of war had changed. "Without a shot being fired, a country risks, if the Communist Party wins, knowing all the effects of defeat . . . From now on, the true borders are those which, in the heart of a formerly unified people, now separate the American side from the Russian side."[5]

The only victory could be the fall of the Communist regime. Aron would not have been surprised that it occurred without a single shot being fired. The leadership had eventually lost faith in the cogency of the economic regime, the political system, and the spiritual convictions that they were supposed to incarnate and defend. The people, of the Soviet Union as well as of the People's democracies, had lost their illusions long since.

With the advance of the Red Army to Berlin in 1945 and the installation of Communist regimes in the countries it occupied, cutting the continent in two, Western Europe felt directly threatened by Communism. According to the leadership of the time, and especially the American leaders who offered financial support via the Marshall plan and then the creation of the OEEC, the organization of Europe was planned in order to resist Communism. The insurrectionary strikes of November-December 1947 and the coup in Prague in February 1948 pushed Europe into the arms of the United States. Régis Debray[6] recalls this dialogue between Paul-Henri Spaak, the Belgian Minister for the Foreign Affairs, and the chief of the Soviet delegation to the UN: "Do you know what is the basis of our policy? It is fear, fear of you, fear of your government, fear of your policy." American senators deliberated for two years before allowing themselves to be convinced that the United States had a new mission to achieve in Europe — to help their allies to overcome their fear of "the Reds." "It is we, the Europeans, who asked for this suzerainty, for fear of losing the cause altogether," Debray concludes. The French were not the least active, nor the English who obtained a condominium with the Americans, allowing them to continue their imperial policy — the last gasps before extinction. Europe admitted being overcome by fear, more than by two world wars. It ceased thinking globally and turned inward on its regional interests.

On March 17, 1948, a treaty was signed in Brussels for military cooperation between France, Great Britain, Belgium, Netherlands and Luxembourg. One year later, it was superceded by the North Atlantic Treaty, signed on April 4, 1949, in Washington, between the United States, Canada and the signatories of the Treaty of Brussels. Denmark, Norway, Iceland, Italy and Portugal were invited to join. The military installations and the responsibilities of the commanders of the military organization of the Brussels Treaty, exclusively European, were transferred and put at the disposal of the new organization — placed under the command of an American general, in fact General Eisenhower. At the same time, the United States, in response to the division of Europe, imposed (over strong French reservations) the creation of a West German state. That changed the course of European construction.

The end of the Korean War dashed the last hopes of organizing an autonomous European defense. Perceiving a reinforcement of the Soviet threat, the North Atlantic Council adopted, on September 26, 1950, the strategy of placing the maximum number of armed forces close to the Soviet lines, right in the heart of Germany. The Americans were ready to strengthen their military presence and to take the lead in an integrated Atlantic command in Europe, provided that Europeans take their share of the burden. Dean Acheson, the American Secretary of State, demanded the participation of the Germans themselves and proposed to set up twelve divisions, which would not constitute an autonomous army, but would be integrated into the allied operative apparatus and be placed directly under American command. But the German government refused a step that would perpetuate the discrimination resulting from the Reich's defeat, and claimed equal rights for the new German State. German rearmament became, consequently, inevitable.

The public forgot that it was specifically to avoid this prospect that René Pleven had proposed (on October 24, 1950) an alternative plan for the European Defense Community (the EDC). Germany would regain its rights only to be more thoroughly dissolved into a larger organization, on the model of the ECSC[7] inaugurated by Robert Schuman on May 6, 1950. As there can be no defense without political authority, "the creation of a European army would be tied to the political institutions of a united Europe." But the construction of Europe was not the last step. Also, this plan did not go so far as to provide Europe the means with the means for its own defense. The European army, on the contrary, would be available to NATO (Article 18 of the draft treaty). On December 20, 1950, the five governments signing the Brussels Treaty decided, in this sense, to amalgamate the military organization with NATO rather than merely placing it at NATO's disposal. In exchange for giving up having its own army, Germany's occupied status would come to an end, through an agreement signed in

Bonn on May 26, 1952. Hardly formulated, the plan ignited passions in France. In addition to the Communists who saw this, not without reason, as a war machine targeted against Moscow, General de Gaulle opposed any plan that would make France, "of all the great nations which have an army today, the only one to lose its own." The harsh debate raised by the Treaty was enough to kill it. Chancellor Adenauer, who was not in its favor in any event, did not have to intervene.

The EDC did not come to fruition, but the problems which underlay it remained, even in the Maastricht Treaty. To prevent Germany from regaining its sovereignty, did France have to give up its own by dissolving itself into a greater entity? Could Europe, under cover of NATO, rely on the United States for its defense and, at the same time, claim to have a European defense? To reconcile national sovereignty and collective security, wouldn't it be simpler to go along with an "Atlantic solution with a European face" as proposed by the British government? The latter was essential.

Germany was invited with Italy to join the Brussels Treaty, which was profoundly changed, and at the same time to becoming a member of NATO. It got what it wanted: recognition of its sovereignty — albeit still limited — and participation in the defense of Western Europe, with equal rights. France retained its sovereignty, but it gave up its dream of submitting the German army to its authority. To the Belgians, Dutch and Danes, who had suffered two German invasions in 50 years, the American presence in Europe was a reassuring, longlasting neutralization of Germany. If they needed a protector, the European leaders preferred the Americans to the French. It was a question of dignity as much as of effectiveness.

Thus, from the beginning, the attempt to organize a European defense stumbled on the determination of the various governments of Europe to defend their national sovereignty and, for some, to have the peace guaranteed by the Americans. The British were no less attached to their sovereignty, but in contrast to the French, they had clearly decided against any European integration that would be incompatible, in their eyes, with their will to be a world power. Moreover, they did not seek to control Germany, whereas this control was the obsession of the French leaders. Neither did they wish to see the French sitting at the head of a continental federation that would cast the power of Albion in the shade. Before it was a model of European defense, the EDC was a model of misunderstanding. Confronted with the Soviet threat, Europeans finally preferred "the defense pact" suggested by the Americans to "the unification pact" of the French.[8]

Forty years of managing European security have not alleviated the misunderstanding. The Franco-German reconciliation and the bonds gradually woven between the two countries in the field of defense have not strained the Atlantic Pact. Neither the building of nuclear weapons nor France's "Lone Ranger" policy, initiated by General de Gaulle, convinced our partners of the need for Europe to take its defense into its own hands. Both are results of the failure of this strategy and the inability to reform NATO, substituting a 3-way leadership for the American-English condominium. The independence of French defense policy (that is, its autonomous ability to decide its doctrines, to define its weaponry and their deployment, to determine the ways and means of mobilizing its armed forces) has been a constant of all French governments since the Liberation. General de Gaulle's policy was not a change of course. It followed this logic to its natural conclusion: a withdrawal. Short of securing a reform of NATO, which it still requests of the Americans, France left the integrated command. But the Atlantic Pact remained.

The Elysée Treaty, signed on January 22, 1963, between France and Germany, is the perfect symbol of the misunderstanding of European construction. It was born from the debates on America's will to protect Europe in all circumstances. But it was ratified only at the cost of Germany reaffirming Europe's defense being integrated in NATO. The failure of the Fouchet plan for European political union, the initiative for which has been attributed to General de Gaulle and to which we will return later, was largely ascribable to the French president's hesitations in relation to his European partners' demands. They rejected the French bid to direct the European concert. Actually, French policy bumped up against NATO.

Following the crisis caused in August 1961 by the construction of the "Berlin Wall," the American and the Soviet governments opened negotiations. The worries this caused gave rise to the French-German reconciliation. On the one hand, MacNamara's declaration of the strategy of "graduated response" gave reason to fear an American disengagement in Europe. On the other, the American proposal for a treaty on the non-proliferation of nuclear arms definitively prohibited the United States from giving the FRG full proprietorship of any such weapons (at that time, the government in Bonn had not given up the idea of eventually holding nuclear arms). By the end of the meeting in Nassau between Kennedy and Macmillan in December 1962, the Americans had proposed to extend to France the same offer it had given Great Britain: Polaris rockets in exchange for abandoning the construction of their own nuclear warheads. Paris interpreted this as an American desire to dampen European nuclear ambitions. General de Gaulle took this as an opportunity to revive his plan for an autonomous European defense (under French leadership). He proposed to the German government, as the Treaty would stipulate, "to align their doctrines on the strategic and tactical level with a view to developing common plans." Including, apparently, nuclear power, although the General never intended to share with Germany neither the secrets of nuclear technology, nor the decisions.

The question of ulterior motives, on both sides, was never raised. Certainly, the General made a step toward Bonn but, as George-Henri Soutou wrote on the basis of his research in both countries' archives, "the plan was (also) to make it possible for France to control Germany's strategic affairs, and to supervise and control its nuclear ambitions in particular."[9] Nevertheless, the French-German reconciliation showed all signs of going full-speed ahead: official visits, a triumphal reception for General de Gaulle in Germany, a French and German military parade at Mourmelon and a mass in the Cathedral of Rheims during Adenauer's visit to France. In this context, not being able to prevent the signing of the Elysée Treaty, President Kennedy set out to have it scrapped. He encouraged the German Parliament to add a preamble once again positioning the "common defense within the framework of NATO." The very European Jean Monnet, who was highly successful as an intermediary, was pleased "with this preamble and with the unanimity of the Bundestag (which) put things back in order, with the Treaty, thus understood, losing its character as an exclusive political alliance to become an administrative expression of the Franco-German reconciliation decided twelve years earlier with the Schuman plan"[10]! Might as well transform a treaty into a dishtowel! De Gaulle stuck it in a drawer, where François Mitterrand, by then president of the Republic, found it in 1983.

"If you want to know my true value, consider that I do not strike bodies alone, but the heart and the spirit; I am the first true psychological weapon."[11] André Glucksmann, writing *La Force du vertige*, was thinking of those carriers of death that were avowed to be weapons of peace — rockets and other missiles with nuclear warheads — but he may as well have been referring to the Elysée Treaty. Today, with the Communist regimes demolished and the Soviet Union self-dissolved, one can hardly imagine the significance played by the debate over deploying Pershing II rockets against the SS 20. Since the installation of the Soviet rockets close to Europe's dividing line, these famous rockets, about which Glucksmann wrote "the Gospel," had acquired the status of fatal weapons. In less time than it takes to write it, they could strike any nerve center, city or military target, in Western Europe, with diabolic precision. But this only applied to Europe, introducing the famous "decoupling" between the United States and Europe, so much dreaded by the Europeans.

To understand the conflict that then ensued in Europe, we need to go back some 25 years. The first Soviet intercontinental ballistic missile, launched in 1957, changed the face of American strategy. Having lost its monopoly on intercontinental launchers, the United States lost their invulnerability at the same time as the impunity that, heretofore, had been guaranteed by their distance from Soviet launch sites. The American military was prompt to recognize that the threat of massive reprisals to any attack, even conventional, had lost any credibility. No American president would take the risk of exposing New York, Chicago or Washington to nuclear reprisals to defend Hamburg or Munich. "Dear Henry," as Henry Kissinger, Secretary of State under Nixon, likes to be called, found it easy to make fun of "one of those theories that sound so impressive during a university course, but are absolutely useless for a political leader faced with reality."[12] Restoring the credibility of their nuclear force then became an American obsession. If they could not restore their invulnerability, then "second best" would be to achieve technological and numerical superiority. The arms race was launched. But the Vietnam War and Congress, while cutting back on ever-greater requests for appropriations, forced them to consider de-escalating. On May 26, 1972, President Nixon and the First Secretary of the Communist Party of the Soviet Union signed the first treaty on the "limitation of anti-ballistic missile systems." Others followed.

In wishing to protect itself at all costs, the United States left Europe exposed. The USSR stepped into the breach. In the wake of Chancellor Willy Brandt's Ost-politik, founded on the recognition of the Oder-Neisse border, the Americans had accepted the proposal which the Soviets had been suggesting since 1954, to hold a conference on European security (convened in Helsinki on July 31 and August 1, 1975). But while the diplomats produced the American-Soviet summits, making it seem that détente could be synonymous with the limitation of intercontinental missiles, the military worked on miniaturizing the weapons of mass destruction, increased their precision and the mobility of launchers. With shorter ranges, these missiles could cover only Europe and were not included in SALT[13] negotiations. By deploying them the Soviets invented, according to Glucksmann,[14] "winnable continental nuclear conflict," of which Europe would be the only theater of operations. German Chancellor Helmut Schmidt, a former Minister of Defense, kicked up a fuss with the American leaders, but they remained insensitive to Europe's concerns. Thus, on October 13, 1977, he presented a violent indictment at the Institute of Strategic Studies in London. On December 12, 1979, the member states of the NATO integrated command made "a double decision:" to modernize NATO's medium-range nuclear missiles (Pershing II) and to open negotiations seeking bilateral limitations. Political leaders and staffs were reassured. But the presence of nuclear missiles, and the prospect that the center of Europe could one day be transformed into a theater of operations, inspired the German population with a rather understandable terror. Pacifism was born.

For three years, Europe experienced an odd sort of war. The protagonists were the pacifists, whose philosophy was summarized in the catch phrase, "better red than dead." By the hundreds of thousands, they demonstrated in the principal German cities and attacked the police force around American bases in Germany. Media campaigns replaced the armies' agendas and antinuclear sit-ins took a page from handbooks on passive resistance. By putting the Westerners on the defensive, the Soviets had, in fact, changed the terms of nuclear war. Of Yuri Andropov, who succeeded Leonid Brezhnev in the Kremlin, Glucksmann, in *La Force du vertige*, wrote, "(he) did not wage war, but he put to the test the leaders' and the populations' determination; he tried a mental battle." His objective was "to obtain, without anything in return, the right to observe, then to veto, the nuclear armament of Western Europe."[15] Strong in their advantage, the Soviets refused any serious negotiation and dismissed various American proposals. At the same time, they allowed the Germans the hope that they might realize their dream of unification against the demilitarization of the heart of Europe.

Although France was not involved in NATO's decisions, Mitterrand, who had decided in 1979 against any decoupling between Europe and the United States, felt that nothing would be worse than to give in. While "the West has pacifism," he liked to say, "the East has missiles." Since the Soviets did not want to negotiate, deployment of the Pershings was inescapable, and the deadline of December 31, 1983, would have to be met. Invited to give a speech before the Bundestag on the 20th anniversary of the Elysée Treaty, which he wished to reactivate with the new German chancellor, Helmut Kohl, Mitterrand said, without mincing words: "Today's equilibrium, like it or not, is based on deterrence . . . A convincing threat of deployment is the only basis for negotiation. Whoever would take a chance on decoupling would upset the balance of forces and thus the maintenance of peace." Helmut Schmidt and Helmut Kohl both appreciated this support: one was bitter over not being able to collect its fruits any longer; the second delighted to silence the social democrats rallied around the pacifist cause a few months before the general elections that were going to give him more than a decade and half of power.

The Bundestag speech sealed a friendship and a relation of confidence between Mitterrand and Kohl that was never broken. After the reaffirmation of the anchoring of the franc in the EMS, two months later, the French President found there a support for the deployment of his European policy. But he soon came up against the same limitations that had blocked General de Gaulle: the integration of Europe's defense in NATO.

Mitterrand was realistic. He had no ambition to reform NATO, no plan for revising its chain of command. He only called for "a clarified alliance," i.e. confined in its role of defending Europe and not claiming to impose its views on the rest of the world (what the experts call "out of area").

Furthermore, he had no illusion regarding the Germans' choices, however much their leaders might wish to cooperate. In the long commentary he added to the 1986 publication of his principal speeches on foreign policy, he wrote: "When the second reflex of a Germany under threat pushes her towards France, the first will have already precipitated her towards America. No one should be astonished nor complain about that."[16] To change this situation is not within the capability of French policy, whatever effort it might make. The refusal to decouple the United States and Europe, which all the French governments approved, did not forbid Europe to take its own security in hand. But since NATO offered its services, many countries did not see any interest in a European defense and prefer to depend on the Americans, rather than their neighbors, to provide for their armament — and that, in spite of uncertainties of the American strategy in Europe. Even the collapse of Communism did not change this point of view.

The French governments' will to create preferential ties with Germany was consistent since shortly after the Second World War. It contributed in no small part to the distorted view of history — General de Gaulle's, which Raymond Aron says "accustomed the French to mistake its enemy"[17] (by making the United States an adversary), more than any other. De Gaulle recognized that "nothing was more justified and, perhaps, more salutary than the American aid" in setting Europe back on its feet and that "the institution of NATO was an almost inevitable consequence."[18] But "the protectorate of Washington" was no less "hateful" in his eyes, and he did not intend to submit to it. Also, as he writes it in his *Mémoires d'espoir*, "as of September 14, 1958, I raised the flag."[19] It would be hard, after that, to reproach the French for not having a faithful memory.

Asked why the decision was made to equip the country with a national deterrent force, the French will answer you in good faith: the general will to ensure a French defense independent of the United States. No one seems to remember that originally it was intended to ensure France absolute superiority compared to German rearmament. However, the EDC, while placing the signatories countries under a common responsibility, prevented France from obtaining nuclear weapons. Pierre Mendès-France, who opposed ratification of the Treaty, also wished not to keep the United States from being the only judge of when to use nuclear weapons in any possible European conflict. Within a few weeks, the dream of a European defense disappeared: on October 3, 1954, at the conference of London in preparation for the Paris accords, Chancellor Adenauer confirmed his country's voluntary decision to forego developing and manufacturing nuclear weapons (although in spirit, that was valid only temporarily). Three weeks later, on October 23, the agreements were signed in Paris restoring sovereignty to the FRG, rearming it, integrating it into NATO and promising the Allies' support for reunification. On December 26, Pierre Mendès France, then President of the Council, took the decision to equip France with nuclear arms, "the last guarantee, considering the new status of the FRG." However, recalls George-Henri Soutou, Pierre Mendès France "forbore to formalize it in the immediate future for reasons of political opportunity."[20] The General was thus able to appropriate it and distort its original objective.

Despite the failure of the EDC, de Gaulle did not attempt to remove deterrent strike force from the domain of Franco-German relations. But he did not go as far as to meet the German requests for nuclear cooperation in manufacture and materials. Similarly, in 1966, when he decided to leave NATO, he chose to remain in the Atlantic Alliance in order to "maintain French military control over the FRG."[21] His successors would employ the same language with respect to Germany: "We wanted to cooperate with the FRG, but at the same time we wanted to maintain superiority over it,"[22] stressed Soutou. Even Mitterrand, who would take Franco-German cooperation the furthest, particularly in the field of the information exchanges on strategic concepts and the design and manufacture of conventional armaments, would not stray from the policy that was set in place forty years earlier: *You don't share nuclear force.* European construction had not only broken down over the fierce will of the European countries — not only of France, Great Britain and, the FRG, but also Belgium, the Netherlands and others — to preserve their national sovereignty, it strengthened this desire and made any European defense unthinkable for a long time.

In his critique of pacifism, Glucksmann spells out the problem that lies at the heart of European defense: "We are depriving the Germans of the right to defend themselves, without asking whether they need it. Logically enough, they anticipate our refusal and are very strongly set against nuclear weapons."[23] Germany claimed this right vis-à-vis the Soviet threat by demanding to be treated on an equal footing; fear of German rearmament pushed France to oppose it, while secretly hoping that the Germans would rely on France and its nuclear deterrence to ensure their security. The German were prepared to wait patiently for this demand to be satisfied, but not to close off their options for the future. While they waited, they relied on NATO. The response to the problem raised by Glucksmann, for the last ten years, has lain not with Germany (unless it would reconsider a "definitive renunciation of any nuclear weapon) but with France. For the Germans to take their defense into their own hands, the French must give up any pretension to hold an unspecified military superiority over their neighbor, and thus re-open the basic question: deterrent force. But is such a break with the past conceivable, without a corresponding, decisive step being taken in the construction of a European defense — without raising the question of the Franco-German misunderstanding?

Maybe a wall is easier than prejudice to tear down. The earthquake that shook Stalin's conquests and his heirs did not reach the western part of the continent. The very prospect of German reunification instinctively resuscitated old fears. Nobody can forget the scene at the Council of Strasbourg, one month after the fall of the Berlin Wall, when Margaret Thatcher pulled a map out of her handbag showing Germany's various borders over the last century, stressing that they "were not entirely reassuring for the future."[24] In the Hague, in Brussels, in Copenhagen, feelings toward the German unification, though more discrete, were hardly different. For his part, Mitterrand hid neither his concern nor his irritation over the chancellor's initiatives,[25] taken without informing his partners, and his refusal to make a clear statement recognizing the Oder-Neisse border (for purely electoral reasons). Kohl's attitude contributed to the conflict. His political intuition impelled him to rush history. He felt that Germany "deserves, after several decades, its partners' confidence to take single-handedly and in sovereignty the decisions expected of her"[26] and delayed the meeting of "the four powers" who were victorious in 1945 and of both Germanies. The dissolution of the USSR turned the European countries' attention back to what had been clear in the immediate post-war period, and that everyone had hoped would go away: the notion that Germany is the kingpin of security in Europe. But how could that be expressed, without stirring up German national feeling, without ruining the "confidence" so patiently achieved? As with the EDC, France believed it found an answer in the revival of the idea of a unified European defense. But President Mitterrand did not dare, any more than did General de Gaulle, to propose to our partners extension of "the sanctuarization" of the French territory to all of Europe.

Can the debate be avoided? Certainly not. "Today's world requires that we give new contents to our security policy and our strategy. Anyone who follows Cartesian logic places an analysis of the situation at the beginning of this process."[27] The remark is from the German Defense Minister. The French, themselves, are not always Cartesian. In 1989, they preferred to go around the obstacle. Rather than defining the contents of what could be a European policy of defense and security, they opted for a "strong" political action that affirms the maintenance of Germany in the European Union. That was to be the purpose of the Maastricht Treaty (which was not, at the time, en-visaged as including the treaty on economic and monetary union). European integration against German reunification — just as, follow-ing the German defeat, the French had sought to drown Germany in a larger unit to avoid any reconstitution of the Reich and any attempted drift toward the East. Once more, ulterior motives controlled European construction, to the point of obsession. But each found this to be in his best interest. Chancellor Kohl needed to show that he was firmly an-chored within Europe so he could have his hands free to handle the German reunification; President Mitterrand relied on the ineluctable to fan the flames of his European policy.

The image of Mitterrand and Kohl shaking hands at Verdun was securely immortalized by the magic of photography, but the agreement did not coincide with the meeting. If European integration is moving, it is crabwise, like two old crabs experienced in political life. At the European Council in Strasbourg, December 8 and 9, 1989, Kohl made clear from the outset that he agreed that an intergovernmental confer-ence, preparatory to the treaty on economic and monetary union, should be held before the end of 1990 (but after the German elections), as the French President had been suggesting for several weeks. "But this commitment had a price," say Pierre Favier and Michel Martin-Roland, two journalists accredited to the Elysée. "The German delega-tion quietly let it be known that, in return, the Chancellor expected the Twelve to formally support reunification."[28] Otherwise, Favier and Martin-Roland continue a little later, "he would be obliged to put his plan for reviving the political union back in his briefcase, given Mitter-rand's refusal."[29] The French accepted the German proposal only after weakening "its federalist excesses" and reorienting it to reflect a com-mon defense and security program. On March 28, 1990, in full polemic on the question of borders — the resolution about the intangibility of borders was only submitted on March 5 — the Chancellor proposed that the Twelve plan an intergovernmental conference on political un-ion that would meet parallel to the monetary conference. However, the merger of the two treaties would only come later, when it appeared that the treaty on political union was too insubstantial to accommo-date the revival of European construction, which was essential if Ger-many was going to become reunified. Likewise, the substance of such an agreement would be discussed later, when the Cartesian logic of analysis would be imposed upon all parties concerned.

Instead of Cartesian logic, historical affinities, maintained by public opinion and special interest groups, set the context in the short term. The collapse of Communist regimes and the dissolution of the Warsaw Pact left Europe without an enemy at its gate, but not without conflicts along its internal borders and within its bosom. At the moment when governments were striving to reach a consensus on the procedures that would govern the future foreign policy and mutual security — "FPCS" in European jargon — they were at each other's throats over the conflict that was tearing apart Yugoslavia. The ink was not yet dry on the Maastricht Treaty when reunified Germany staked out its unilateral position and imposed its law in what it regards as its traditional area of influence: on December 19, 1992, it unilaterally recognized Slovenia and Croatia.

There were grumblings in Paris. But President Mitterrand chose to support Franco-German solidarity in spite of the issue. "French diplomacy," notes Jean-Pierre Maury, "only managed to disguise its retreat: the common foreign policy will conform to the law . . . which will be defined as the occasion arises."[30] The Twelve's inability to agree on a solution to conflicts flaring up on its doorstep or, worse yet, to those destroying States within its bosom, belies the objective laid down by the European Council shortly after the Treaty took effect: stability and peace in Europe. In Yugoslavia as in Northern Ireland, each State treated the conflict as an internal problem that did not relate to the Community as a whole. The only hopes of peace and a resolution came from the United States. With or without the Soviet threat, with or without the Berlin Wall, the American presence remains the only guarantee of peace in Europe. In this context, there can be a European defense only under the sovereign wing of NATO.

Cartesian logic, which calls for analysis before working out the solutions, was invoked by Volker Rühe, the German Minister for Defense, during a conference held in Paris at the suggestion of the French minister Pierre Joxe.[31] Talking about a "dramatic gain in security," he defined the four fundamental changes brought about by the collapse of Communism: Germany is no longer within the reach of a State capable of strategic offensives and conquests; the dilemma of German security (the contradiction between persuading her to give up nuclear protection at the risk of becoming a nuclear battlefield) was dissipated; Central Europe became an area of strategic calm; and finally, Germany, the European country with the greatest number of land borders, is now surrounded by allies and partners.[32] The conclusion, and the only conclusion, is that Europe's security must rest on "a flexible system, including all the possibilities offered by the United Nations, the CSCE, NATO and the WEU. None of these institutions can, nor should, replace the others." He doesn't count on European forces or institutions at all. On the contrary, he adds, "It is in our vital interest to have the United States participate in European processes. What we need is a new partnership among equals and an American partner who contributes responsibly to the shaping of the new Europe." Is the time right for creating a European defense protective? Why not. But, the German minister immediately added, "This should definitely not be regarded as competing with NATO." Four years later, "the Franco-German concept of common security and defense," defined by the agreement signed in Nuremberg in December 1996, added nothing to what was said that day. France took steps toward re-integrating with NATO, if only during that period and dropped since then, and admitted that the European security and defense identity is developing within the Alliance.

And what is a German Cartesian? It is one who deduces from the disappearance of the Soviet threat, "the clearly identified threat," that it is pointless to have nuclear weapons on European soil. Having definitively given up nuclear weapons, he dreams of having his neighbor, and equal, do the same. Since everyone admits that "the supreme guarantee of the security of the allies (thus of Europe) is ensured by the strategic nuclear forces of the Alliance," the *French deterrent force becomes useless*, at least in its land-based component. If there is no more need to have missiles directed toward the East, then what is the point of having Hades rockets, with a range of 500 km, which can only fall on Germany? Keeping them would have meant acknowledging the French desire to hold its neighbor in subjection, to strike, as Glucksmann says, the German "heart and soul." Psychology was returned against those whom it had formerly defended. Recognition as equal partners, required by Chancellor Kohl, assumed that the Hades missiles would disappear. Mitterrand started the process by "freezing" the missiles and suspending deployment. Elected president, Jacques Chirac decided (with Bonn's approval) to dismantle them. Without any democratic debate, they did away with any land-based deterrent force, retaining only the naval and air components.

Does French deterrent force still have a future? Imperceptibly, doubt has crept in. It was never seen as serving any goal but defending the national "sanctuary," and it could only be used with the Americans' agreement. Using it against a threat coming from within Europe has become almost impossible. In addition, the violent reactions to the last French nuclear tests, and the demonstrations in Germany against nuclear waste storage, even of civil origin, show that the antinuclear ideology is a powerful political force in Europe that is making nuclear weapons increasingly nonviable. The recent priority given to disarmament by the French government can only accentuate this phenomenon.

Lastly, the Americans' efforts to get Moscow's agreement on enlarging NATO to encompass the Central European countries will lead them to promote the denuclearization of these countries, not without ulterior motives in regard to France. "All these commitments," writes Vice-Admiral Duval, the long-time director of the *Revue de la Défense nationale* and a top expert on nuclear affairs, "converge towards doctrines of 'no first use' of nuclear weapons (in other words, towards negating the concept of deterrence, or at least towards the idea that nuclear force deters only nuclear force), which limits their scope considerably."[33]

During the debates over military planning for 1997-2002, the vice-admiral was astonished by the silence relative to the doctrines and the missions foreseen for French deterrent forces. By law, "nuclear deterrence remains a fundamental element of our defense strategy." But a malicious spirit could add, "Does France still have a defense strategy?" Even the military is wondering. The political leaders seem to have settled for an implicit renunciation without even trying to negotiate any *quid pro quo* at the European level. By exposing the ulterior motives behind the French strategy, the fall of the Berlin Wall evaporated the illusion of military superiority over Germany via nuclear force. It did not, however, pave the way to a purely European defense. A "major event" indeed.

Unless the 1990's are the turning point, they will be remembered as the decade of the dupes. This time, the post-war period clearly is over. With the passing of time, we will understand Mitterrand's reticence and Thatcher's hostility toward German unification, and President Bush's eagerness to support Helmut Kohl. The former were worried about the risks of destabilizing Gorbachev, but could not follow their logic to the end of its course. Such a course would tie German unification to a security treaty negotiated in due form with the Soviet Union, which would have associated it with security in Europe. The American President, on the contrary, played on Gorbachev's weakness and imposed American conditions for the reunification of Germany, within a NATO that was to be maintained and strengthened. The way toward enlarging NATO, while isolating Russia a little more, was open.

Someday, it will seem astonishing that such major events, which upset the conditions of European security from top to bottom, were carried out without any strategic reflection. Sweeping aside his predecessor's reservations, Jacques Chirac, hardly elected President of the Republic, charged blindly ahead, putting France back in the midst of NATO's integrated command without having sought the least concession in return. Not being able to detach the other European countries from NATO, he hoped to improve the chances of building "a European defense identity," even if, initially, it had to be done under American conditions.

But every step forward held its share of disappointment for Chirac. The elimination of obligatory military service made it more difficult to integrate French and German soldiers within Eurocorps, which was, in effect, reduced to nothing by the dissolution of the First Armored Division. Also, the creation of a European Defense and Security Identity within NATO, decided by the Atlantic Council in Berlin on June 3 and 4, 1996, did not recognize the autonomy of European intervention (the United States reserved the right of veto on the use of NATO's European forces). And the dismissal of military obligation did not lead to the reorganization of the European commands desired by France. As an immediate consequence of the directives for arms policies and cooperation, the head of German armament, Martin Guddat,[34] produced a set of obligatory rules of competition: no government subsidies, the acceptance of restructuring, and adherence to purely political criteria for the export of materials. The French would rely on the future European arms agency, Occar, while the Germans prefer to remain free of their alliances, as shown by German DASA's failure to come to terms with Aérospatiale for the manufacture of satellites and missiles.

Faced with the American refusal to reform NATO's European command structure, the French government stalled its return to the integrated structures of the Alliance. But it has not changed its strategy. What does France want? If it is a question of thinking national under America's protective wing, if France's European partners refuse to take the leap that would make them equally emancipated from any oversight, then the NATO framework is not only sufficient but actually more appropriate. Let's not forget that the Atlantic Alliance is as much political as it is military. General de Gaulle disputed the fact that the strategic and operational command is in the hands of the Americans; he never withdrew France from the political bodies of the alliance. Furthermore, for all those who are opposed to the prospect of political integration within a European unit, NATO offers an indisputable advantage: it "absolutely preserves the principle of national sovereignties and makes it possible to eliminate the thorny question of European political integration and delegated sovereignty."[35] In addition, for many countries too small to organize their own defense, and for the most part hostile to nuclear power, NATO is a guarantee of the ongoing American military presence in Europe. With or without the Berlin Wall, it prevents us having to think about relations with a newly sovereign Germany.

That proposition is not weakened by either Tony Blair's (as Prime Minister of Great Britain) acceptance of the principle of a European Defense Identity, nor by the Western intervention in Kosovo. Whenever their security is jeopardized, the Europeans continue to prove (as they did with Bosnia) themselves to be incapable of undertaking military operations, even in a conflict that is modest in scope, without a political decision and full participation by the American armed forces. The glaring insufficiency of European defense capabilities is not only due to the dedication of a smaller budgetary amount (and unequal from country to country) but above all it is the consequence of a choice of armaments that derived from strategic concepts that are not well-adapted to the challenges hat arise in Europe now that the Berlin Wall is down. Europe cannot do without NATO. While the Franco-British summit at St. Malo (December 1998) and the European Council in Cologne (June 1999) finally brought military cooperation into the equation, it will still be a long time before Europe is capable of autonomous intervention. Furthermore, Europe will also have to review from top to bottom (under pressure for the U.S.) its approach to the enlargement (which it began to do after the Kosovo crisis) in order to resolve the dilemma posed to countries such as Turkey by the dissolution of the Union of Eastern Europe (of which they were members) into the European Union (from which they will continue to be excluded).

To design a European defense policy would suppose the existence of a European political power, and a European forum for debate where the essential consensus could be forged as to what the continent's security should look like. But are we really surprised that an agreement between heads of state could be signed without the public opinion of the countries concerned being informed — not *a posteriori*, but indeed as a prelude? Did any European deputy contest the fact that the European Parliament, which should represent the European citizens, is kept at arm's length? Does any European wonder what is the meaning of "a common concept of Franco-German security," when what is needed is a properly European concept? Who cares that the relationship between Europe and Russia, which now, as before, determines the future of peace on the continent, is decided in Washington, with the risk of bringing more instability than security?[36]

Germany had briefly considered fomenting for the European Union to have a permanent seat in the UN Security Council. France's and Great Britain's refusal to give up their seats quickly convinced Germany of the "inopportunity"[37] of this position. Now, like Italy, it claims a seat for itself. The Atlantic Alliance was conceived by Europeans a half-century ago so they would not have to take their security and their defense into their own hands. That is the only fact that the fall of the Berlin Wall did not upset, or even scratch. It is the only one that renders the idea of a European defense pointless. However, Mitterrand wrote in 1986, "The idea of Europe cannot be dissociated from the idea of defense. At present, it is only an Atlantic defense."[38]

Notes

1. A brand of cars from the old GDR.
2. Helmut Kohl, *Je Voulais l'unité de l'Allemagne*, Paris, Fallois, 1997.
3. François Mitterrand, *De l'Allemagne, de la France*, Paris, Odile Jacob, 1995, p. 13.
4. Margaret Thatcher, *10, Downing street, Mémoires*, Paris, Albin Michel, 1993, p. 633.
5. Raymond Aron, *Le grand schisme*, quoted in his *Mémoires*, Paris, Julliard, 1987, p. 287.
6. Regis Debray, *Les Empires contre l'Europe*, Paris, Gallimard, 1985, p. 46.
7. European Coal and Steel Community.
8. I refer to the distinction introduced by Jean-Pierre Maury, in *La Construction européenne : la securité et la défense*, Paris, PUF, 1996.
9. George-Henri Soutou, *L'Alliance incertaine*, Paris, Fayard, 1997, p. 209.
10. Jean Monnet, *Mémoires*, Paris, Fayard, 1987, p. 551.
11. André Glucksmann, *La Force du vertige*, Paris, Grasset, 1983, p. 24.
12. Quoted in Andre Fontaine, *Un seul lit pour deux rêves*, Paris, Fayard, 1981, p. 234.
13. SALT: Strategic Arms Limitation Talks — discussions on the limitation of the strategic weapons.
14. André Glucksmann, *op. cit.*, pp. 68-69.
15. André Glucksmann, *op. cit.*, pp. 68-69.
16. François Mitterrand, *Réflexions sur la politique extérieure de la France*, Paris, Fayard, 1986, p. 94.
17. Raymond Aron, *op cit.*, p. 449.
18. Charles de Gaulle, *Mémoires d'espoir*, Paris, Plon, 1970, p. 211.
19. *Ibid*, p. 214.
20. George-Henri Soutou, *op. cit.* p. 35.
21. *Ibid*, p. 291.
22. *Ibid*, p. 363.
23. A. Glucksmann, *op. cit.*, p. 138.
24. Margaret Thatcher, *Mémoires , op. cit.*, p. 662.
25. See Mitterrand's account, *De l'Allemagne, de la France, op. cit.*, also those of Pierre Favier and Michel Martin-Roland, *La Décennie Mitterrand*, T 3: *Les Défis*, Paris, Le Seuil, 1996 and Hubert Védrine, *Les Mondes de François Mitterrand*, Paris, Fayard, 1996.
26. Hubert Védrine, *op. cit.*, p. 437.
27. Volker Rühe, "De nouveaux contenus à la politique de sécurité et à la stratégie," in *Un Nouveau débat stratégique*, Colloque de Paris, September 29 - October 1, 1992, published by La Documentation française, Paris, 1993.
28. Pierre Favier and Michel Martin-Roland, *op. cit.*, p. 206.
29. *Ibid*, p. 244.
30. Jean-Pierre Maury, *op. cit.*, pp. 252-255.
31. *Un Nouveau débat stratégique*, proceedings of the Colloque de Paris, *op. cit.*
32. However, it took Helmut Kohl, definitely very concerned with his electoral interests, a little more time than his minister suggested to erase the after-effects of the latter: in order to assuage the former Germans of Sudetenland, he delayed signing a peace agreement with the Czech Republic until January 1997!
33. Marcel Duval, "Perspectives d'avenir de la dissuasion française," Revue de la Défense nationale, December 1996.
34. Cf. *Le Monde*, January 31, 1997.
35. Nicole Gnesotto, "L'Europe, pilier politique de l'OTAN," *Libération*, October 8,

1996.

36. Michel Rocard was the only French leader to have raised this question, which he did in two articles published in *L'Express,* March 13 and *Le Monde*, April 19, 1997.

37. Joint note of the Ministries for Foreign Affairs, *doc. cit.*

38. François Mitterrand, *Réflexions sur la politique extérieure de la France, op. cit.*, p. 101.

Chapter 3

The Specter of Davos

In his famous novel, Thomas Mann called it "the magic mountain." A curious magic: actually, the air of the high summits is lethal to the men of the plains below. At the time where the writer set his tale, Davos was famous for its sanatorium. Yet, already, the small village of Grisons was attracting the high society of all Europe. Today, Davos is a winter sports resort. A Swiss tourist bureau brochure suggests that Davos preserves all its "winter magic," worthy of "important guests" who, as a result of globalization, now come from all over the world. Her celebrity owes less now to her snow-covered slopes than to the "World Economic Forum" which has been held there annually since 1971. The air is equally harmful to those hardy visitors who arrive there with visions of old Europe, only to depart converted into pure liberals.

Every winter, between two ski slopes, the participants of Davos can dream of a "capitalism in its pure state," removed from the debris of official regulations and the wage demands that they will inevitably find upon their return home. Seen from the Swiss mountains, which stubbornly abstain from European construction, Europe is nothing more than a battle lost before it has begun. What good is it if it cannot provide anything that the European states do not already have, in excess? For the apostles of Davos, governments play a secondary, if not redundant, role. A European government would be somewhat superfluous. Isn't the economy global in scope, and doesn't it ignore borders? Aren't the barriers that States put up absurd at a time when capital circulates freely and causes labor to move to where profitability is the best, not where people live? Then what is the point in building Europe?

In Davos, liberal thought rules the day, and the epic of the market-as-king is underway. From the heights of this new Olympus, each celebrates in his own way, and all proclaim that the people and the States are condemned to adapt if they do not want to be sidelined by history. Of course, that may entail some human breakage and thus some concern. Thus, the organizers are quick to dampen their followers' sometimes-overheated enthusiasm. "The globalization of the economy entered a critical phase," they declared the day before the Forum of 1996. "The growing reaction against its effects threatens to have a very destructive impact on the economic activity and the social stability of many countries. Revolt is not far off."[1] But the warning had a goal: to bring the controversy to the forefront, to convince people that it was impossible to avoid adapting to globalization, and to persuade them that they had more to gain by going along with it than by challenging it.

The light of the mountain peak dazzles more than it enlightens those who reach the summit. It reflects the surface of capitalism; it does not penetrate it to any depth. The litanies heard in Davos repeat the old saws that everyone believes: "Competition from Southeast Asia, with its low wages and its lack of social legislation, causes a massive relocation of employment." "Billions of dollars are circulating around the planet every day looking for the least bit of appreciation." "The amount exceeds the reserves of all the large central banks together." At Davos, they can be sublimely unaware of the strikes paralyzing South Korea (one of the notorious dragons ready to devour the West), and the great demonstrations by the German trade unions, which have kept employers from reconsidering their funding of sick leave. But how is it that the financial crisis that shook the Asian currencies and stock exchanges in 1997-1998, did not manage to shake their certainty? As it did during the October 1987 stock market crisis, the *sang froid* of the Fed and the central banks of the G-7 kept the Asian, Russian and Brazilian crises from transforming into a system-wide crisis with incalculable consequences. But the magnitude of the shock underscored the instability that is inherent in a monetary organization ruled by the market alone, where exchange rate arbitrage inevitably feeds speculation.

Nobody in Davos will take the chance of putting the present into perspective, to see whether the history of capitalism confirms or denies, the great innovation of globalization. It never occurred to any of the organizers to invite the historian of capitalism, Fernand Braudel, during his lifetime. Today, still, such an invitation would seem absurd to them; but he would have had much to teach them and much to bring to us. For worldwide markets and globalization are not all they are cracked up to be. A new phenomenon? Certainly not. Simonde de Sismondi, a Swiss economist and historian from the early 19th century, was already referring to "the whole universe as a market," and "of that part of mankind that trades together and now forms just one market." A few decades later, Karl Marx affirmed that "the tendency to create a worldwide market is encompassed within the concept of capital." Braudel, at the end of his long and meticulous research covering several centuries since the origin of capitalism, is categorical in approach: "There have always been global economies or, at the very least, for a very long time."[2] Not that every person on the planet was involved; "the global economy affects only a fragment of the universe — a piece of the planet economically autonomous, basically self-sufficient, and on which its connections and its exchanges confer a certain organic unity." So it was yesterday as it is today. Although the contemporary world-economy is not exactly the same as it was in centuries past, it still includes only a portion of humanity and excludes from her prosperity — but not her tyranny — whole sub-continents in Africa, South America, Asia, and even at the Russian borders of Europe.

Is globalization, then, a change of scale for this world economy, and does it indicate that the economies are more open to trade? This question launches many controversies. For Paul Hirst and Grahame Thompson, Cambridge professors, the answer is negative: "The high current degree of internationalization of the economy is not unprecedented. In certain respects, the contemporary international economy is *less* open and integrated than the regime that prevailed between 1870 and 1914."[3] That is also true of migratory movements and direct investments. In the 1980s, developing countries attracted less than 20% of foreign capital, compared to 30% at the end of the 1960s.[4] Capital remains, in fact, concentrated in the developed economies, which are already well-supplied — 90% of European investments are directed to them . As for trade, the answer is more complicated. If one compares the percentage (in GDP) of the average of imports and exports in 1996 with 1913, only Japan is less open today than before the First World War: 10% in 1996 against 15.7% 83 years earlier. The European economies, whose trade had strongly contracted during the crisis of the

1930s, regained their former openness and then some: 29.9% against 22.3% for Great Britain, 22.6% against 17.7% for France, and 22.9% to 17.5% for Germany.

Actually, it's all a function of the time frame you look at. In the second half of the 20th century, the economic growth and the increased openness are manifest; however, on the scale of capitalism's long history, the European and Japanese economies merely erased the protectionist consequences of the 1930s. That took a half-century to achieve. *The American economy was the only one of the major economies to experience a change, as the 20th century waned, in its relationship to the global market,* which may explain the fortune of the idea of globalization. Its openness, which hardly exceeded 5% of the GDP before the First World War or after the Second, has doubled today to reach 12.5%. The U.S. economy, long autarchic, has thus gradually become global. In addition, this opening was accompanied by important developments in the structures of the exchanges and by products and geographical areas: The share of raw materials has been reduced considerably compared to a century ago, while that of manufactured goods and services has become heavily predominant. Developing countries thus were marginalized in the new world economy.

However, the appearance of openness in the European economies is misleading. While the economies individually may have become more open, that is by no means true of the European economy as a "bloc." The Americans are not wrong to see this as a "fortress" on whose portals globalization is battering in vain. From 1960 to 1996, the share of imports within the GDP increased from 12.4% to 21.4% for France and from 16.5% to 25.7% for (Western) Germany, and the average within the European Community's economies went from 19.2 to 27.8%. A similar trend holds true among exports: they increase from 14.5% to 23.8% for France and from 19.7% to 29.7% for the average of the Community economies. The bulk of this progress is not due to an overall opening; it takes place exclusively between European countries.

With the rest of the world, non-European exports are absurdly stagnant, measuring 8.6% of the GDP, while imports recede from 9.8 to 8.7%. In thirty years, the European single market has gradually become a reality but, overall, the European economy has remained relatively closed to the outside world. In fact, it is much more closed than it was at the beginning of the century. The result is a true *inversion* of the geographical structure of trade: in the 1950s, two-thirds was directed outside of Europe, in particular toward the countries producing raw materials, and only one-third toward Europe. Trade is now conducted in such a way that two-thirds involves European countries, and is even more highly concentrated between industrialized countries. The developing countries' share fell from 29.5 to 12.8% of the total for imports and 27.4 to 14.2% for exports.

So much for the "globalization" vaunted at Davos. "The world economy is not truly 'global.' The 40,000 multinational firms indexed by the United Nations produce only 8% of the world GDP. Trade, investments and financial flows are concentrated within the triad of Europe, Japan and North America, and this tendency seems likely to continue."[5] Rare are the groups that can be described as worldwide: Ford, Coca-Cola, Sony, Nestle; maybe twenty in all. The true change is not an invisible globalization, but a recombining of the national economies into vast "regional ensembles:" the European Community; NAFTA (the United States, Canada, Mexico); Mercosur (the countries of southern Latin America), and ASEAN (Southeast Asia). The same thing happens every time: the economies within each regional block become increasingly interdependent. Even the bankruptcy of the Asian model, which causes the Asian countries to turn inward, will further reinforce the trend.

The Third-World countries have remained at the outskirts of this evolution, except for some advanced ramparts of liberalism at the borders of Asian Communism. The importance of the latter should not be overestimated, either. The proliferation of products manufactured in Taiwan, Korea or Hong Kong into supermarket chains magnifies the penetration of Asian goods well beyond reality. Imports from these countries, concentrated on popular consumer goods — from the T-shirt to the bicycle — barely represent 1.5% of the internal demand of the European countries. That amounts to 10 times less than intra-European commerce and far behind the competition from Japanese products, which extends to home furnishings and industrial machinery with a strong technological component.[6] The consequence, obviously, is considerable: competition takes place mainly between countries at the same level of development, and thus with comparable wages and social protection. International competition does not exploit the wages of the least developed countries but, rather, it is based on productivity, innovation and education in the three areas of the triad.

Capitalism likes summits; it is the apex of the economy. In this sense, too, Davos suits it well. "Capitalism implies above all a hierarchy, and capitalism sits at the top of that hierarchy, even if it created the hierarchy itself," Braudel wrote. It has always "settled at the strategic points that control the key sectors of accumulation."[7] Between the 16th and 17th centuries, this was "long-distance" maritime trade. In the 19th century it was "big" industry and today it is "high" finance. Capitalism chooses the niche where it is easy to concentrate a considerable mass of capital to be mobilized based on anticipation of a greater profit. Capitalism does not fall into different periods, progressing from merchant to industrialist to financier. It is always all of those at the same time. It is characteristic of capitalism not to be specialized — to go from international trade to stock market speculation, from real estate to international tourism, computers to health care. *Globalization is the essence of capitalism.* It does not exist without that. It gives capitalism the mobility that enables it to get out of a sector as quickly as it went in. The economists speak of "seizing opportunities," common sense sees the hand of the speculator. In fact, without speculation, capitalism would not exist.

Pension funds, which manage the retirement money for employees in the U.S. and Great Britain,[8] are today capitalism's diamond tip, "the highest stage," as Braudel would have said. They inaugurate the new form of financial capital from America, "Labor's capital" — in other words, *financial capital from wages.* On the ground floor are the headquarters of the corporate networks, the "head offices" that mobilize the resources of the myriad companies that they control and of which they manage the economic activity. Twenty years ago, "big companies" would have been embodied in towers bearing their names, and the general management would have occupied the highest floors. The manager was a king in his empire, as it was defined in those days. Cash flow was the only law in firms that developed by internal growth. It ensured the self-financing of investments, and if it was deemed necessary to look for external capital, the firm simply went to the bank. Europe followed suit, more or less, but preserved its own characteristics of financing, dependent on the State in France and Italy, and the banks in Germany. It seemed as though nothing could shake up this organization, called "the Industrial State" (J. Galbraith) and "the managers' era" (P. Drucker), and written up so prolifically by American authors. The shareholders were relegated to the background, and the heirs of Carnegie, Rockefeller and other empire builders were reduced to the role of philanthropists.

Change came when there was an abrupt shift in the balance of power between the shareholders and management. Rising interest rates, caused by the dollar crisis and inflation, set the ball rolling. By sharply increasing the cost of credit, it forced the companies to look to the stock exchange to find new capital. However, after a fifteen-year lull, the stock markets at the beginning of the 1980s were particularly attractive, bringing the financial markets back into favor. This reversed companies' development strategies. After the internal growth of "the Glorious Thirty" (the post-War boom years), external growth was spurred by the practice of buying up competitors' market share. This resulted in a wave of corporate buyouts and mergers with Wall Street serving as midwife. It was, briefly, the reign of giant takeovers and junk bonds — debt issued by predatory companies to finance the purchase of their prey — a realm of dubious (because it was highly speculative) debt, offering hopes of huge returns based on the undercapitalization of the companies and not on their intrinsic value. Grand Metropolitan's raid on Pillsbury, Philip Morris' against Kraft, KKR against RJR-Nabisco — each for sums amounting to several billion dollars, filled the headlines. During these years, takeovers exceeded the rate at which new shares were issued and caused a demand for securities, which sent the stock exchange to a new high. Speculation was the sovereign of Wall Street.

In a few years, power changed hands. Managers, once all-powerful, were now relegated to the lower levels (of capitalism), and the financiers moved in. Profitability became the watchword. The goals of the designated operatives were motivated by financial reorganization — "thinning" the payrolls, starting with middle management; "wage compression," except for those of the new leaders, which reached new heights; "cuts" in businesses to keep only the most profitable The "big corporation" was cut up and parceled out into a variety of "profit centers," as far as the division of labor and the developing communication technology allowed. The majority of non-financial investments was devoted to this "rationalization." The office towers, a symbol of the previous age, were emptied, creating an unprecedented real estate crisis. The era of the managers was over; the *third age of capitalism* had begun.

The rise toward the summit of the "magic mountain" leaves no one untouched. The employee, whose retirement is managed by pension funds, is dispossessed of his earnings. For a promise of higher returns, he puts his holdings into someone else's hands. On its way up, this money is metamorphosed into "pure capital," money becoming money whose only goal is its own growth as capital, property of an anonymous capitalism that takes charge of maximizing its value, the source of the promised returns. This is not a new phenomenon. Since the end of the 19th century, public companies have dissociated the holder of the funds from the process of enhancing their capital value. But Davos is located at another height altogether. Compared to the shareholders' hilltops, it is the Himalayas. The public company, which replaced purely family capital, had mobilized all the capital that was available for savings. Nonetheless it remained captive to the fraction of savings directed toward the stock exchange, which is strongly dependent on corporate profits. The pension funds break this barrier. They uncouple the accumulation of capital funds from profits and tie it directly to wages and salaries. Now, the only limit is the level of the wages, the proportion of employees covered by retirement funds and the percentage withheld to finance the pensions. In effect, from now on, the realm of capital has no limit but wage policies.

And yet, the trade unionists are told to keep out. These employees have given up all rights over the sums they contribute to the pension funds. American teachers have no more say over how their fund (TIAA-CREF) is managed than do California civil servants or Scottish widows. The contribution is established by collective agreement; how the fund is managed is not. Fund managers do not have to answer to the employees; they make their own decisions.[9] To this group, the Alpine universe of Davos is fatal. Like Hans Castorp, Thomas Mann's hero, the employee must accept that he is "leaving behind him the world of trees with leaves, and probably songbirds; and this thought of suspension, of impoverishment, seized him with giddiness and a light nausea, so that for two seconds he covered his eyes with his hand." When he reopens them, the money that he worked so hard to earn with his labor will have disappeared from view. The idea of invisible management of the contributed sums is incongruous. The doctors of Davos handle everything, in the interest of their greater profit and, incidentally, the good health of the pensioners.

Under full deregulation, liberal capitalism now thrives in its homeland only on the basis of contractual saving, imposed by the collective conventions that govern American workers' employment contracts. While the habitués of Davos swear by "less government," the pension funds owe their takeoff to the very specific protection granted them by the American Congress. In 1974, Congress passed the so-called ERISA law (Employee Retirement Income Security Act), which strictly regulates the management of these funds in order to guarantee the commitments entered into as regards to payment of the retirement benefits. This security provision supported their growth. From 1980 to 1993, the share of capital that is centralized by pension funds doubled in the United States, going from 34.6 to 68% of the GDP. The American funds alone represent three quarters of the sums thus collected worldwide. The English funds, second in size with 15% of the world's assets, also experienced exponential growth, going from 28 to 73% in the same period. Moreover, unlike the German or French pension funds, they are up to 46% invested in stock for the U.S., 63% for the British; thus they constitute the principal shareholders of the companies listed on the stock exchange. To escape the rigors of regulation, financiers created mutual funds, which have sky-rocketed: from $134 billion in 1980 to $2.6 trillion in 1995 (or 60% of the assets in pension funds).[10]

These funds are far from being masters of the universe: their internationalization is both recent and weak, hardly more than 5% of managed assets. And, if some French or German companies are targeted, they are few. In this the degree of change depends on the time frame considered. Compared to the mode of corporate organization and management of the years that accompanied the growth of the "Glorious Thirty," the pension funds mark a rupture. But put in perspective from the historical point of view, they represent a return to the practice of financial capitalism at the end of the 19th century. In fact, they broaden its scope by investing wages and transforming part of them into capital.

Labor's capital entails three consequences. First, unlike the traditional shareholder, who is isolated and solitary and who submit to the general movement of the stock exchange, labor's capital leads the market due to the size and the regularity of the sums that it controls. These sums cause a continuous growth in share prices, which in turn enhances the value of the sums invested. In the second place, it exerts the *global* financial constraint of maximizing company profits, as a result of the obligations imposed by ERISA. This places constant downward pressure on wages, through lower rates of pay and fewer benefits, as well as staff reductions (the sadly celebrated "downsizing"). Fund managers have no need to involve themselves in defining strategies or in questions of internal organization to be heard. The threat of a massive disengagement of the capital is enough to make the managers keep an eye on results, if they do not want a brutal wake-up call. Thirdly and lastly, the need to make a certain amount of pension payments every month makes them more demanding of dividend payments, whereas traditional shareholders can place their bets on the middle or the long term. Consequently, external growth has become, to corporate management, what internal growth was in "the era of the managers": a source of legitimacy.

Internationalization and globalization live in the realm of the circulation of goods and money, where the major changes, those which lie at the heart of the productive process, are invisible. Once again, as at the end of the 19th century, the circulation of capital claims to dictate its law to labor. Adam Smith was the first to draw attention to the link that exists between trade and division of the labor. Smith observed that, while the division of the labor creates wealth, it is nothing but "the necessary consequence . . . of the tendency that leads (men) to traffic, to barter and exchange one thing for another."[11] Nevermind that the nature of the correlation between trade and the division of labor remains debatable. What is important here is that the dismantling of the work process, the effects of which Smith observed at the beginning of the 19th century in a straight-pin factory, improved the comparative advantage that England derived from its labor and allowed her to become an exporter of pins. The division of labor led, shortly, to an explosion in manufacturing and a reorganization of production, with companies subcontracting certain parts of the manufacturing to others. But the whole process remained a national affair with no effect other than improved competitiveness for trade outside the country. With the help of concentration, "national champions" appeared which, having become leaders in their sectors, went off to conquer the world, or at least its markets. This was the time when "what was good for General Motors was good for America."

The tale has been told many times. To avoid repeating the experience, let us simply join Robert Reich,[12] who was a Harvard professor before becoming Labor Secretary under President Clinton, in saying that this era is over, and we must focus on today's situation: companies organized as "networks," crossing borders. The process that got us here is secular. Contrary to the utopias of the 1970s, the crisis of Taylorism did not lead to a recombining of work. On the contrary, it gave birth to an even more thorough division of the labor. This conforms to the same principle that Smith identified in the manufacture of pins ("to reduce each man's task to some very simple operation and make this operation the sole occupation of his life") and in which Marx saw the engine of his "relative appreciation" — the art of earning more profit without paying less wages: "to produce the virtuosity of the worker in detail by reproducing and by pushing to the extreme the separation of the trades, to tighten the pores of the working day by devoting it to one continuous operation."

The engineer F. W. Taylor was not satisfied to systematize this principle, as is generally believed. He made a qualitative jump: he took away from the workman "the choice of how to perform each element of the work, unconsciously learned by observation," and entrusted it to "a scientific department" that would prepare the work "so higher levels of output and quality could be achieved."[13] However, transmitting the instructions still required human intervention. Mechanization, then automation (foreseen by Marx), then the creation of the assembly line by Henry Ford, reduced that in part. But no one imagined that human thought could be transmitted other than orally or in writing. A real revolution was at hand. However, until these last decades, it remained unthinkable.

The nature of the revolution? To replace man with a machine. After human strength and the virtuosity of his movements, it is his word, his communication, that is seized by matter, transformed into machine attributes, reduced to instructions that can be reproduced indefinitely without the least human intervention. Now it is not only the workman who is expelled from the process of work; it is also the supervisor and the foreman — all whose functions consist of regulating, overseeing and control. The need for the hierarchical organization disappears when there is no longer a need for human transmission of commands. The implementation of the most complex tasks can be completely entrusted to the computer and can be decentralized, while still being thought out, organized and supervised in a centralized way. With computing and telecommunications, intelligence not only becomes "matter acting on matter," it is converted into goods. After having successively invested in land, currency and labor, "elements which are not produced for sale" and which, however, "function as commodities,"[14] capitalism has now extended its influence, and its empire, to human intelligence. The digital revolution made possible this ultimate "takeover." But it is the market that gives him its (unfortunately) revolutionary scope and transforms our societies into an "information society."

A new organization of work consequently becomes possible, combining and furthering, to an unknown degree, the twofold principle of dividing and recombining tasks. It integrates what Marx could only have smelled in the air: the expulsion of human effort from the process of management itself. The goal is always the same: to make each part of the chain of work — however small it may be — as productive as possible. Some tasks that used to be closely tied to production — adjusting the machines, moving the parts, passing along orders, monitoring the workers — are controlled by computer and are carried out by robots; others are isolated and given to specialized services or outsourced to other companies. Major enterprises, which separated different trades but integrated them under one roof, have broken up into a multitude of companies. Now, the head office will, at best, control their capital, and at worst it will reduce them to the state of suppliers or subcontractors, imposing its own conditions of price and output. Today, a car manufacturer controls only the design, assembly and marketing of the vehicle. But the new model is designed, tested and prefabricated virtually on computer. The various elements used in actual production are out-sourced. Seventy percent of the parts used in the construction of a vehicle are produced by subcontractors and suppliers: Renault uses more than 500 subcontractors, 75% of them concentrated in France and 99% within Europe. Sometimes, subcontracting is even conducted by subsidiaries shared with manufacturers that are otherwise direct competitors — for example, engines, gear boxes, transmissions, and semiconductors.

No branch of industry escapes it, whether traditional — textiles, cars, petrochemicals — or more recent — electronics, computing. Service industries that tie in with this fragmentation of the process of production are also affected. They are automated, only to be recomposed on a compartmental basis. Know-how is "confiscated" in management software; activities that corporate management used to consider strategic and confidential, such as accounting, are standardized and can be completely out-sourced. This results in greater "professionalization" of each unit of production, whose return depends directly on the economies of scale that it allows. This requires a certain volume of production, which results in companies serving wider and wider geographical areas from one base. In politically fragmented spaces like Europe or Southeast Asia, this reorganization, which takes advantage of the borders, implies sizable trade volumes between countries. It is estimated that trade within multinational firms, in the mid-1980s, represented approximately a third of the trade in the manufacturing sector. This phenomenon is most notable in Europe, where it exceeds 40%, and where it contributed significantly to the growth of intra-European trade — twice greater than that attained with the rest of the world.

The firm-as-network did not arise directly from this. It came into being only with the revolution in communications, which made it possible to extend this logic of compartmentalization even further. Transport, with the development of container shipping and aviation, has drastically reduced time and costs; add to that the emergence of telecommunications, which cancels time and space. The deregulation of these latter, agreed within the WTO under pressure from America in February 1997, should accelerate the drop in prices. Geographical fragmentation, which started the so often denounced trend of relocating, is the consequence. Actually, the developed countries are both the first victims and the principal beneficiaries of a trend that remains internal to them. Automobile production is typical; it is still monopolized by the industrialized countries. Among American manufacturers, production is split between a little more than 50% in North America and one-third in Europe; for the Japanese, the ratio is about two-thirds in Japan, a little less than a third in North America, and a few percent in Europe. In both cases, production corresponds approximately to the sales distribution of each. European manufacturers produce between 85 and 98% in Europe and sell between 70 to 85% of their vehicles in Europe, with two exceptions. Volkswagen and Fiat produce and sell only about 60 to 70% in Europe, and are more established in Eastern Europe and Latin America. The world economy (in terms of automobiles) remains very much an economy of the triad of industrialized countries, and each one remains deep-rooted in its country of origin.

Consequently, cooperation becomes a *sine qua non* of competitiveness. Competitiveness is now based not on wages, but on the ability to mobilize the entire "company-network." The smallest error, the least defect or lack of coordination, can compromise a good production run. A routing error, for example, brings down the whole organization running on just-in-time distribution, which aims to eliminate inventories whose costs are just as high as interest rates. The firm must thus categorize its profits by relating them to the risks incurred. Telecommunications cancel space and time, but not travel (or the transfer of funds). If travel is too random, it becomes counterproductive. Profits must also be gauged against overall costs. The less reliance there is on direct labor, especially the unskilled, the more marginal wage cost becomes. The search for "zero defects" demands a lot of the employees and encourages further professionalization.

Complexity, as Edgar Morin would say, generates new "comparative advantages" founded on the capacity to articulate a segmented process. This becomes the supreme competence, that which qualifies corporate leaders and distinguishes the management. Bringing together "professionals" and combining their skills become the decisive factors of competitiveness. Woe to him who has no skill. Where once he would have been able to do everything, in today's world, he is useless. Unemployment and rejection are his lot. As for the low-wage countries, they find a place in the vacant interstices of complexity. The transfer of certain segments of activity, like the relocation of reservations management or invoicing services to India, is sometimes spectacular, but it relates to only a small, non-strategic part of the business. Many plant relocations will have proven to be only an intermediate stage in the recombining that is under way, and which proceeds principally *within* each area of the triad.

This era has ended. The marginalization of direct costs, under the effect of new technological breakthroughs, changes the perception of the spatial organization of production. The sectors that most symbolize manufacturing relocations — electronics, the apparel industry, etc. — are beginning to return as robotization makes headway.[15] Thus, in the textile sectors of household linens, upholstery fabrics and automotive fabrics, Germany, in spite of its high wages, has remained the leading worldwide exporter. Germany even surpasses Italy, which still does well thanks to its design capability. These two alone cover 20% of world exports. With 40% of global exports, the whole of Europe is far ahead of Southeast Asia, which has approximately 25%. The light of Davos blinds us to the essence. Contrary to the generally accepted view, the recombining of work has not been mostly to the benefit of

Southeast Asia and the low wage countries. Of the more than 3 million unemployed in France, nearly 300,000[16] are due to trade with the low-wage countries, a figure that economists agree is a maximum. This result should not astonish economists, who know that wage costs are meaningless if they are not related to the productivity of labor. In fact, this ratio is favorable to the developed countries. Their high productivity (of labor, and of all the factors of production) compensates for their high wages, and a broad competitive advantage ensures them, except for some segments of production (which are liable to be moved) where the level of productivity remains low.

Once again, we should repeat: let's stop confusing low wages with productivity, and cease giving fiscal encouragement to unskilled workers instead of providing skills to the workers who lack them and preparing them to work with the most modern equipment. The challenge facing Europe is technological. Moreover, it shows how large a gap exists between the growth rate of the telecommunication and computing industries on both sides of the Atlantic: 2.4% in Europe to 9.3% in the United States, involving a deficit of more than one million jobs.[17] Any technological revolution involves job destruction and job creation, but it also transforms what people must do to acquire skills. It does not drive out employment, only unskilled employment, which does not correspond to any "profession," however low the skill level may be. Driven out of agriculture, today unskilled labor is expelled from industry and migrates toward the service sector, which offers lower wages. But at the same time, the recombining of work processes is accompanied by the creation of high-skilled jobs.

Thus, of 7.8 million net jobs created in the United States from 1989 to 1995[18], two-thirds are high-pay jobs for managerial staff in the service sector (private and public) and a third are sales positions or low-pay service jobs. Company investments in computing, which doubled during this period (whereas purchases of other capital equipment increased only by 37%) alone created 400,000 jobs. In spite of weak job creation, the same phenomenon can be observed in Europe: fewer jobs for physical laborers, more for employees in sales and services, and still more in the intellectual professions and at the executive level. As computers become more widespread, jobs that require no training will become increasingly scarce. In other words, the unemployment that plagues the unskilled workers is not so much the result of overly high wage costs or overly rigid labor markets relative to Western Europe's high level of productivity, but of a wide-ranging professionalization of employment, even for the least qualified, which drives out the employees with the least training. And they are proportionally more numerous in France, and no doubt in Europe, than in the United States, due to the late transition to compulsory secondary education.[19]

Is this the end of work? The American economist Jeremy Rifkin proclaimed it so.[20] The French philosopher Dominique Meda ponders "a value in the process of disappearing."[21] Both are mistaken, as fear of technology-based unemployment is not new. In the last century, the silk workers of Lyon revolted against the introduction of the weaving looms which "ate" their work. Technology has always abolished employment on a large scale, starting with agriculture, which it literally decimated. At the same time, it never ceases to create employment, also on a large scale. If this idea is in itself accepted, then shouldn't we produce machines that replace men? Doesn't the scale tip heavily? If the changes in employment were only negative, it would be indisputable. But then the consumer goods that have appeared since the last century, and that are so much a part of our daily life, would not exist.

Capitalism would instead have its head in the stars — thanks to the launching of satellites — but its feet in the pasture, as in the Middle Ages. Most of the peasants driven out of their fields did not find work in the agricultural machinery factories. They went to the automobile assembly lines, which they had never heard of before. Others, in great number, became teachers or policemen. Technology "poured out" (to use Alfred Sauvy's expression) the jobs it destroyed into the new activities which it created. Labor did not disappear; it emigrated to previously unknown lands that have, in one century, revolutionized our daily life. Are we sure that this trend is over? When one sees the high hopes capitalism pins on the development of personal computing, the Internet and new multimedia accessories, one has every right to doubt it. Moreover, this sector is not the only one to generate new employment. Travel became an industry unto itself in just two decades — the first global industry. And the health sector could soon double that of education, which for a century has accompanied technical progress.

Thus goes the market. It is not acting on Europe from the outside, on the pretext of some globalizing effect that we cannot resist without giving up our values. It operates internally and primarily inside of the individual and our social structures. The market seizes man's body and spirit. It changes his relations with individuals and with society according to the immutable logic of the monetary principle of self-regulation, which claims to dominate everything since it is self-sufficient. What good are rights, institutions and states that protect the individual if the market takes their place? Such is the new misunderstanding that the construction of Europe must introduce. How can we create new institutions, how can we ensure a European right of the individual, how can we conceive a freedom that is not merely the freedom of circulation proclaimed in the Treaty of Rome, that could stand as our defense against the market? Europe does not have to adapt to the world market, as firms must do; it has to define man's place in this new world. It must design suitable European ways of organizing life together, to find out whether the market is his new sovereign or if, faithful to that "spirit" which since the time of Athens has been shaping "European man," his goal still is to be the master of his destiny.

The answer does not lie in the winter magic of Davos. Mann's novel is not only about self-recognition; it is about the cultural disintegration of the era, which led to two world wars with Europe as the epicenter. Castorp believed he had reached freedom by removing himself from the real world. But the war has reduced his freedom to nothing and brought our hero back into the world of the living, and precipitated him onto the battlefield. If those who hold the responsibility to lead societies believe they can find the solution by escaping from the realities of the "flat country," they are preparing for us the same tragic destiny. The new novel of Davos is not only that of the annual lessons on liberalism that are given there every year; we should also read the account of social disintegration under the battering ram of the market. There is just time enough to drive out the shadows of the *magic mountain* and create Europe "from below." This construction, such as it is, will be with us for a long time. Does it correspond to that which it "could be," — that is, to the highest aspirations of Europeans?

Notes

1. Klaus Schwab and Claude Smadja, *International Herald Tribune*, February 1, 1996.
2. Fernand Braudel, *Le Temps du monde*, *op. cit.*, p. 12.
3. Paul Hirst and Grahame Thompson, *Globalization in Question*, Polity Press, Cambridge, Blackwell Publishers, 1996, p. 2.
4. François Chesnais, *La Globalisation du capital*, Paris, Syros, 1994, p. 49.
5. Paul Hirst and Grahame Thompson, *op. cit.*, p. 2.
6. RAMSES - 1995, *Synthèse annuelle de l'économie mondiale*, Paris, Dunod.
7. Fernand Braudel, *op. cit.*, pp. 50-51.
8. In particular in the United States, where retirements are collectively underwritten by corporations for their employees through private fund management organizations.
9. Michel Aglietta had already underlined this point in *Régulation et crise du capitalisme*, Paris, Calmann-Lévy, 1976.
10. Richard Farnetti, "*Le rôle des fonds de pension dans l'essor de la finance globale*," François Chesnais, *La Mondialisation financière*, Paris, Syros, 1996.
11. Adam Smith, *Recherches sur la nature et les causes de la richesse des nations*, Paris, Gallimard, coll. "Idées," 1976, p. 47.
12. Robert Reich, *L'Economie mondialisée*, Paris, Dunod, 1996.
13. Frederic Winslow Taylor, *La Direction scientifique des entreprises*, Paris, Marabout service, 1967.
14. Karl Polanyi, *La Grande transformation*, Paris, Gallimard, 1983, p. 107.
15. A Belgian industrialist relocated his tee-shirt factory to Roubaix when he realized that it took him seven minutes to produce a shirt in India as against only two minutes in Europe. "What I gain in India thanks to a cheap labor, I lose elsewhere (in productivity, quality, tasks that are still performed manually in India, slow communication, transport time...)," in *Libération*, February 20, 1997.
16. Claude Vimont, *Le Commerce extérieur créateur ou destructeur d'emplois*, Paris, Economica, 1993.
17. Study carried out by the office of Booz-Allen and Hamilton, cited in *Le Monde*, February 4, 1997.
18. US Bureau of Labor Statistics, Monthly labor review, June 1996.
19. Arnaud Lefranc, "Quelques éléments de comparaison des taux de chomage français et américain," *Economie et statistique*, February 1997.
20. Jéremy Rifkin, *La Fin du travail*, Preface by Michel Rocard, Paris, La Découverte, 1996.
21. Domenica Meda, *Le Travail, une valeur en voie de disparition*, Paris, Aubier, 1996.

CIVIL LIBERTIES, WITHOUT CITIZENS

Chapter 4

The Right to Sell, as a Doctrine

March 20, 1996: Standing before the House of Commons, Stephen Dorrell, Her Gracious Majesty's Health Secretary, solemnly announced that the microbe responsible for "mad cow disease" was, apparently, being transmitted to humans. On the same day, the Minister for Agriculture, Douglas Hogg, made public the report drawn up by the renowned London Medical School showing the relationship between bovine spongiform encephalopathy (BSE) and Creutzfeldt-Jakob disease. Thus, the British government made the news public, after keeping it quiet for more than ten years. What inspired it to take this step? Was it a sudden concern for public health, fear of scandal, or a desire to make Europe contribute to the massive and inevitable destruction of British livestock? Before the question could even be raised, all of Europe was trembling.

In a few weeks, the "mad cow" crisis became a cataclysm. The market collapsed, consumption and exports outside of Europe plummeted, tripe was prohibited. . . the meat industry was badly hurt. But despite its magnitude and its cost to European taxpayers, it was not this aspect of the problem that had Europe quaking. The Commission's embargo on British livestock was not enough to escape the storm and an investigation from the European Parliament. The biggest concern was that the storm that shook the European Union raised questions about European construction itself: giving freedom of movement primacy over public health, and professional lobbyists primacy over the definition of health policies; the tendency to keep things under cover and the confusion over responsibilities within the Commission; the lack of control of national veterinary services and the privatization of the British services.

From the first day, the Commission and the national governments tried to circumscribe the crisis and to play it down. They stood in the way of any threat to European construction, and more specifically to the Commission's great task that is the achievement of the "single market." For how can we dissociate the genesis of this crisis from the implementation of the "Single European Act?" The flashback is too cruel. While the governments adopted and signed the treaty creating the "single market" in spring 1986, the first cases of BSE were diagnosed in November of that same year. A few months later, while the parliamentary debate over ratification were going on, to the general indifference of the public, the transmission of the disease to humans, for the first time, began to seem likely. Thus, in the shadow of the Single Act, which the centrist Jean-Louis Bourlanges had described as a "miraculous moment" and the Socialist Jean-Pierre Cot called, "the zenith of European construction," a nightmare was unfolding. For the national and European leaders, it was necessary at all costs to keep the "mad cow disease" crisis from re-opening the Treaty of Rome.

Yet, how can we not open it? How can we not raise questions about a treaty that, in the name of freedom, sabotages the first "security," life itself? One day we are looking at "mad cows," the next day we see convoys of waste being hauled across Europe. Every European initiative seems to bring its own shocks: the freedom of broadcasting television programs damages cultures; the deregulation of the public services hinder equal access by every citizens; the freedom of service provisions counters the right to work. The "mad cow disease" crisis is by no means one specific dysfunction of the European institutions. Jacques Delors, who chaired the Commission during these ten years, is not wrong in saying that they only implemented the agreed texts, and that the Commission could not be held liable for negligence. But the claim that they were not responsible is worrying, in itself.

Few can dispute that if Europe wants to be a single space, then circulation must be unfettered by borders and national regulations, and protective measures must not stand in the way. That is how national markets are formed. The Treaty of Rome posed the principle of free circulation: freedom of movement of goods, services, capital and people. "Four freedoms" that work together as one and control all the Community actions. Its object being limited to the creation of a common market, the freedom of circulation made good sense. The Single Act has no other objective but to apply this in an integrated fashion. But how could the governments, which have changed hands many times in 30 years throughout the Community, think that these "four freedoms" contained *all* freedoms? This confusion is the source of a profound misunderstanding.

Furthermore, shouldn't we ask whether everything that circulates is actually part of the market? If Europe wanted to be faithful to the tradition of human rights, the answer would have to be "no." Man, his ideas and culture have a purpose different from trade. The question arose very early in European construction. The Italian government confronted the Commission in 1968, in connection with a law relating to the protection of artworks. The Italians maintained that the rules of the Treaty of Rome applied only to everyday usage or consumer goods, not to goods that were not the product of a commercial intention, such as works of art. In accord with the Commission's position, the European Court of Justice, sovereign authority on the interpretation of the texts, disagreed. The term "merchandise," says the judgment of December 1968, "applies to goods that are appreciable in monetary terms and are likely, as such, to be the basis of commercial transactions." That the primary purpose of artistic creation is not trade, that the quality of a work is appreciated differently than in monetary terms, doesn't count for much. If it might form the basis of a commercial transaction, then it is reduced to the level of merchandise and subject to the laws that govern its free circulation, excepting for "imperative requirements of the general interest" (Article 36). The principle being clear, the Commission could only decline the Italians' request. For thirty years since it has applied the rule methodically and consistently, with the vigilant support of the Court of Justice. Let us look at some examples to determine its outcome.

First, let us consider waste. The convoys of German nuclear waste, on their way to be treated at the French center in the Hague, and from there back to Germany for storage in Gorleben, have been the target of public demonstrations that constantly make the news. Other convoys, smaller but just as harmful, transport industrial and hospital waste. Until recently, nothing has stopped them. However, the Community has been concerned about this question since the 1970s, well before the environment became Community policy with the Single Act. In 1975, a first European directive regulated the disposal of spent oils; in 1984, a second was applied to the monitoring of trans-border transfers of hazardous waste; in 1987, it was the Court of Justice's turn to make a judgment on the disposal of animal wastes. In all three cases, the Community intervention was concerned only with the same economic problem, namely the circulation of waste at the time of their "elimination." At the time the Commission was not empowered to protect the environment; but everything that crosses a border inside Europe is within its jurisdiction. Anything that relates to "borders" relates to "free circulation."[1]

First, we should question whether or not waste is merchandise. *A priori*, no. It is not "produced" for the purpose of being sold; it is the refuse left over from human activity. But insofar as its disposal requires suitable storage processes, recycling or destruction, it causes monetary transactions to take place. At that point it acquires the status of merchandise. That is what the European Court of Justice ruled on several occasions.[2] Consequently, the provisions relating to freedom of circulation are applicable, and thus it becomes impossible to protect oneself from other countries' waste. Thus, a state that obliges its own nationals to dispose of or to recycle the wastes that they produce has no right to prohibit the entry onto its territory of waste coming from countries less concerned with environmental protection. Worse, the development of treatment plants effectively becomes a gravitational force, and the country is likely to become its neighbors' "garbage dump." It cannot force them to set up equivalent installations, even if transporting the waste presents mortal danger for human life and the environment, as is the case with nuclear power.

The Directive of 1975 had ignited a hope: it made the required allowance of intra-Community trade "secondary to the objective of environmental protection." However, it was implemented in a way that contradicted the intention: "What won out was the concern for avoiding any partitioning of the markets, rather than any concern for ecology."[3] The 1984 Directive confirmed this commercial interpretation. It allows exceptions only for hazardous waste, whose traffic endangers the environment and health on the one hand, and public order and security on the other. But the Commission, supported by the Court of Justice, always looked with suspicion on the exceptions presented by the states. Even nuclear waste had no special status, in their eyes. It made no difference that a chapter on the environment was introduced into the Single Act, based on the principles of "prevention and correction, primarily at the source, of attacks on the environment, and of the pollutant-payer." Freedom of movement took precedence over protection of the populace.

A judgment made in July 1992 is proof. The European Court reaffirmed, against the Belgian government, that any waste constitutes merchandise and that, consequently, the Treaty did not permit any prohibition on depositing foreign waste on one's own territory. The decision was justified on the basis that the Court felt it had to anticipate the future economy of waste treatment. In fact, it considered the distinction between recyclable and non-recyclable waste to be "founded on doubtful elements, likely to change over the course of time with technical progress."[4] Actually, it was looking at economic considerations: allowing for the possibility that things that are not recycled today, for reasons of profitability, may become recyclable tomorrow when costs can be brought down or financial incentives are put in place. It didn't matter that this jurisprudence contradicted the environmental policies of the member states as well as the Commission: the Court is sovereign and its judgments apply directly to the states. A directive cannot change the principles of the Treaty of Rome, except by revising the Treaty to amend the aforementioned principles. But nobody ever proposed that. The freedom of circulation takes precedence over any other consideration.

The absurdity of these doctrines flies in the face of the objectives tied to environmental policy. In a presentation to the European Parliament in January 1989, when his mandate as head of the Commission was being renewed, Delors stated the priorities on this matter: "safeguarding the ozone layer, the greenhouse effect, regulation of toxic waste and fighting against tropical deforestation."[5] By autumn of the same year, the Commission had translated its "waste" policy into a few operational principles: to prevent the creation of waste, to take care that those produced be re-used and, in the event that re-use is impossible, that they be disposed of according to ecologically acceptable methods. Moreover, the Commission asked that wastes be required to be treated at the nearest plant, and accepted restrictions on the transportation of those waste shipments that would not be handled at the closest treatment plants. At the end of 1989, as part of the Lome IV Convention, the Commission and the member states signed with the ACP (Africa-Caribbean-Pacific) states an agreement prohibiting "any direct or indirect export of waste from the Community to these countries." The result: the Third World would not be Europe's garbage dump. But Belgium and France could be their neighbors'!

The member states were subject to two international agreements — the International Convention of Basle, from March 1989, and the decision/recommendation of the OECD in January 1991, obliging states to minimize waste production, to limit the cross-border transport and to ensure the self-sufficiency of their disposal. Then a new directive came, on March 18, 1991, to consolidate the provisions. Given the reservations and delays brought by certain member states to adopt this text, the Commission had the Council of Ministers transform it into a regulation, a provision more constraining since it applies directly to the states. However, its goal was by no means to support an environmental policy. It aimed to strictly limit the Community's scope to only intra-Community traffic, by excluding the internal traffic within the member states. Since this procedure left them out of any discussion, the European Parliament highly denounced both the method and its finality. The Commission paid little attention.

Thus, what is valid between the countries is not valid within each one of them. Firms are required to dispose of the waste that they produce, but they are free to choose the method: to implement nonpolluting techniques or to dispose of the waste produced — if need be, by having them treated abroad. The decision will be based on profitability alone, and environmental policy will give way. As for the citizens, they can still protest by lying in the road, as they did at Gorleben, to try to stop convoys that plow across Europe in every direction, laden with cargoes, one more hazardous than the next.

Foodstuffs offer another example of how policies have been misconstrued in connection with health. For thirty years, the Commission has been putting out more and more regulations relative to food products: banning or authorizing preservatives, coffee and chicory extracts, products containing cocoa, the manufacture of beer, fruit juice, jams and marmalade. The list is like one of Prévert's poems, only longer and less poetic. It had dozens of European directives, adopted "to harmonize" the manufacturing methods. But its actions were by no means motivated by an interest in gastronomy, consumer protection or public health. As with waste, they arose from the sole principle of "freedom of circulation." The Treaty of Rome gives it the mission of assuring that "national" standards are not obstacles to this freedom, or disguised protection.

The European Court of Justice, too, gave it a free hand. Since 1979, it has used the judgment known as "Dijon Cassis" as a precedent. That conflict pitted the distributor of the famous "Dijon Cassis" against German legislation, which required a minimal alcohol content for a product to be marketed as a fruit liqueur. Since the legal limit was higher than that of the French product, the German law incontestably prohibited the distribution of French fruit liqueurs in Germany. The Court judged, logically, that in the absence of "a valid reason," especially of a medical or tax nature, goods "legally produced and marketed in a member state" must be free to be distributed in any other state. In the absence of a common regulation, the cogency of the national regulations was to thus be allowed. But they could not be applied to imported products.

Another famous event, settled in 1987, had to do with the German law on the purity of German beer. The Court denied that beers produced under given conditions and incorporating different elements could be prohibited from being marketed in Germany under the name of beer. The court judged, not without reason, that consumer protection, invoked on the German side, was not the question and could be ensured by other means, such as by providing objective information on the contents and the manufacturing methods.

In these affairs, writes Professor Molinier, the Community authorities sought to avoid allowing "one state's legislation to crystallize its consumers' habits and to preserve the advantages acquired by national industries which are adapted to satisfy them."[6] The protectionist intention was often clear, but the European Court's decisions led to a paradoxical result: making two legislations co-exist within the same territory. The states reacted by adding exceptions, sometimes in the name of public health, sometimes for the sake of security or environmental protection. To preserve the free movement of goods, the Commission's only alternative was to work toward eliminating technical barriers, which constitutes one of the aspects of the Single Act.

The adoption of the Treaty known as the Single Act marks a real turning point: From then on, the Commission could impose a single standard for the manufacture of a product on all the member states. Initially, it had planned to bring the industries into alignment, by product (electric lawn mowers) or by family of products (construction machinery). But very quickly, it became clear that it was impossible to carry out this work within the intended timeframe. Therefore, it settled for working out a harmonization limited to the essentials, and left the technical specifications to the organizations. For the industrialists, the Single Act was a gift. What many of them had lost with the Treaty of Rome, through increased competition from imported products manufactured according to standards different from theirs, they sought to regain on this occasion. The effectiveness of the lobbying thus prevailed over consumer protection and quality guarantees. From this point of view, the Single Act is, indeed, as Delors says, "a qualitative leap."[7] But not in the usual sense. The chocolate war proves this without any ambiguity. Should the name "chocolate" be reserved for products based exclusively on cocoa butter, or should it be extended, as groups like Nestle and Cadbury demand, to chocolate products which incorporate up to 5% of other vegetable fat content? In this standardization, where the economic considerations precede, the consumer is the one who loses.

However, while the Single Act confers on the Commission full powers to eliminate national standards, this does not cover "imperative requirements" cited by the Court in connection with the "Dijon Cassis" matter. Public health and the public environment, security and order remain within the national states' jurisdiction. Subsidiarity applies. Thus, products can circulate while being subjected to different health code regulations. This dichotomy creates the same distortions as in the case of waste treatment. Lacking jurisdiction on health and safety matters, the Commission looks askance at these concerns of the national governments. The Commission sees them as attempts to thwart the elimination of national regulations. Also, it creates exceptions in the definition of standards, but each time a state invokes them to prohibit the importation of a product considered to be dangerous, the Commission threatens to lodge a complaint with the Court of Justice. If the State insists, it has to go to court.

The genesis of the "mad cow" crisis must be understood in this context. If, since 1988, following the prohibition of the British government to feed cattle with bone meal, the other governments had been obliged to make, without delay, the same provisions and to destroy any contaminated livestock, the BSE would have died early. Europe would not have experienced a crisis, eight years later, of unprecedented proportions. But at the time, the directive on the production and the marketing of feed had not been written. It dates back only to 1990; it went into effect only in 1992, and the details of implementation concerning the animal meal go back to 1994!

The Commission should have recognized, in the name of "an imperative requirement" for public health, that the member states were well founded to refuse the ground meal entry into their territory. But the opposite occurred. Henri Nallet,[8] then Minister for Agriculture, reports that in August 1989, when the French authorities decided unilaterally to close the British borders to these meals, the Commission threatened France with a suit before the European Court of Justice for obstructing "free" trade. After long negotiations, a minimal compromise was found, specifically comprising a ban only on imports from Great Britain and limited to meat or offal coming from a farm where cases of disease had been observed. Under this provision, the English bovine bone meal remained *prohibited in Great Britain and authorized for export on the continent!*

Since they were legal, exports of bovine meal thus continued normally to flood the continent. Moreover, nobody at the time was agitating to have them banned. When it came up, Philippe Lemaître says, quoting the spokesman of the commissioner in charge of agricultural affairs, "every time, the member states voted against it."[9] Public health, within the jurisdiction of the individual governments, was set aside in favor of the requirements of the free circulation of products, the Community's domain. Fraud took care of the rest — fraud on the English side, as to the origin of the meal, and supported by the fact that the veterinary services are private; fraud on the part of buyers on the Continent, in using as bovine feed the stuff that was bought for feeding pigs and poultry. Moreover, on both sides of the English Channel, the professionals let Brussels know that controls were not within their jurisdiction (in fact, it is hard to see on what basis the Commission would have been able to establish controls, since it does not have jurisdiction in regard to public health). The freedom became the fox's freedom in the hen house.

Were Community authorities very concerned with public health? Since 1974, the Study Committee "For a European Health Program" has been wondering. "Europe," it wrote, "has until now been a matter of trade, finance and investments. It is time she made an effort to seek the quality of life we hear so much about, and especially health considerations, because if there is any form of wealth that the nations of Europe must endeavor to preserve in common, that is it."[10] And yet, health has remained a secondary objective and, notes Maryse Cassan, it makes only a cameo appearance in the Single Act. The European community of health is only that of health professionals, of the drugs and the agro-alimentary products for which we are certain to ensure, ever and always, "freedom of circulation." Brussels defends itself in vain. The facts prove that it continually ignored the defense of public health, although it had the duty "to prevent the propagation of diseases liable to affect citizens' health."[11] Thus, according to the October 9 and 10, 1990, minutes of the standing committee on veterinary affairs, they did not hesitate to recommend "minimizing this BSE affair as an example of misinformation." And to add, "It is better to say that the press tends to exaggerate."[12] An attitude that conforms to the Commission, convinced that putting public health and consumer protection at the forefront is only a pretext to justify setting up barriers to the free movement of goods — in short, an intolerable attack on the single market.

The "mad cow" crisis underscores the paradox of subsidiarity. When it is under fire, the Commission invokes subsidiarity while feigning regret, to justify that it is not legally competent to deal with matters of public health. The rest of the time, the Commission and the Court of Justice assume jurisdiction over everything. They deny member states the right to invoke subsidiarity to protect their citizens, for fear the states only use it to give an advantage to their national industries. Seven years after Henri Nallet, Philippe Vasseur (his successor at the Ministry for Agriculture) reviewed the prohibitions within the Council and as a preventive measure unilaterally declared a general embargo on animal feed made from cattle, sheep and goats. The Commission immediately condemned and threatened France. "The member states," declared the Commission spokesman, "can take more severe measures only with regard to their national producers. They are not entitled to do so, unilaterally, with regard to imported products" (September 13, 1996). The Commission does not deny that preventive measures are necessary, but "they should be taken at the level of the European Union." It may be regrettable that such and such government is against it, but that does not authorize a country unilaterally to protect the health and lives of its citizens against epidemics imported with foreign products. *Thus, a country cannot prevent another member state's laws, or lack of laws, even if they are in contradiction with its own, from applying in its own territory, in effect flouting the concept of sovereignty.*

Can citizens go along with such a concept of Europe? Are we naïve to hope for the priorities to be reversed, placing health before freedom of movement? The Community does not need to have broader jurisdiction in order for health to be defended. What is necessary is that where national jurisdiction is recognized, it should be exercised fully, and questions of intra-Community commerce should not be allowed to limit it or even, as in the "mad cow" crisis, to render it meaningless. Lacking the power to sanction the then president of the Commission, the European Parliament threatened to censure his successor, Jacques Santer. He escaped only by promising to reform the structures of the Commission. But that would not be enough to put Europe on its feet. As long as the treaties that decide who is responsible for health provisions within the European Union are not modified, Europe will be prey to new "tremors."

Public services (utilities) offer a third example of misunderstanding — even more interesting since the Commission was late in getting involved in this area. Public services encompasses the postal services, telecommunications, transport, electricity, gas and water. These activities have a common characteristic: They require *networks*, which are essential to guarantee an adequate correlation between supply and demand, along complex and changing routes. The quality and the extent of the infrastructures are thus indispensable to the effectiveness of these services and the satisfaction of the "user-clients." All of Europe is familiar with public services. The public monopoly, be it a national company or a local or regional authority, is the most widespread form. But public utilities can also be concessions with private firms. In fact, that was the principal form of utilities in France at the beginning of this century, an expression of the radical will to reconcile the principle of equality and the freedom of enterprise (with the support of the Conseil d'État*). In contrast to Germany, where the local public services, distribution of water and heating, were always covered by public controls, in France they were largely privatized and were "conceded" to large corporations that carved out their own territories. But every-

---

*The French Council of State, a body of 200 members, serves as the highest authority to which legal matters may be referred; it is also a consultative body to which bills and rulings are submitted by the government before being sent to the Council of Ministers.

where public utilities meant the same thing: they were *a way of organiz-*
ing an activity to guarantee every citizen equal access at identical prices.

The European authorities do not debate the need for public services, but they apply a completely different definition to these two
words. Let's not get caught up in an artificial semantics quarrel. While
the Treaty of Rome does not expressly use the term "public service,"
apart from the specific case of the provisions relating to the common
policy on transport, it does address the concept. The point is, not all
the countries use the same term. The Anglo-Saxons call them *public
utilities.* The standard provision of the treaty, Article 90, refers to "firms
in charge of managing services with general economic interest." What
is different is that the relationship is inverted between what has traditionally founded the public utility and the market. The utility's mission
of general interest justifies allowing the participating enterprises,
whether public or private, restricted competition — that is the basis
for the formation of monopolies.

The Treaty of Rome reverses this proposition. It poses a principle:
that the public utility enterprises are liable to the rules of competition
and freedom of movement in the provisions of services. It adds a restriction: "The application of these rules should not cause the enterprises to fail to achieve, in principle or in fact, the particular mission
which was assigned to them." In other words, the Treaty acknowledges
that competition cannot be allowed to prevent a state from requiring
an operator to cover all of a territory or from imposing a level rate
schedule. On the other hand, these requirements do not provide for any
sort of monopoly.

For twenty years, the Commission hardly used the full powers
that the Treaty confers it to manage the implementation of the stated
principle and to dismantle the public monopolies. Several reasons explain this relative disinterest: at the time, a very strong consensus
reigned in the member states as to the role of public firms in handling
public services; intra-Community interventions were rare, apart from
transport, which is governed by specific provisions of the Treaty; telecommunications were covered by international agreements that were
considered to be more appropriate; and finally, administering public
services was considered to fall exclusively within the domain of the
member states, all of which held to the principle of equal access to public services for all the citizens, as a guarantee of national cohesion. In

addition, when the Court of Justice judged in 1964 that electricity was indeed "merchandise" (which is obvious, although it remains impossible to inventory), the Court did not draw any conclusion as to the administration of the production and the distribution of electricity. Each state remained free to entrust it to a public monopoly, or not. Liberalism had yet to conquer the governments.

The Commission's attitude changed radically in the early 1980s, for reasons that are ideological, economic and legal. The philosophy of deregulation, which President Carter applied to the U.S sectors of electricity and air transportation and which was systematized under the Reagan presidency, was immediately echoed in Europe by Margaret Thatcher's privatization policy. At same time, in a budgetary context that was increasingly strained, many countries began to debate the administration of public services, its effectiveness and, specifically, how rates are set and how new activities are developed. Lastly, the adoption of the Single Act made it seem more legitimate for the Commission to get involved in sectors from which, until then, it had largely been excluded. It was open season on monopolies.

In a few years, the new schema was in place.[13] In 1980, the Commission adopted a first European Directive on the "financial relations between states and public enterprises," (i.e. government subsidies); in 1982, a complaint by British Telecom led the Commission to make its first incursion into telecommunications sector; in 1984, it intervened in express mail services. From 1985 on, things snowballed. The Commission published a series of "Green Books" on the policy it intended to follow to liberalize the domestic postal markets, energy, transport and telecommunications, and began drafting the corresponding legislation. The dismantling of the public services was under way. No one knows where and when it will stop.

The doctrines of the Commission contain two postulates that reinterpret the Treaty of Rome. *Competition is the rule, and public services are the exception.* Thus, the Commission's policy boils down to eliminating monopolies and strictly limiting the field where state intervention may be considered inevitable. The Court of Justice confirmed these doctrines in two judgments that consolidate the Community legislation. The first, handed down in May 1993 and concerning the monopoly of the Belgian post office, admits "the possibility of balancing profitable and less-profitable sectors of an industry, which would consequently justify limiting competition."[14] But having made this statement, the Court immediately limited its scope, stressing that "the exclusion of competition is not justified when the specific activities in question cannot be dissociated from serving the general economic interest." In other words, while you can't "skim," you can "segment."

The second postulate goes back to April 1994, in connection with the distribution of electric power to a Dutch community.[15] This led the Court of Justice to define for the first time the criteria of "serving the general economic interest:" equal treatment, continuity of service, public transportation. In fact, the Court was satisfied to use the definition given by the Commission, in its 1992 "Green Book" on postal service: a service referred to as "universal," but actually reduced to the minimum. So much for the principle of equality. The general interest was defined ever more narrowly, limited to "a basic service offered to all, throughout the Community, at accessible prices and with a standard level of quality." Another Green Book (on telecommunications) "recommends" that public service do nothing more, or less, than to offer "preferential or subsidized rates to indigent or unprofitable clients." Beyond that, competition is king. Before he became the French Minister of Industry, responsible for public services, Franck Borotra, in a crusade against subsidies, had denounced the tendency to limit the concept of public services to those activities[16] "which can be provided only at a loss" and for which specific public financing must be provided. Once he found himself heading up the Ministry, from 1995 to 1997, he became, like his European colleagues, a zealous propagandist in its favor.

Thus, at a time when the German railroads were divided into one company to handle the infrastructure and one company to take charge of development, the unprofitable secondary lines were transferred to regional administration. Thus companies that wanted to build some particular high-traffic route were relieved of any obligation for developing secondary routes. In the same way, during the liberalization of the French domestic air routes, the competition introduced on profitable lines (Paris-Nice, Paris-Toulouse) was not tied to any obligation to serve the lines with low potential traffic. As a result, if universal service could no longer be financed out of fare equalization, it would have to be financed through subsidies or specific taxes on profitable activities, a solution that the Commission always resisted. Alain Juppé's government ended up going along with this thesis and made an about-face. Instead of integrating the concept of "public utility" into the Constitution, as he had promised during the transportation strikes of December 1995, he wrote "universal service" into the law, while the telecommunications sector was being opened up to competition. Minimum service became the new rule. The result wasn't long in coming. Faced with protests by the local councilors of regions whose air service was threatened by the complete liberalization of the sky, effective as of April 1, 1997, the French government announced that these lines will be "eligible for subsidies" out of the state budget.[17] The Commission wants to prohibit support for public enterprises, but deregulating public services leads to subsidies for private companies. So much for liberalism.

With the adoption of the directive on energy in December 1996, after those on telecommunications and rail transport in 1991, the Commission, in barely ten years, achieved its goals: to break up the public services in Europe, and to abolish the public monopolies that had built the wide-area infrastructure networks. Before the end of the 20th century, the development of these networks would be rocked by competition, and those who had run the utilities would be forced to give access to competitors who never had to invest a cent to build them. The states would retain their prerogatives only over the maintenance and the extension, if necessary, of the infrastructures — in other words, the heavy investments that the private firms were unable to finance, as shown by the resounding financial failure of the Eurotunnel. They would no longer be able to use ticket sales to support the modernization of the networks nor to finance the debt that such a project entailed, which likely would have reduced the volume of investment. As for the citizens, reduced to the state of clients, they would have access only according to their incomes, relegating "the poorest and the least profitable" to organized begging. That is a curious way of defending "the European social model." Unless public charity is the supreme form of solidarity.

The 1993 and 1994 judgments of the Court of Justice by no means mark "a jurisprudence turning point"[18] that would moderate the deregulatory ardor of the Commission, as some in France wanted to believe. They did not give recognition to the legitimacy of public utilities, since that was already incorporated in the legislation since the Treaty of Rome. Resuming the traditional criteria to define the general interest would no longer help to thwart the minimalist conception of universal service as developed by the Commission. On the contrary, the

European Court cemented the legal basis of the deregulation of the public services so dear to the Commission. Borotra could well claim that "more and more countries are taking up the principles of public utility advanced by France." But it is *at the price of a disavowal and a complete inversion of philosophy, reducing a citizen-oriented administrative concept to a simple "safety net" within a commercial service.*

In some cases, it took years of negotiations to have the directives adopted by the member states. But the Commission finally imposed its law, even on those governments that most resisted the deregulation of public services. If need be, as in the case of the European Directive on energy, it did not hesitate to threaten to haul them before the Court of Justice on the pretext of eliminating an obstacle to gas imports. All the resisters were overcome and forced to accept the dismantling of the public monopolies. Some, like EDF [Electricité de France], lent powerful support, before becoming a victim itself. Wishing to force open the doors of neighboring countries to sell its surplus electricity, while retaining its monopoly, the French firm enabled the Commission to obtain a decisive victory over the member states — by making them give up their sovereignty in a domain that heretofore had been uncontested. Now, that is a real jurisprudential "turning point." A policy turning point.

Admittedly, the decision to keep these firms public — or, conversely, to privatize them, as governments were attempting to do, more or less, throughout Europe — was up to the member states. The Treaty of Rome is absolutely clear on this point. It "does not prejudge in any way the ownership structures in the member states" (Article 222). But Leon Brittain, an ardent protagonist of competition, is pleased to note, "in the case of deregulation, the Commission has the right to act."[19] And it did not lack opportunities. However deregulation, associated with the prohibition of subsidies to enterprises, which limits the possible sources of capital investment, makes the public status of the enterprises untenable. Tomorrow, the only activities remaining in the public domain will be those that are "of general economic interest" to be sure, but are operating at a deficit, as well. Public enterprises will no longer be considered a viable alternative form of management. Their employees understand this perfectly, and despite the assurances made to them, have protested against the European directives. But these movements have been too sporadic to stop the steamroller that is the Commission.

The Commission has, besides, sensed the danger of going too far. In the autumn of 1996, without any change as far as its operations, the commission gave out a communiqué on "the services of general interest in Europe"[20] that purported to be a defense and an illustration of "the public services." The Commission recognized that "European societies are attached to the services of general interest which they set up. These services meet fundamental needs. The function they perform, cementing the society together, exceeds the level of material concerns alone. It comprises a symbolic dimension. The general interest services offer the community models and help make up the citizens' sense of membership in the community. Thus, they are an element of the cultural identity of each European country, down to the very gestures of everyday life. Solidarity and equal treatment are the objectives." Who wouldn't subscribe to such a declaration? "Universal" service is supposed to correspond to this mission, even while becoming part of the context of the "creation of the extended market and the introduction of increased competition." Never does the text mention "minimum levels of service," only "flexibility" of the universal service. It is only in the context of telecommunications that the text hints at the unspoken, by specifying that "the universal service aims to supply a broad range of basic services . . . at a price accessible to all, including those in social difficulty." Enough hypocrisy and double talk! It didn't change a thing, when it was written into the Treaty (Article 3) on the occasion of the 1996 intergovernmental conference that the Union's objectives include "a contribution to the promotion of the services of general interest." The Commission does not defend "the values common to European societies." It destroys them in the name of a concept of solidarity reduced to the bare bones.[21]

France tried the sounding board. "Public utilities in France are an intellectual and institutional construct which will have to be remodeled in order to meet our needs during these changing times,"[22] write the authors of a report on public services, inviting a renewal of the vocabulary and the practices of management and regulation. They affirm in vain that "it is not European construction that imposes the modernization of the networks;" they readily admit that "Europe crystallizes the change, and impresses upon it a dynamic that to some extent escapes even those who started it on its way." If it is only a question of adapting to the evolution of the market and of technology, the public utility enterprises did not wait for the construction of Europe before they began. Whether we look at civil nuclear power, the Minitel (which for a long time was unrivaled in Europe) or the TGV [high-speed trains], French public enterprises have demonstrated an entrepreneurial spirit that is admittedly seldom found among her European homologues. And if EDF was not more diversified, it is not for lack of ambition but because the Juppé government opposed it due to pressure from private companies. As for their debt, indeed excessive, it is not the fault of their management; it is the product of the policies of the successive governments, which, since the end of the 1970s, have used these firms as "cash cows" for the state budget.

Do the inevitable changes really require us to abandon the public service as citizens know it? No one has proven why we have to reduce public services and dismantle the public monopolies. No one has shown how the missions of the public utilities are better assured when they are reduced to activities and services for sparsely populated areas and for impoverished populations, rather than when tariff leveling ensures the economic equilibrium of the whole. Nor has it been shown why subsidizing private firms is preferable to tariff equalization. The supposed superiority of deregulation has never been proven. Unless the economic optimum consists in privatizing the income-producers (the profitable networks) and making the taxpayer support the inevitable deficits of the "minimum service." In that case, it is less a question of adapting than of "metamorphosing," giving up the general improvement in well-being and economic efficiency that was promised, at the cost of formidable social and civic regression that inevitably produces winners and losers.

The firms, which lobbied hard with Community authorities in favor of the deregulation of the public services, are the big winners of this battle. They have ended the system of rate equalization, which, they maintained, obscured the "true costs." In fact, equality of treatment is contrary to this concept. Indeed, it postulates that the tariff should be the same, whatever the volume or rate of consumption. "True costs," conversely, make it possible to establish a sliding rate scale that corresponds to the quantities consumed. Thus, deregulating the energy market will allow "eligible customers," those who consume more than 40 GW/hour, to buy their electricity from the producers, therefore adding the latter to the competition to reduce prices. And in telecommunications, it means reducing prices for long-distance calls, which are used primarily by businesses.

For private individuals and small firms, the "true costs" will increase the price, and there will be no more equalization to spread it around. Every example points in the same direction — toward Great Britain, where the public services were privatized in anticipation of European deregulation, such as the deregulation of German telecommunications. In England, the prices have gone up, and are likely to continue in the future. In France, the privatization of water has caused an average price hike of 9% per annum since 1991! The Commission was careful not to make the least evaluation of how these privatizations affect the consumers. The price increases don't quite help to illustrate the prediction that privatization is a boon for Europe. It is hard to justify an inflationary effect after preaching fiscal stability. As for the citizens, they have lost the chance to dispute the decisions made by firms which, having become private, can avoid any political debate. By promoting privatization, the Commission has driven back both democracy and citizenship in Europe. Are we then surprised that the people do not see this European construction as a reflection of them, and that they feel they have been fleeced by the political leaders' promises when they talk about a "Europe close to the people"?

The situation for employees is both the least well-known example and the most alarming. "Social Europe" is a recurring theme in the European construction, expressing both hope and regret. The hope of getting beyond the purely economic dimension of the European market and the regret that good intentions are regularly shown to be not enough. What are we really looking for? Alignment of rights and rates of pay? "Attenuation of the destabilizing effects"[24] of the single market? The fight against intra-European business relocations (now symbolized by the Hoover Group's decision to transfer its vacuum cleaner plant from Dijon to Scotland) or the extension of collective bargaining to the level of Europe? No one, to tell the truth, is very sure. However, that is not for want of having discussed it endlessly and writing innumerable action plans, memoranda, charters and social protocols, and even an impressive number of directives.

Here too, the question of a social Europe was posited right from the start — beginning with the freedom of movement of laborers (Article 48). In 1968, European directives and regulations adopted measures to ensure the full effectiveness of the relocation and foreign stays of workers from the member states, and their family. These provisions were intended to ensure "treatment equal to the local workers" with regard to the conditions of employment and pay, social protection and taxes, and trade-union rights. This approach is not neutral. In the social field as elsewhere, Europe tackles the problem not from the point of view of the basic rights that the Community should accord its nationals, but instead from the point of view of movement between member states.

However, a trend began in the 1970s that hinged on the search for common rights. Europe oscillated between two objectives that the governments considered equally undesirable, for opposite reasons. On the one hand, the idea of a harmonization that would pull up the countries with the least social rights worried the latter; on the other hand, the idea of "a minimum base" that would be required of all made the most advanced countries fear that they would never be able to cut back on social rights. The Commission's problem was in that it had no clear basis to start from. The European social model, like the public utilities, pre-existed European construction. In every country the employees had a set of rights and protections, acquired over the course of many battles, collective bargaining and, sometimes, political majorities, which contributed to forging the citizenship in each country. But, even more than in the public services, the social models were highly heterogeneous in the level of protection as in the forms of organization: more governmental in France and Italy, more contractual in Germany and in the Benelux countries. In addition, apart from the problems arising from intra-European immigration, the social rights were, clearly, within the jurisdiction of the national governments.

The only grounds where real progress could be made toward a harmonization were that of sanitation and work safety. Again, we are talking about very specific measures of protecting workers against hazardous substances such as lead, chemical agents, vinyl chloride and ionizing radiation. The social protocol annexed to the Single Act did not achieve any decisive progress with regard to the Community's scope of activity, except for the introduction of a "workers' right to information and consultation," which caused Britain to block the protocol. The idea of European minimum wages never even came up. The only innovation was the decision to settle these matters by majority vote. This immediately resulted in an increase in the number of directives on labor conditions relating to exposure to carcinogenic agents, asbestos and noise, as well as specific measurements relating to video screens. Similarly, several laws were passed to bring into alignment the safety requirements applying to manufacturing equipment and machinery. But nothing came into law that touched upon the essential.

As soon as one gets to the heart of social relations — the wages, social security, the length of the workday, workers' representation — Europe has seldom gone beyond solemn declarations. "The Community Charter of the fundamental social rights" adopted by the European Council of Strasbourg, December 9, 1989, remained a dead letter. Nor did the social protocol appended to the Maastricht Treaty produce, in areas however limited, all the anticipated results. Of the 28 draft directives having to do with the Council's areas of competence, only 16 were adopted by the end of 1993. Great Britain's refusal (until the Labour Party came to power in April 1997) to subscribe to these texts, regularly invoked in order to get around them, does not entirely explain the Community's social impotence. Admittedly, in fields where progress seemed possible, especially in connection with the famous Vredeling Directive relating to the consultation and participation of employees in a European business council, the British opposition directly caused the delays in having it adopted. But Great Britain should not be the tree that hides the forest. France, which likes to be at the forefront of the battle for the "social charter," seldom goes beyond words. It has hardly encouraged its companies, private or public, to set up any real consultation of the workers at the European level. Besides, why would French firms do more for society at the European level than they do at the national level? It took the brutal closing of the Renault plant in Vilvorde, in Belgium, to put an end to French doubletalk. Integrating the "social charter" into the Treaty, as agreed in Amsterdam, constitutes some progress, but it will not change much in the short term.

European social policy is a political failure for more fundamental reasons, too, reasons that are intrinsic to the way Europe is being constructed. They are due once again to the concept of Community law. The principle of "the same wages for the same labor at the same place," reaffirmed in the 1991 Directive on "temporary workers," was in conflict for quite some time with the policy of freedom of movement of migrants, combined with the freedom of the provision of services. In countries like Germany, where the wage policy, including the minimum wage, is entirely based on collective bargaining conventions that affect only national firms, firms from other member states have an advantage. That is how we found Portuguese civil engineering companies sending Portuguese workmen to work in Germany — for Portuguese wages! Not until the business leaders joined in the public outcry from the union of construction workers, confronted with this unfair competition, was a new directive on "temporary work assignments within the context of providing services" adopted on December 16, 1996. This directive recognizes that only the terms of labor and employment of the territory where the labor actually takes place are applicable, whether they are defined by legislative provisions, laws or conventions. It was high time.

European law holds other surprises. Thus, we have the Court of Justice's decision prohibiting late night work for women, issued contrary to the Treaty's provisions on non-discrimination between men and women. The Commission not only was not moved, but it promptly took action against the five countries, including France, that had adopted such legislation. In the domain of social protection, the Commission has, of its own initiative, set to work on a directive that disputes the monopoly that benefits the social security providers and seeks to introduce competition among the insurers. And among the Commission's future objectives appears the idea that "the Welfare state must now evolve toward an optimal balance between public security, and private collective and individual security."[25] As with the public services, deregulation and competition in the provision of social services are trying to penetrate the member states using the Commission as a door. At a risk of dissolving further the cement of social cohesion and citizenship.

It is also true that this failure derives from the contradiction between the implicit objectives of social Europe and the "strategic objectives" for the construction of Europe, that is, the single market and the economic and monetary union. "The populations [may] wish for a Europe less dominated by economic and technocratic considerations," but, for the Commission, the European social policy is nothing but a "cover story."[24] It is hard to see how, in these conditions, governments that have committed national policies of flexibility of employment (and Great Britain is not alone), would subscribe at the European level to policies that would reinforce the rights of the employees.

The Commission itself acts no differently than the member states. Not because of technocracy, but because it is implementing treaties that never made employment and welfare a priority. Admittedly, among the missions assigned to the Community is "a higher level of employment and social welfare,"[26] but this objective is listed only in the section about principles. Neither the economic and monetary union, nor the powers entrusted to the Commission regarding competition, mentions any employment target (although price stability is mentioned). Needless to say, the rare attempts to add this ended in failure. Left out of the Treaty, employment is also ignored by the Council of Finance Ministers (Ecofin) and the Commission when it deals with mergers and acquisitions, and public services. Should we be astonished, like the commissioner for employment and social affairs, that "Europe's social policy is entering a critical phase"?[27]

"Is a return to full employment possible?," the Commission's Green Book asks, rhetorically. The only certainty we have is that it is not possible within the current framework of Community institutions and legislation. While full employment might figure in the list of goals for a social Europe (and how could it not, when Europe counts more than 11% of its active population as unemployed?[28]), it will not happen as long as employment lacks the same essential force in the European construction as competition and price stability. Simply adding the social charter and the protocol on social policy to the Amsterdam Treaty will solve none of the problems arising from the implementation of the legislation already approved. Neither the Finance Ministers nor the Commission would see any new obligation in that. The resolution adopted in Amsterdam, at the request of Jospin's government, tries to go further, proclaiming that it is "imperative to give fresh impetus to placing employment at the top of the Union's policy agenda." But can such a statement help, when it is contradicted a few lines further down by the need "to give more attention to European competitiveness as a precondition of growth and employment"?[29]

If Europe really wants to make employment its top priority, it should reverse the hierarchy between employment and stability. First, the European Council should adopt, as the Commission has proposed,[29] a goal of reducing the unemployment level not for each state, but for the whole Community. For example, to bring it down from 11% to 7% or 6% into four or five years. All the authorities, the Councils of Ministers and the Commission, would be expressly invited to do everything within their power to reduce unemployment all over Europe. In the second place, fundamental social rights should become "common social rights." They exist in each member state, which should facilitate their adoption at the European level; and the European Parliament should be accorded the power to define the common terms according to which they would be implemented.[31] This would create a European public space with freedoms anchored in the life of each one. Thus, a basis of rights would be built, which would apply simultaneously and directly to the whole European territory and would serve as a rampart defending us from the market.[32]

Notes

1. The following discussion is based on the article by Nicolas de Sadeleer, "La Circulation des déchets et le marché unique européen," published in *la Revue de marché unique européen*, 1-1994

2. In particular: in 1983, in connection with the introduction in France of an obligatory system of collecting and disposing of waste oils, which had the consequence of prohibiting their export; in 1987, in connection with a Netherlands law relating to wastes of animal origin; in 1992, in connection with Belgian legislation aiming to ban the import of waste in Wallonia.

3. S. Soumastre, quoted by N. de Sadeleer, *Art. cit.*

4. Ruling of July 9, 1992, Commission c. Belgium.

5. Speech before the European Parliament, January 15, 1989, in Jacques Delors, *Le Concert européen*, Paris, Odile Jacob, 1992.

6. Joel Molinier, *Droit du marché intérieur européen*, Paris, LGDJ, 1995, p. 77.

7. Jacques Delors, *Presentation de l'Acte unique au Parlement européen*, February 15, 1987.

8. *Le Monde*, June 15, 1996.

9. *Ibid.*

10. Quoted in Maryse Cassan, *L'Europe communautaire de la santé*, Paris, Economica, 1989, p. 1.

11. *Ibid*, p. 151.

12. This report, dated October 12, 1990, was revealed by the monthly magazine *Que Choisir* of February 1991 and was published by the *Le Journal du Dimanche* on June 30.

13. See the Commission Report of the plan chaired by Christian Stoffaës, *Service public-question d'avenir*, Odile Jacob, Paris, 1996.

14. This ruling, named Corbeau, set a residential mail distribution company against the royal control of the Belgian post offices, aff. C 320/91, ruling of May 19, 1993.

15. This ruling, called 'the Community of Almelo,' was between the community and a Netherlands regional electricity distribution company that benefited from an exclusive purchase clause prohibiting the local distributors from importing electricity, aff. C 393/92, ruling of April 27, 1994.

16. Franck Borotra, *Rapport de mission sur le service public*, Dec. 1995.

17. Statement by Anne-Marie Idrac, State Secretary of Transport, in *Le Monde*, 29 March, 1997.

18. Christian Stoffaës, *op. cit.*, p. 312.

19. Leon Brittain, *L'Europe qu'il nous faut*, Paris, Plon, 1994, p. 105.

20. Communication from the Commission of the European Communities, *Les Services d'intérêt général en Europe*, Brussels, 11 September, 1996.

21. According to Professor R. Kovar, "Le Peau de chagrin, ou comment le droit communautaire opère la réduction des monopoles publics," *Revue Europe*, July 1992.

22. Christian Stoffaës, *op. cit.*, p. 352.

23. Daniel Lenoir, *L'Europe sociale*, Paris, La Découverte, 1994.

24. Commission des Communautés europeénnes, *Livre vert sur la poltique sociale europeénne, options pour l'union*, Brussels, November 1993.

25. *Ibid.*

26. First part, Article 2 of the treaty establishing the European Community.

27. Padraig Flynn, The Objective of the Green Book on the European Social Policy, Introduction to the *Green Book on the European Social Policy, Options for the Union, op. cit.*

28. Chiffre 1997.

29. *Résolution du Conseil européen sur la croissance et l'emploi*, Amsterdam, June 16 and 17, 1997.
30. *Propositions de lignes directrices pour les politiques de l'emploi des Etats membres en 1998*, Communication of the Commission, Brussels, October 1997.
31. See below, Wishing for Europe.
32. Cf. André Gauron, *Les Remparts du marché*, Paris, Odile Jacob, 1991.

Chapter 5

The Single Market Society

Competition is to the Treaty of Rome what light is to the Bible. It brightens it, regenerates it, gives it meaning. Not only is it seen as a more effective way for markets to operate, it is the spearhead of a political plan to dismantle and reorganize European societies. As Noël Monnier wrote, "as an intellectual concept, the single market has nothing to do with socio-economic reality — a true market — which would be established gradually after being tested and modeled at length and collectively, then adopted. In this sense, it does not have a history of its own."[1] It is the affirmation of an ideology. It is the embodiment of the liberal postulate of the superiority of the competitive market. It is "the best possible form of organization," and it would be a sin to deprive Europe of it.

Toxic waste, food, public services, social rights — we run into the same misunderstanding. The public believes that Europe exists to create "well-being," but every day they find new evidence that it is only a machine for creating competition, to the point of making that the very essence of European construction, the ultimate purpose of integration. The greater market that the European Union proposes to create only makes sense in terms of this objective. Originally, competition was only to be the means by which Europe would ensure the free movement of goods, services, capital and people within its bounds. It soon became an end in itself. How could the public not be distraught, given this inversion of objectives?

Is Europe a victim of its legal structure, of the role that it has given to one major institution, the Court of Justice of the European Communities? As a judiciary power beyond the control of any democratic mechanisms, the national governments and the European Parliament, it is dragging Europe toward what can only be called "a market society." Its philosophy of competition is based on the purest sophism. "Real competition implies the existence of an effective competition," says a judgment dating from 1977. "That is, sufficient competition for the fundamental requirements and objectives of the Treaty to be achieved and followed, and, in particular, the formation of a single market under conditions similar to those of a domestic market."[2] In short, competition can exist only if it is effective. The Court does not dispute the existence of "a different type of objectives" (for example, the environment or welfare policies), nor that in meeting those objectives the Commission will have to apply "certain restrictions on competition." But the restrictions are acceptable only when they are "essential to the achievement of these objectives and do not serve to eliminate competition from a substantial part of the common market." In other words, competition can only be restricted in such a way as to continue to allow competition!

In taking this principle of competition to the extreme, says Jacques Delors, the realization of the single market will "metamorphose"[3] European societies. While holding to the goal of a unified market, the President of the Commission sought more than a "revival" of Europe. He wanted to instigate a major transformation of the nation-states. He says it directly enough. "The lack of drama should not mask the fact that ours is a revolutionary undertaking, (and) we are giving birth to a different kind of Europe." Like any "revolutionary undertaking," the single market implies violence. But, unlike previous attempts at unifying European, through religious or military means, it is not using force. This violence is to be democratic, almost peaceful. Its weapon is the law. For the Europe of the single market is "a creation of the law." Even, "the Community based on law."[4] The law's central role in the construction of European arises from the principle declared by the Treaty of Rome (and already contained in the ECSC Treaty), namely: *Community legislation is an autonomous legal order that is mandatory on member states.*

The European Court of Justice has spelled it out very clearly since 1962. "In contrast to ordinary international treaties, the Treaty of the EEC has instituted a free-standing legal order which is to be integrated into the legal framework of the member states when the Treaty takes effect, and which is binding on their jurisdiction; by establishing a community of unlimited duration, endowed with its own institutions, . . . and particularly with real powers, the member states have limited, albeit in restricted fields, their sovereign rights, and have thus created a body of law applicable to their nationals and to themselves." The Court would be both the invisible master behind the scenes and the vigilant guard.

This choice is fundamental. It establishes the Community legislation's supremacy over national laws and prevents the latter from voiding the substance of the former. This point has become commonplace. But we often overlook the breadth of its impact, which is stressed by the various departments of the Commission. "Given the autonomy of the Community legal order, the Community's judicial concepts are always defined according to the requirements of Community legislation and the objectives of the Community."[5] This autonomy applies not only to the legislation, it is the foundation of the independence of the European judiciary bodies, the Commission and the Court of Justice, which interpret it and guarantee its execution. They can place injunctions on the member states to apply Community legislation and, in the event of refusal, they can impose sanctions. They thus have real executive power, to which the national law must yield. If there is only one federal power in Europe, it is the Court of Justice.

There is autonomy, but also unity. Implementing Community legislation is not the responsibility of European institutions alone. It is incumbent upon the national political, administrative and legal bodies. National governments and parliaments must "transcribe" the European directives into the national legislation (laws and regulations). For their part, the national jurisdictions must conform to the Community legislation when pronouncing their decisions, even if "incidental title" would otherwise apply. Community legislation takes "precedence" over the national law. Thus there is unity of the integrated legal order comprised by the Community and the national authorities. As always, problems of interpretation (sometimes delicate) arise *de facto* and *de jure*. But there can be no conflict between the national law and the European law.

The European law takes precedence over the national. The Court of Justice said it most clearly. "Any national judge, operating within

the scope of his jurisdiction, is obligated to apply the Community legislation in its entirety and to protect the rights that it confers on the individual, and not to apply any possible contrary provision of the national
law, whether adopted anterior or posterior to the Community rule."[6]
Moreover, national judges are increasingly consulting the European
Court of Justice on their own initiative before ruling on matters where
Community legislation may pertain.

Any other solution would have been impracticable. The national
laws are too dissimilar and it would have been impossible to bring
them into alignment beforehand. They inevitably would have con-
flicted with the Community legislation and very quickly would have
become irrelevant. This becomes clear if we look at the obstacles that
the member states have thrown in the way to limit the scope of the
autonomy of the European legal order, and to thwart its unity. They
range from delays in getting the European directives transcribed into
national law, to the national courts' reticence to fully apply the Community standards. This has been particularly true of French courts. It
took 18 years for the Supreme Court of Appeals and 32 for the Conseil
d'État (the administrative jurisdiction) to acquiesce in admitting the
precedence of Community law. On the basis that they were not competent to judge whether the law was in conformity with the Treaty,
they refused to assess the legality of a text adopted *ex post facto* to the
European Acts. If they were so inclined, they always have the option of
giving a "Gallic" interpretation of the Community legislation, i.e. favorable to France, in particular when national authorities are in question.

Without there being a European State, the Community legislation
(while it may be a form of positive law) is not "legislated" law like, for
example, the French, Belgian and German laws, which are bodies of law
emanating from the States. It is a law "derived" from the Treaties, developed by and for the purpose of implementing those Treaties. The
European legislature — that is, the Commission and the Council of
Ministers (of the member states) — is not the source of the law in the
sense that they do not have the sovereign power to produce laws. That
is held by the Treaties, and there is no way to get around that. The legislature lacks general jurisdiction that belongs to any state — i.e. the
sovereign power to modify laws, including constitutional law. Thus,
they cannot of their own accord extend their scope of influence. Although the heads of state and of governments hold sovereign power at

the national level, at the Community level they have to adopt a new treaty (and get it ratified) to supplement and extend the precedents. It took adoption of the Single European Act to create the single market, then the Maastricht Treaty to carry out the economic and monetary union. Like institutional reform, integrating the legal pillar into the Community's sphere of influence assumes that a new treaty will be drafted to supplement and amend the precedents. As positive law, Community law is thus similar to American contract law, a "law without a State, made by the judges and the lawyers," according to Laurent Cohen-Tanugi's definition.[7] Except that this is not, by definition, a "law without a State": a "system of rights and obligations between decentralized units which ensure the distribution of power and the self-regulation of the society."[8] On the contrary, European law denies power, and supercedes the existence of the State.

Community legislation is original in another sense, too. It organizes the self-regulation of society solely on the basis of the market. The innovation is not so much the inversion of the relations between law and state as the fact that it ties the law to the market. The source and the subject of the law are no longer the individual, as in "natural law," nor the state, as in "legal positivism." The market becomes the source and the subject of the law. Indeed, at the European level, we are not looking at a simple law of competition, as the member states know it. Rather, the European legislation places *all of the laws* governing relations between people *under the rubric of commercial relations.* It does not deny individual rights or civil freedoms. But since those are only national in jurisdiction, and since Community legislation is superior to the national legal corpus, individual rights and civil freedoms are subordinated to the market. The law no longer protects individuals against the market; it subjects them to the market.

European societies, which claim to embody all the humanistic values of the "State of law" and which made that a condition of membership in the Community, then in the European Union, have established at the European level an antihumanist body of law. Although they exalt the law as a rampart against state totalitarianism, they have invented a supranational legal order that founds the totalitarianism of the market. Even the most liberal of nation-states never went that far. Never did anyone dare to establish the principle of competition as absolute master that nothing can stop, not even the national laws in-

tended to protect individuals. At the level of Europe, freedom of movement of cattle fodder, of waste, or the provision of "human" service is
higher in the eyes of the law, whereas in the states, they are subordinated to public health, the environment and public welfare. It took the
"mad cow" crisis, and unilateral prohibitions on marketing bovine meal
on the part of various states, for the Commission to admit, in the words
of the judgment handed down, that "certain restrictions on competition
are acceptable because they are essential to the achievement of the objectives of a different nature" (health protection) that the Treaty additionally ascribes to the Community.

Let us say it a little differently. What is the State? The expression
of the general interest, which the political body is responsible for defining. If there is no State, if there is no place where different objectives
and policies clash — and that can only happen in Parliament — there is
no way to define the general interest. Then only private interests exist
and regulate the laws of competition. We can see how this plays out,
for example, in the public services. Until the Single Act, the Commission had no authority to commit to the deregulation of the (national)
structure of the public services. The nationally defined general interest
could then prevail in each country. With the extension of jurisdiction
recognized by the new treaty, the Commission has not only the power,
but even a mandate allowing it to dictate that public services be
opened up to competition. Even though that flies in the face of the
principle of equal access to these services, which used to prevail
throughout the European States.

The concept of "general economic interest" is certainly recognized
by the Treaty of Rome, but it is strictly tied to those enterprises that
acknowledged (before the Treaty?) a mission of serving as a public utility. But the concept in itself does not exist, for lack of a legitimate political power to discuss it and define what would be a *European* general
interest. The fact that the Community derives its legitimacy solely
from treaties, and not from any legislature democratically invested by
the universal vote, makes this concept impossible. "In the persistent
absence of any real governmental power, the Community policy of competition spontaneously tends to play the part of an interim government — permanently installed in Europe, which thus functions in extreme liberalism," wrote Noël Monnier. Not because of any deliberated
plan, but because of "an intrinsic tendency of the Community, in its

current institutional configuration, to express itself only through an unlimited promotion of the commercial system alone."[9]

In the absence of a European state, competition is less a policy than a principle of action. Monnier outlines the exceptional conditions established within the institutions of Europe that favor competition. Competition "is based from the outset on a set of pre-existent rules, well-established and generally perceived as technical matter. The fact that it pertains to multiple sectors gives it a range of application that is potentially vast, and finally, implementation would not really require any financial investment."[10] In short, the Commission finds itself in a situation where it can "go quickly, unilaterally, everywhere, and for free." No other principle in the Treaties is that strong — not even the principles on justice or employment. So what if competition has a particularly high cost, especially in terms of inequality and unemployment? Its dynamism and its force for autonomy are overwhelming, and those who use it as the lever of European integration have the means of shattering the national states. That is their dream as Europeans. For the citizens of Europe, it is already a nightmare.

One last factor makes competition's pre-eminence absolute: lobbying. The special interests have moved in everywhere that there is no firm policy. It's no surprise that Jacques Delors finds "economic middlemen more active than the politicians."[11] They have no trouble making their views heard, making their specific interests prevail, since they are in place for the long haul. While the European directives and regulations are being drafted, they are consulted, met with, and especially listened to. In Brussels, representatives of economic interests are more numerous, and effective, than the members of the European Parliament. This system, deeply alien to "the State of law," is, on the contrary, consubstantial with the societies based on "law without State." As Laurent Cohen-Tanugi says, in connection with American society, it expresses "the dynamism of the civil society and its capacity for initiative, compared to governmental action."[12] How can everyone who is hoping to promote civil society against the State, through European integration, not welcome this with open arms?

In this race for civil society, which, as Adam Smith said, makes "our dinner depend not on the benevolence of the butcher, the beer merchant or the baker, but on the care by which they attend to their own interests,"[13] everyone does not start with the same chance of having influence. Corporate lobbying is obviously more effective than that of the consumers or conservationists. The first is divided and subdivided into many specific cases to discuss, standards to be defined, directives to be promulgated. They have powerful financial support to "help" the Commission make its decisions and to keep it from getting bogged down in the task of standardization, which it had taken on (a task that it ended up delegating to the professional organizations). Lobbying by consumers' associations and the conservationists is more general. In many sectors, it is non-existent. Who would think of consulting them over questions of manufacturing and distributing cattle feed? Veterinarians are consulted, but where is the public to stand up for its right to health and to serve as a countervailing power? In France, Germany, Great Britain and the Netherlands, it is the politicians, both in the Parliament and in government, who look after the public interests. In Brussels, they are not consulted.

The imbalance between the enterprises and the trade unions is even more evident. Formally, they are institutional partners of the Community, organized within the Confederation of European trade unions, members of the European Economic and Social Council. But did anyone ever see the Commission asking its opinion on questions about ensuring the freedom to offer services? Freedom of movement is provided by law. It is derived from the Treaty of Rome, and the Single European Act that extended it to the financial services and insurance. Who at that time considered the opportunity this offered to the Portuguese business, to excuse itself from German collective conventions and apply the Portuguese wage structure? If lobbying expresses the dynamism of the civil society, it is that of a society reduced to just one actor, the firm. Negotiation, on which the pluralist liberal society is founded, is, in fact, excluded.

The European leaders have said it repeatedly. "The single market is a means for achieving a greater ambition, a real societal plan." But, is brandishing "the European model of society" — the way others have "jumped around like billy goats bleating 'Europe, Europe, Europe'" — enough to protect Europe from the "metamorphosis" that competition is foisting upon it? Don't we see that they only talk about this "model" in order to be able to circumvent it more easily? Invoking the model of society this way makes believe that the sovereignty of the States is being preserved, and affirms the primacy of political decisions over the market — prerequisites of the expression of the general interest and the collective solidarity to which the public is justly attached. Competition does not exclude a state guarantor of solidarity when such exists. But the plan for society, which the Community legislation promotes, is in direct conflict. It leads to an Americanization of European societies, bringing into being a society where generalized competition becomes the rule, with corporate competition on a global scale, competition among individuals, and competition of the nation-states that are condemned to disappear and where solidarity cannot exist. Is this the society we want; is this the market-based Europe the public is looking for? To say that the misunderstanding is complete would be an understatement.

Before the Single European Act went into effect, anything was still possible. Michel Albert, a former commissioner, wrote the book *Le Pari européen*[14] at the request of the European Parliament, presenting the conditions that would lead to revived growth in Europe. He denounced "non-Europe," but establishing a greater unified market was not his point. His concern was the lack of a collective body that could define Community objectives and formulate a European general interest. He called for policies on industry and research, for an energy policy and regional policies, and, finally, for a European employment policy. Albert maintained that a recovery would not result from simply intensifying the economic integration. It would require a change in the design of European construction, giving policy questions priority over the market; thus institutional reform would have to come first.

Lord Cokfield, a European Commissioner, used "non-Europe" to refer to something else in his "White Book on the Achievement of the Internal Market," which formed the gist of the Single European Act. He had in mind the technical, legal and tax barriers that hinder freedom of movement. He estimated the cost at no less than 200 billion euros per annum (something like $210 billion).[15] One can just imagine what a "burden" this "monstrous bill" imposes on European competitiveness! Conversely, removing these obstacles would allow Europe to enter "a new world," with "320 million consumers and millions of businesses as the primary beneficiaries, as it would reduce their costs and prices." The Commission saw in this "the prospect of a new burst of progress," and, "for the first time in two decades, a significant reduction in chronic unemployment." There was no room for doubt, and the details did not matter. The skeptics had to be convinced, with every song and dance. "Yes," pronounced the Commission, "success is within hand's reach."

In this Europe freed of all kinds of borders, competition clearly held every virtue. It "will cause a shock in sales prices; will start a "virtuous circle" based on the dynamics of lower prices and increased demand, which will simultaneously provide enterprises with the opportunity to increase production; and, in the final analysis, come up to a European and world standard of competitiveness." As if businesses had been waiting for the Single European Act before competing on the global market! In addition, "under the combined influence of the opening of the public markets and the regeneration of the economy, the public deficits will be reduced." If we do not make this move, thundered the Commission, it will mean failure. There is no other choice. "Watch out!" warned its president, who was "not inspired by any ideological consideration, but relied, quite to the contrary, on the evidence."[16]

Addressing a European Confederation of Trade Unions worried about persistent, widespread unemployment, Delors spoke of a shining future that could only nourish hope "Fulfilling the 1992 program should bring economic and social advantages, including 4.5% additional growth and the creation of almost 2 million new jobs."[17] The Commission's experts said that would be "insufficient to reabsorb all the current unemployment, (but) would nevertheless make it possible to reduce the rate by about 1.5%." This is why, the president of the Commission continued, "it should immediately be added that if the corollary policies are implemented, taking full advantage of the flexibility offered by the greater market, the community would derive addition of growth of 7%, and 5 million new jobs could be created." Which would take the sting out of unemployment.

Unfortunately, evidence can be deceiving. Prices did not go down — the only decrease occurred in 1990-1992 and it related to the industrial prices of goods like aluminum, glass and basic chemicals (which are related to a global cycle) and budgetary profits did not materialize. The single market did not cause the "virtuous circle" as promised. Admittedly, growth created 9 million jobs in Europe between 1985 and 1992, but that was due primarily to the resumption of demand induced by German reunification, which has nothing to do with the Single European Act. No; when the target date of 1992 was finally reached, Europe was mired in a recession of unprecedented scope. The public deficits grew deeper and unemployment spread. Did it take the work of forty of Europe's most prestigious institutes and research centers, the efforts of more than 300 researchers, and interviews with more than 11,000 firms, to achieve this? "We are only talking about potentialities," Delors carefully specified to the congress of the trade unions. But it was about potentialities he believed in and which led him to tell the Commission that, with the single market, "tomorrow, nothing will be the same."[18]

Everything stayed the same. The dynamics of Community legislation on competition continued its insane progress, to the general indifference of the public. Having conquered Europe through the arteries of the European market, competition drew no special attention. It penetrated to the heart of the states via intra-Community trade, for example, with waste management and foodstuffs, as we have seen. When it came to the public services, whose markets are by nature national, it took a political process of deregulation on the part of the Commission to allow competition to progress. Similarly, in a completely different field, that of taxation on savings, the 1988 attempt at harmonization stumbled over the political incapacity to solve the question of the status of non-residents for nationals of a member state whose capital is deposited in a country other than that in which he lives. The existence of a well-established, specific, derogatory regimen prevented the Community from imposing a single Community-level levy, which would have been less favorable to (European) non-residents.

The decision to foster the single market was not inevitable from the start. The idea that economic integration should one day give birth to a politically united Europe never achieved unanimous support. The governments held back for years, drafting innumerable plans for reforming the institutions. But none was likely to attract all the votes. Some parties felt that creating "a real political entity," a European Union, was necessary to pull Europe out of its slump; others rebelled against the idea. It was impossible to come up with an acceptable plan. The Single European Act resulted from this failure. Since he became president of the Commission in January 1985, Delors sought to surmount this problem and made it his absolute priority to achieve the single market. In his first presentation to the Parliament of Strasbourg, January 14, 1985, he challenged the European deputies. "Would it be presumptuous to announce, and then to carry out, the decision to abolish all the borders inside of Europe between now and 1992?"[19] With that, the Single European Act was launched.

In June 1985, over opposition from the British among others, the European Council in Milan approved the objective of "an internal market, a space without borders," as well as the convocation of an intergovernmental conference. When that conference first met, in September, the Commission put on the table a draft of a complete chapter on the "internal market," addressing the 300-odd decisions necessary for the abolition of borders as listed in the "White Book on the Achievement of the Internal Market" written under the authority of Lord Cokfield. The decisions are grouped into three chapters: the elimination of physical barriers, the elimination of technical barriers, and finally, tax harmonization. They cover every sector, without exception, where such barriers exist. The Commission was thus empowered with a broad scope. Furthermore, it took on the right to control mergers and acquisitions for any transactions that might be assumed to affect the European market. Whereas in each individual country an agency or a commission independent of the government had handled the oversight of mergers and acquisitions, it now became the exclusive jurisdiction of the European Commission.

The monetary question remained. The Commission and several governments, including France and Belgium, felt that completing the internal market should go hand in hand with completing the monetary union. Great Britain was opposed. Germany, after consulting with the British delegation, had the monetary question deferred to a later date — but on the condition that a decision should be made immediately to liberalize the capital markets, and thus to remove any control over exchange rates, by December 31, 1986. The outlines of a compromise were taking shape. Finally, the Council adopted only the principle of monetary freedom and left to a later Council the charge of adopting a timetable — the end of exchange rate controls was finally set for July 1, 1990. The Single European Act could be adopted. After being ratified without difficulty by the national Parliaments, it went into effect, as planned, on July 1, 1987.

Margaret Thatcher was hostile to the idea of an intergovernmental conference, but chose to take part in it nonetheless. There wasn't much risk for her. While a simple majority could convoke the meeting,

a unanimous vote was required for any resulting decisions. As she relates in her memoirs, she was above all interested in "one paramount
goal: to create a single common Market,"[20] as she considered that
"British companies are among those most likely to benefit from an
opening of other countries' markets." Under the guise of a liberal ideo-
logue, the British prime minister was a pragmatist who knew how to
separate the essential from the auxiliary. "The price to pay for arriving
at a single market, with all its economic advantages, consisted of a su-
per majority vote within the Community. The single market also implied an increase in the Commission's authority. "There was no way
around that," she later acknowledged. She fought hard to prevent this
principle being extended to "vital sectors of our national existence, including taxation, immigration control, the fight against terrorism and
crime, the drug war, and sanitary measures that make it possible to
keep out carriers of dangerous diseases" (but not to forbid their export!). The British Prime Minister had accepted what she had refused
earlier, the abandonment of the principle of unanimity. But Thatcher
estimated that she had sufficiently locked down the provision. She had
made the minimal concessions necessary, in her eyes, "to create and
maintain the market single, and not to be used for other ends."[21]

The law was absent from this debate. Or, more exactly, it was
reduced to a technical problem introduced at the end of the conference
at the request of the Court of Justice itself. The Court wished to see a
jurisdiction of first authority created and the procedures of appeal improved. This reform would simplify its own encumbered state and
make it easier for plaintiffs to initiate a claim, which could only benefit
the national states. But this reform was far from being trivial. As one
attentive observer said, "the combination of the new decisions concerning the Court added up to a remarkable reinforcement of the Community's autonomous decision-making powers,"[22] on top of the extension
of jurisdictions conferred on the Commission to encourage competition.

The Single European Act did not invent competition, or the
autonomous nature of Community legislation. But it was a watershed.
Powerful in its monopoly over initiative, from which the Parliament
remains excluded, the Commission could transform the "White Book
on the Achievement of the Internal Market" into "a railway timetable,"
to quote François Lamoureux,[23] a close collaborator to Delors. In a

presentation to the European Parliament, the president of the Commission had clearly announced his intention "to fully use his right to take initiatives to fulfill his priorities." The Commission, he added, "will not hesitate to withdraw a proposal if it believes that its contents are too distorted, or if it senses an explicit or implicit refusal to debate."[24]

The Council of Ministers was thus forewarned. In the final resort its decision remains sovereign, but since it can only act on the basis of texts that the Commission submits, the Council either accepts the texts with some minor amendments, or there will be no text until a more favorable political climate develops. The President of the Commission stood up fourteen times in a row to present the same draft of one directive (relating to customs clearance for small parcels). The machinery for creating directives was launched. Only time would tell how explosive it could be.

Although neither of the two protagonists would be willing to admit it today, this result would have not been achieved without the involuntary complicity between Delors and Thatcher. They were set against each other in every way, because of their reciprocal hostility (as described in *Memoirs from 10 Downing Street*, and because of their different views of Europe. The first dreamed of a politically unified Europe, the second only wanted a greater market, unified and opened to the world. One was a federalist; the other was rabidly in favor of national sovereignty. But they were equally obstinate, which polarized any possible compromises around their respective positions. However, to succeed, both their plans had to remove the obstacles of regulations, subsidies and other state interventions. Both wanted deregulation, even if to Delors it was for the sake of European integration, and to Thatcher, for liberalism.

What does it matter that their intentions were different? Their objective was the same, to make the single market a success. And they were united in their crusade against the state, too. If we want a stronger Europe, said Delors, the states must give up their economic powers; if we want a single market, echoed Thatcher, we must remove the national states' ability to interfere. The "Iron Lady" was right. In giving the "President of Europe" the powers he sought, she did more for the market than for Europe. Behind a public show of disagreement, seldom has convergence been so great. And it is not by chance if, in circus of turning the European Directives into national law, Great Britain grasped the brass ring. No credit to her: her Europe triumphed. Jacques Delors repeated that "through the Single Act, the Twelve are engaged in making the Community much more than a simple free trade zone."[25] But the Europe defined by the Single European Act is diametrically opposed to the great concepts of Community revival that the most enthusiastic Europeans were promulgating in the early 1980s. Statements of purpose, intended to drum up support, are not enough. The political leaders are also responsible for the misunderstandings that they create.

Notes

1. Noël Monnier, "Politique économique et raison communautaire," in Cartelier et al., *Critique de la raison communautaire*, Paris, Economica, 1996, p. 22.
2. CJCE October 25, 1977, Metro S.B.-Grossmärkte, in Joel Molinier, *op. cit.*, p. 15.
3. Jacques Delors, *Le Nouveau concert européen*, Collection of the principal speeches given by the president of the Commission between 1985 and 1991, Paris, Odile Jacob, 1992, p. 118.
4. Klaus-Dieter Borchardt, *L'ABC du droit communautaire*, Brussels, Documentation européenne, 1993, p. 33.
5. Klaus-Dieter Borchardt, *op. cit.*, p. 56.
6. CJCE, March 9, 1978, Simmenthal ruling, cited by Henri Nallet, "Droit communautaire et droit national ou la nostalgie de la loi républicaine," *Après-demain*, October-November 1997.
7. Laurent Cohen-Tanugi, *Le Droit sans l'Etat*, Paris, PUF, 1985, p. 57.
8. *Ibid*, p. 10.
9. Noël Monnier, *op. cit.*, p. 23.
10. *Ibid*, p. 30.
11. Jacques Delors, *op. cit.*, p. 118.
12. Laurent Cohen-Tanugi, *op. cit.*, p. 144.
13. Adam Smith, *op. cit.*, p. 48.
14. Michel Albert, *Le Pari européen*, Paris, Le Seuil, 1983.
15. Jacques Delors, *1992 le défi*, Report from the research project on the cost of not unifying Europe, directed by Pablo Cecchini with Michel Catinat and Alexis Jacquemin, the Commission européenne, Paris, Flammarion, 1988.
16. *Ibid*, p. 41.
17. Speech made during the CES congress in Stockholm on May 12, 1988, published in *Le Nouveau concert européen*, *op. cit.*, p. 73.
18. Jacques Delors, *1992 le défi*, *op. cit.*, Chapter X.
19. Jacques Delors, *op. cit.*, p. 30.
20. Margaret Thatcher, *op. cit.* p. 462.
21. *Ibid*, p. 462.
22. Jean de Ruyt, *L'Acte unique européen*, Brussels, Edition de l' University de Brussels, 1987.
23. *L'Europe de l'acte unique* à Maastricht, in *Le Monde*, February 18-19, 1996.
24. Jacques Delors, *Le Concert européen*, *op. cit.*, p. 46.
25. Center for European Studies, Brussels, November 30, 1989, in *Le Nouveau concert européen*, *op. cit.*, p. 151.

THE MONETARY ILLUSION

Chapter 6

Genesis of a Misunderstanding

"Europe will be unified by currency, or it will not be unified." In 1949, the economist Jacques Rueff, the father of the French monetary reform of 1958, stated what would become the creed of every French government. Forty years later François Mitterrand echoed him, declaring that "the Economic and Monetary Union is the necessary route toward political union."[1] Since the beginning of the construction of Europe, France conceived of economic integration as the means of making Europe. The common market, the single market, the Economic and Monetary Union were to be stages in this inexorable drive toward political union. If a politically unified Europe is the final goal, the only possible means is to build the economic and monetary foundation step by step. President Mitterand intended to take this vast enterprise, begun by President Pompidou with the creation of the European currency "Snake" symbol and continued by his successor with the creation of the European Monetary System, to its conclusion. Michel Rocard added the citizen dimension: "What could be better than the unification of the currency symbols to create that feeling of shared membership that politics fails to inspire?" he asked. If that is true, then "how" it is done is less important than the goal, and the adoption of the "single currency" is more important than the conditions necessary for it to be viable.

"In the year 2000, we will still be able to pay in marks."[2] Hans Tietmeyer, President of all-powerful Bundesbank, the central bank of Germany, was not the type to have doubts. One year after the "passage to the single currency," set for January 1, 1999, by the Maastricht Treaty, nothing was to have changed for the German citizen. He would continue to use his national currency, just like the Frenchman, the Dutchman and every other European. The European Council, held in Madrid in December 1995, decided that would continue until 2002. However, no date appears in the Treaty. As far as Tietmeyer was concerned, that could go on until the political union would be achieved. The Germans' conviction was as deep-rooted as that of the French, but held to the opposite sequence: "Without political union, there can be no monetary union." The existence of a "single currency" and a European central bank could only "crown" a long process of political and economic rapprochement. Currency would not be the precondition.

And then, there was Great Britain. Margaret Thatcher's position was not dictated by the anti-European feelings that her colleagues in the European Council readily offered. "We carry on the European cultural tradition," she recalled in a speech made in Bruges, "as much as any other nation, (and) our destiny is in Europe."[3] Rather, her hostility to the idea of a single currency arose from doctrinal considerations. "The value of a currency is none other than that which the market determines." The "Iron Lady" thought that the politicians should give up defining the exchange rates between the currencies. Thus, the key was not to decide whether there should be a European central bank, but to immediately apply freedom of movement of capital. As for the single currency, "it would be sufficient to expand the usage of the ecu," created by German Chancellor Helmut Schmidt at the same time as the EMS. That could be accomplished by having the state issue its loans in ecus — which, indeed, the British Treasury did, although Germany remained reticent.

The scene thus being set, there was still some room for finishing touches that could temper or even neutralize certain distinct positions. By conviction as much as by function, Pierre Bérégovoy (who negotiated the Treaty of the EMU, for France, as a minister for the Economy and Finances), was in favor of a more pragmatic solution, preferring to fight unemployment and to organize Europe to stand up to the dollar. In 1987, he proposed "to give the ecu public status and, to that end, to create a European central bank with the ability to issue currency, and debt. We will not get there in a day," he acknowledged. "That is why we must organize, immediately, a common management of the European currencies vis-à-vis the dollar and yen, separating the management of the external parities from the intra-Community parities."[4] François Mitterrand let it go, but his advisers expressed their reservations: "The Germans won't want anything to do with this." They were already dreaming of a "single currency."

On the English side — by chance or as a function of Thatcher's decisions? — its doctrinal hostility was beaten down by the pragmatism of the successive Chancellors of the Exchequer.[5] From 1987-1988, Nigel Lawson, then John Major, stabilized the pound sterling in relation to the mark and supported joining the EMS. Thatcher saw this as the equivalent of "abdicating to the Bundesbank all control over monetary policy," which she found totally unacceptable. The disagreement with the prime minister, which erupted in June 1989 at the European Council in Madrid, quickly turned into a political crisis. Lawson had to resign. Finance Ministers are not the ones who set their countries' foreign policies, in London anymore than in Paris.

There were conflicts in Germany as well, between Bonn and Frankfurt, where functions ran counter to convictions. Chancellor Helmut Kohl's attachment to "the political and economic unity of free Europe" was extremely solid, but his first priority was political union and he was happy enough to use some of the Bundesbank's positions as arguments to cool Mitterrand's monetarist ardor. For his part, Karl-Otto Pöhl, President of the Bundesbank, was no less European than the Chancellor. In spite of his colleagues' reservations, he declared himself "very much in favor of strengthening the EMS and progressively transforming it into an economic and monetary European Union." But only to announce, in short order, "the conditions which must be met if monetary stability is to continue to be assured in the future." The roles were thus distributed: the Chancellor should set the goal; the Bundesbank should make sure that the process is conducted in conformity, not with its wishes, but indeed with its requirements. For both had one and only one concern: the German investor.

"The Germans are a nation of savers who live below their means; the Americans are a credit-card people and live beyond their means."[6] Coming from Schmidt, this report was a warning. For if his country is obsessed with monetary stability, it was less because of the hyperinflation of the 1920s than the monetary reform of June 1948, which replaced the reich mark with the Deutsche mark. Imposed by the Americans on a vanquished and occupied country, the parity between the old and the new currency was one-to-one for wages and pensions. But when, in October, it was time to convert the savings accounts, the parity was only 6.50 Deutsche marks for 100 reich marks. Thousands of individuals and some large investment portfolios were ruined. A half-century later the memory of this reform, imposed from outside, is still strong. German investors have enough political weight so that no leader forgets them, neither in Bonn nor in Frankfurt. In Germany, to defend the currency is to defend savings, and vice versa. And, more important yet, not to let the monetary policy depend on anyone other than the Bundesbank.

But who, in April 1988, was paying attention to the former chancellor's proposals? The German economy was a monster of virtue, at the time. Sustained growth, negative inflation, a small budget deficit, sizable foreign surpluses and the discount rate (the central bank's floor) at 2.5% when the Bank of France's was over 10%. What more could be wanted? When, at the end of June, the Bundesbank followed in the footsteps of the Bank of England and moved its intervention rate to 3% to recuperate the liquidity injected in the wake of the stock market crash of October 1987, the experts applauded its wisdom. It wasn't until interest rates started to rise — again and again throughout the summer, countering the downward trend started in France — that people began to be concerned.[7] The risk of renewed inflation then obsessed the Frankfurt authorities and worried the investors who had been accustomed to price stability and even, for a few years, a slight decline.

The German savers are as well organized as they are well defended. As members of the Investors' Defense Association, or through their representation via the savings bank federations and mutual benefit banks, they have links to the very heart of the Bundesbank. These institutions are strongly represented in the "Buba" council. The presidents of the Länder central banks, appointed by the elected presidents of the Länder, are seated side by side with the members of the board of directors appointed by the federal government. These district banks speak for the savings banks and the mutual benefit banks. There were eleven Länder central banks at the time and they had six members on the board of directors (in theory that can go up to ten) — a clear majority. So far, no one has succeeded in reducing their influence. When, in April 1991, during the reform of the statutes imposed by the German unification, Karl-Otto Pöhl (then President of Bundesbank) tried to limit the number of their representatives, he was isolated by his council and had to give up on the reform.[8]

The concerns of the German political and monetary authorities are thus diametrically opposed to those of the French and English leaders. German investment accounts were calculated in 1996 at 2 million francs on average; the authorities' concerns are in proportion with the questions the investors pose with regard to the future, the day when they will have to give up the mark. The single currency scares them; the investors are afraid it will not be as "powerful" as the mark and they will be, if not ruined, then at least impoverished. They want to be assured — and not only reassured — that when their fortune is converted to European currency, it will not lose any of its value and that they will still be able to enjoy their *pensions* in the sunny "Club Med" atmosphere of countries like Italy, Greece and Spain. And, as always, the fear is inversely proportional to the size of their estates. But how can anyone be sure? Research conducted among investors shows them generally hostile to the thought of abandoning the mark. It will take endless guarantees to get them to agree; and the Bundesbank is there to give the guarantees, and the government to ensure them. All results from this: the interest rate and exchange policies, the design of the EMU, the lack of exceptions. But a German victory will be long in the making. The English and the French will score the first points.

The liberalization of the capital markets set the scene for the first skirmishes. While the Single European Act was being adopted, at the Council of Rome, Thatcher forced the total and rapid liberalization of capital movements to be substituted for the advance toward economic and monetary union. In essence, that turned out to be a stumbling block. Upon his return to the Ministry of the Economy and Finances in May 1988, Bérégovoy found on his desk the draft of the corresponding European directive. It anticipated that liberalization would become effective in two years, on July 1, 1990. Having achieved the liberalization of the financial markets in 1985 and having started to dismantle the exchange controls, he was generally in favor. But following alarmist comments from the bankers, relayed by the ministry, he feared that the differences in tax rates on investments would lead to a flight of capital. This fear was particularly strong since the envisaged liberalization was to apply simultaneously in every country, without any particular protection for Europe.

To limit this effect, the minister proposed linking the liberalization of the movements of capital with the European harmonization of the taxation on investment income, and making the tax harmonization a "precondition" to that one. The Elysée, fearing that the Germans would object to this demand and, on top of the predictable resistance of Great Britain and Luxembourg, could block the launching of the Economic and Monetary Union, called him to order: the tax harmonization could only be "parallel, not a precondition." Mitterrand got Chancellor Kohl to go along with this.[9] But this decision did not go over well with German investors. Although they dutifully pay their income tax, they are a little less disciplined when it comes to paying tax on investment income. A deduction at the source would hit them hard. The response was immediate. Associations took up the cause, and investors sent 100 billion marks across the border to Luxembourg. Chancellor Kohl repudiated his Finance Minister, who had to resign. The plan for a European taxation on investments was buried, and for a long time. The German investors had just given Thatcher her sole victory. But they had already set the stage for the next move, which would seal their fate.

The Economic and Monetary Union was launched in February 1988 by Edouard Balladur, then Chirac's Minister for the Economy and Finances. Speaking on television a few months before the presidential elections, he decided to out-do President Mitterrand on the subject of European unity, so dear to the Christian Democrats. Balladur announced that he thought the time had come to "examine the possibility of creating a European central bank that would manage a common currency."[10] Three weeks later, in Bonn, Hans Dietrich Genscher, the irremovable German Minister for Foreign Affairs, published "a memorandum on a European monetary space and a European central bank." He proposed that a committee of experts be tasked with drafting a plan. It was duly established by the European Council held in Hanover in June 1988, and "charged with studying and defining the concrete steps that would lead to the progressive realization of the Economic and Monetary Union." Chancellor Kohl, who expressed a very limited degree of enthusiasm for the monetary union, allowed himself to be persuaded that, in terms of experts, the committee should be composed of the governors of the central banks with the addition of three carefully selected individuals.[11] The President of the Commission would, himself, hold the presidency. Bérégovoy would have liked to have experts who were a little more "diplomatic" and, undoubtedly, a different president. But he went along, convinced that the opinion of governors like Jacques Delors would in any event be impossible to circumvent. Thus was born "the Delors committee," of which Pöhl quickly became the most influential member and the principal draftsman. He submitted his report one year later, in spring 1989.

Here we must put to rest a legend, born from the confusion that soon cropped up between the Economic and Monetary Union and the Maastricht Treaty, between the single currency and the unification of Germany.[12] The Delors report was submitted to the heads of state and government in April. In June, the European Council (held that year in Madrid) approved the guidelines and the proposed three-stage scenario. At this same council, it was decided that a treaty should be prepared addressing the "Economic and Monetary Union" alone. At the time, when everyone was thinking about the coming celebration in Paris of the bicentennial of the French Revolution, nobody foresaw that in a few months history would accelerate abruptly. President Mitterrand had proposed holding an intergovernmental conference by the end of 1990, but Chancellor Kohl, while agreeing in principle, thought it premature to set a date. Thus, the contents of the future treaty and the various decisions that it implies are not based on the conditions of the German monetary unification, which took place only during the course of 1990. After having imposed his views on that project, the chancellor did not have to yield to the Bundesbank's requirements on the monetary unification of Europe. The scenario was already spelled out; it would be carried out as written.

However, the fall of the Berlin Wall changed the picture: now it was the two Germany's, whose unification was announced less than three weeks after the historical night of November 9-10, 1989, who came to the negotiating table. Until then, the Economic and Monetary Union had been a subject in itself. It abruptly became part of a larger question, to some extent a currency of exchange. For the French President, it was the touchstone of Germany's commitment to Europe; for the Chancellor, it was a pledge of goodwill toward his partner. Kohl, who seized the historic moment, sensed it before anyone else. Based on his own reservations about the monetary union, he took it hostage.

Everything hinged on the misunderstanding that was thus established between Paris and Bonn. Kohl's speech on German unification, November 28, 1989, sent a tremor through Franco-German relations, and the question of borders shook them for several months. The Elysée was full of worries and concerns. Would the Chancellor back off from European construction? The French President asked his partner for a firm commitment to the "single currency." At the opening of the European Council of Strasbourg, Kohl responded by proposing to set a date for the intergovernmental conference, stating "let's have it all ready in 1990 . . . in order to send a clear political message from Strasbourg. . ." in exchange for the Twelve's formal support for the German unification.[3] The treaty on the Economic and Monetary Union was now linked to the effects of German unification on the conduct of European affairs.

This linkage did not inspire any change in the process that was under way. Jean Paul Fitoussi suggests that seeing the German unification as "too insignificant an event to justify any modification of the parities within the EMS... was a dramatic, serious error, with consequences for the present, but also fraught with danger for the future of European construction."[14] But beyond the debate on the franc-mark parity[15] lay a more fundamental question: shouldn't the European monetary union have been completely rethought, both by shortening the expiration terms and by making political union the first, not the last, step toward monetary union? The occasion was missed and, it should be noted, mainly through the fault of French diplomacy.

The Franco-German misunderstanding on the monetary union resurfaced in spring 1990. Mitterrand wanted to accelerate negotiations on the EMU and tried to get Kohl to move up the convocation of the intergovernmental conference by six months. The chancellor adamantly refused. Instead, he insisted that the political union be given more attention and that the plan abandoned in Milan in 1985[16] be reconsidered. Now it was the French President's turn to rein in his partner. A compromise was finally reached during the "informal" council of Dublin in April 1990. A political union was to be conceived between then and December 31, 1992. But only in June was it decided to hold an intergovernmental conference distinct from the one on the EMU. It would meet in spring 1991 and cover institutions and international relations. Actually, there was complete disagreement as to the agenda. To avoid failure, a decision would be made retroactively to combine the two treaties into one, the now famous Maastricht Treaty, and to defer political union to a new intergovernmental conference, the CIG, not to be held until 1996!

The fall of the Berlin Wall did not succeed in reversing the order of French priorities between monetary union and political union. It did not change the Chancellor's either: he remained deeply committed to Europe, but German unification took precedence over European monetary unification. In the short run that goes without saying, but it is valid for the longer term as well. Kohl did not take the same approach to Europe as Schmidt. For Schmidt, the creation of a European currency was to be the (never fulfilled) second stage of the EMS; this was part of his "grand strategy of European integration." Schmidt acted, while Kohl made promises. Schmidt came up with accords to be implemented immediately, while his successor negotiated treaties whose execution was always put off to a later date. The contrast between the EMS and the EMU is striking. The first was created in ten months; the second was in the making for more than ten years. In fourteen years at the head of the chancellery, Kohl made two major monetary decisions with immediate effect: the movement of capital was freed, and the two Germany's were unified monetarily. Two decisions that draw opposite pictures: unification by the market on the one hand, by the State on the other. The first one opening up to the world, the second closing Germany back in on itself. The liberalization of the movements of capital was approved by the Bundesbank, the German monetary unification was carried out in spite of its sharp opposition — proof that for the Chancellor, the creation of a European currency was not a monetary question but a matter of political will. However, Kohl took only measured steps on the European currency, as he did on the question of German unification. In the year 2000, said Tietmeyer, "we will still be able to pay in marks." The Chancellor proved him right

"What people cannot or will not do, the markets will do for them, but painfully and usually chaotically."[17] François Renard, long-time financial columnist at *Le Monde*, said this about the Wall Street crash of October 1987, but it applies admirably to the attitude of the German authorities with regard to the plan for monetary union. Would the Bundesbank do what the Chancellor did not want to do? Judging from the Bundesbank's policy, throughout the treaty's negotiation, the question was more than rhetorical. The Bundesbank's Council never had a unanimous position on the question of monetary union. The deeply European feelings of presidents Pöhl and Tietmeyer coexisted with the monetary nationalism of Helmut Schlesinger — a long-time No. 2 before he took the presidency from 1991 to 1993 — and of the majority of the regional bank presidents. However, they all insisted on the objective stated in June 1988 by President Pöhl: to define "the essential points" that the German government would have to impose via the treaty, before they could agree to move toward monetary union. Even President Schlesinger mentioned it to Pöhl, recognizing that "these points appear in the statutes (of the SEBC) . . . in their entirety."[18]

For four years, the Bundesbank's monetary policy also fed speculations. Admittedly, there were sound economic reasons for raising the interest rates: the October 1987 stock exchange crisis, which caused a fear of renewed inflation; German monetary unification under conditions that the Bundesbank publicly resisted; the Gulf War. . . But the coincidence of certain decisions at the Bundesbank and the various European councils was very disturbing. In June 1988, the Delors committee was created in Hanover; a few days later, the rates started to climb. In June 1989, the Delors report was adopted in Madrid; rates rose again. In September, the Bundesbank moved again, bringing the discount rate to 6% and the Lombard to 8%; these rates were murderous for the European economies, while as of yet the Berlin Wall was still standing and there was no apparent prospect of German unification in the near future. As it does during every election period in Germany (the elections took place in November 1990), the Bundesbank froze its monetary policy for almost a year. Then, rates went up again, synchronized to the negotiations for European monetary union: in November 1990, just before the start of the conference of Rome; September 1991, when a decisive meeting of the Finance Ministers held in Apeldoorn, the Netherlands; December 1991, during the European Council of Maastricht; and finally, July 1992, after the Danes said "no" and while France was voting on the referendum. The Lombard was at 9.75% and the discount rate was changed to 8.75%, their highest levels since the 1930s. This rise would also be the last.

An era was finished. France said "yes" in Maastricht by referendum, if only by a slender margin. The other countries were preparing to ratify the treaty and the Danes were preparing to vote again. The September 1992 monetary crisis led to the expulsion of the sterling and the lira, making Great Britain's and Italy's participation in the monetary union less likely — which must have pleased the Bundesbank. In July 1993, a brutal attack against the franc seemed to jeopardize plans for a moment, until the Bundesbank, under pressure from Chancellor Kohl, agreed to defend the French currency. Since then, for the Bundesbank, the die was cast. The promise of growth evaporated. On the contrary Europe entered a recession and unemployment strengthened its grip. What a way to influence public opinion! Then began a long period of declining interest rates,[19] which, in three years, brought short-term rates back to their early-1988 levels, and even slightly less in real terms. Admittedly, they remained positive, but it would be hard to set negative rates given the Bundesbank's policy of looking out for investors. Meanwhile, the European landscape was profoundly changed.

Did the Bundesbank conduct its monetary policy with the intent to compromise or to put pressure on the negotiations, as people accused it of doing? Was David Marsh (then correspondent with the *Financial Times* in Frankfurt) right in suggesting that, by raising its rates, "the Bundesbank let us know that it would not give up its position without a fight"?[20] The truth is probably neither black nor white. As its leaders tirelessly repeated, Buba only fulfills its mission, which is to ensure domestic stability. Its increasing responsibility for the stability of the EMS, explained Pöhl, should not divert it from its top priority, which was "to pursue a money supply policy, which presupposes managing liquidity to a certain extent, and this management presupposes certain market rates."[21] His successor was even more blunt. Questioned by the newspaper *Der Spiegel* as to whether "the Council of the Bundesbank is only looking for what is good for Germany," Schlesinger answered: "That is its fundamental mission. We must pursue our own original goals as prescribed by the law on the Bundesbank."[22] The creation of the European Monetary Institute in 1994 did not change a thing. The treaty denied it power over monetary decisions. Until January 1, 1999, the beginning of the monetary union, decision-making belonged to the central banks and the national governments — and to no one else. In deciding its interest rate policy, the Bundesbank applied this rule "completely independently," and its leaders decided to apply it right up until the last day.

"If the single currency is as stable as the mark," Pöhl said one day, "I am ready to participate in the monetary union immediately." Tietmeyer would later add: "The single currency will have to be as good as the mark, not only at the beginning of the monetary union, but for the duration." Over the years, the mark's strength with respect to the other currencies had become a gauge of prosperity, and no German political leader would suggest giving up the mark for a currency that would not be as "strong." It would be better to do without the monetary union. The ecu had cost them. Not because of its name, but because of its definition. Its value was based on the weighted average of the currencies making up the ecu "basket," and since the weaker currencies were devalued after its creation in 1979, the ecu's value had also dropped. It was thus both a bad currency and a bad symbol for the future. The euro, creation *ex nihilo*, would be virginal, pure, free of any negative influence. Good-bye, ecu. Long live the euro. So decided the European Council of Madrid in December 1995.

But what does a "strong mark" mean? The mark is undoubtedly strong compared to the dollar. For thirty years, except for 1979-1984, the American dollar has been continually devaluated compared to the mark, from 4.20 marks[23] in 1958 to 2.66 in 1977, to 1.82 in 1988. In the fall of 1996 it went to 1.50 — considerably undervalued — before going up to 1.80 marks during the summer of 1997. The mark is also strong compared to the other European currencies. Since the creation of the EMS, it is the only currency that was constantly revalued compared to all the European currencies. Thus, the German cultivation of a stable monetary policy is, in fact, more a policy favoring an *upward* trend. Its overt purpose is to fight inflation by reducing the price of imported products, in order to balance high domestic wages. But its hidden intent is to enhance the value of investments and purchasing power abroad, during the foreign vacations so popular with the Germans; that certainly helps a monetary culture to take root.

The German leadership had no intention of changing this, neither in Bonn nor in Frankfurt. In their eyes, the stability of the euro, just like that of the mark, implied that the monetary union will not stand in the way of their constant revaluation vis-a-vis other currencies. The euro had to remain free to fluctuate and, contrary to the wishes of the French leaders, no parity could be assigned to it. In a system of total freedom of the movement of capital, one cannot hope to use the interest rate both to control the money supply and to maintain the exchange rate. This is why "the Bundesbank pursues neither an economic policy nor an exchange rate policy,"[24] affirmed President Pöhl. "It pursues a money supply policy — which is not always understood elsewhere," he added perfidiously. Times have changed, but the lack of understanding lingers on.

Governments that spell out an explicit exchange rate target — that is, which announce the parity they intend to defend — give up any purely monetary policy. Their interest rate policy is dictated by that of the country whose currency they follow. "If our partners exclude adjusting the exchange rates as a tool, they have to accept the consequences that that implies as far as both monetary policy and interest rates,"[25] explained Pöhl in an address to the French. By binding themselves to the mark, France gave up any chance to pursue an autonomous monetary policy; it gave this up long ago. It dates back to President Pompidou, who had tied the franc to the dollar, following the suspension of the Bretton Woods system by President Nixon. In 1978, Raymond Barre, then Prime Minister, preferred anchoring to the mark rather than to the dollar. Mitterrand, after having tried to avoid it, did the same. Thus, when the rates go up in Germany, they also go up in France; when they fall, France can reduce hers. But only the Bundesbank has a policy. Not the Bank of France.

Thatcher was, apart from Germany, the only European leader to have been clearly aware of this contradiction. She refused to make the exchange rate an objective in itself. "It is part of our sovereignty." But it is also a pillar of monetary philosophy. She always considered, sometimes in opposition to her own Finance Ministers, that monetary policy should be guided exclusively by the objective of inflation. Controlling the money supply was a means; it could not be an end, for "the monetary indicators are often distorted, misleading and ephemeral,"[26] a view that is corroborated by the practice of the Bundesbank.[27] That was the major reason for her hostility toward the EMS. Even in 1996, the vice-governor of the Bank of England preferred inflation targets to the creation of a new EMS: "Since price stability in each country is a necessary condition to a lasting stability of the exchange rates, one can expect that convergence in the stability of prices will generate a considerable degree of stability in the exchange rate."[28] But this position also sent it off course.

The forced march toward the Economic and Monetary Union, to which the Twelve committed, did not dissipate the misunderstandings that prevailed at its launching. France remains faithful to the motivations that have underlain European construction since the 1950s: to dilute Germany in a greater whole, the better to control it, and to put Germany's industrial power to the service of Europe — and in particular, of France. German unification did not change this intention. The fear of still greater supremacy even reinforced this goal. In this sense, the Maastricht Treaty extends the Treaty of Rome. As Germany's monetary policy becomes more rigid, the EMU looks like a means of "regaining monetary sovereignty" and reversing the trend. In Paris, they are convinced that, while "the Bundesbank took control of Europe" with the EMS, the EMU will make it possible for "Europe to take control of the Bundesbank."[29] If Germany should take advantage of this dream, that doesn't make it any less legitimate. One man took up that task: Karl-Otto Pöhl.

Notes

1. *Le Nouvel Observateur*, July 27, 1989.
2. Hans Tietmeyer, interview published in *Süddeutsche Zeitung* October 20, 1994.
3. Speech given to the College of Europe, September 20, 1988.
4. Interview published in *La Tribune de l'economie*, November 30, 1987.
5. Cf. the account that Margaret Thatcher gave, *op. cit.*, Chapter 24.
6. *Die Zeit*, April 22, 1988.
7. Eric Aeschimann and Pascal Riché described it in *La Guerre de sept ans*, Paris, Calmann Lévy, 1996, pp. 40-46.
8. A reform finally came at the end of 1991. The council henceforth comprises seven members of the directory and nine representatives of the Länder banks, which thus preserve the majority.
9. Pierre Favier, Michel Martin-Roland, *op. cit.*, T 3, p. 70.
10. In the television broadcast *L'Heure de verité*, February 6, 1988.
11. This refers to Niels Thygesen, professor of economy in Copenhagen, to Alexandre Lamfalussy, general manager of the bank for international settlements in Basle (where the committee will meet) and the future president of the European Monetary Institute, and to Miguel Boyer, president of "Banco Exterior de Espana."
12. See for example Jean Pierre Chevènement, *France-Allemagne: parlons franc*, Paris, Plon, 1996 and David Marsh, *La Bundesbank aux commandes de l'Europe*, Paris, Belin, 1993.
13. Cf. the 1st part *supra*.
14. Jean Paul Fitoussi, *Le Débat interdit*, Arléa, Paris, 1995, p. 75.
15. Eric Aeschimann and Pascal Riché give a detailed description of the legend of "the revaluation of the mark." The only time Otto Pöhl mentioned it publicly was October 6, 1989, after the last time the interest rate went up, i.e. one month before the fall of the Berlin Wall. His "request" had been relayed by Count Lambsdorf, former president of the liberal party, who had denounced the "obstructionist" attitude of France. *La Guerre de sept ans, op. cit.*, pp. 133-141.
16. See below, The Political Quarrel.
17. *Le Monde*, October 28, 1987.
18. Interview in *Der Spiegel*, February 17, 1992.
19. The Bundesbank maintains that it did not change its monetary policy from one period to another since it "leads a policy of money supply and not of support for the economic situation." But the continuity of the method is no less likely to entail changing the direction of rate changes.
20. David Marsh, *op. cit.*, p. 15.
21. Press conference with K.-O. Pöhl, January 31, 1991.
22. Interview in *Der Spiegel*, February 17, 1992.
23. In 1948, the allied military authorities fixed the exchange rate at 3.33 marks per dollar; in September 1949, the mark was devaluated by 20.6%, the new parity being established at 4.20 marks per dollar.
24. K.-O. Pöhl, press conference, January 31, 1991.
25. *Ibid.*
26. Margaret Thatcher, *op. cit.*, p. 558.
27. Otmar Issing, number two at the Bundesbank, admitted in an interview given to *Frankfurter Allgemeine Zeitung*, July 26, 1996, that the money supply (measured by the aggregate called M3) "is largely determined by the behavior of the banks and the financial services" and in particular by the trends in the various forms of investment. However, they vary from one country to another, which can only

make more complicated still the interpretation of the aggregates of money supply at the European level.

28. Declaration by Howard Davies to the Economic Forum of Alpbach (Austria),
August 29, 1996, *Le Monde*, August 31, 1996.
29. Pascal Riché, Charles Wyplosz, *L'Union monétaire d'Europe*, Paris, Le Seuil, 1993.

Chapter 7

A Monetary Janus

The man who watched over the cradle of the future Economic and Monetary Union European in spring 1988 was there as a result of his abilities, his authority, his charm and good-natured nonchalance. However, the fairies had jinxed his first steps. The 1929 crash on Wall Street poisoned the year of his birth; the ensuing crisis condemned his father, an office worker, to long layoffs. Then his mother died at the end of the war; he worked nights from the age of fifteen in an office sorting mail for the English army. Nothing in his difficult childhood destined little Karl-Otto to become the all-powerful President of the Bundesbank one day.

Then, he got a lucky break. An apprentice journalist for the Social Democrat party, he got a scholarship to finish his baccalaureate, then found a job as a sportswriter to pay for his studies in economics at the University of Göttingen. Meanwhile, he stayed with the SDP and, when Willy Brandt became Chancellor, he joined the Ministry of Finance and quickly became Secretary of State for Helmut Schmidt, then for Karl Schiller. At 48, he was appointed vice-president of the Bundesbank and became President about three years later, in 1980. There he remained eleven years, until May 16, 1991, when he announced that he had decided to leave. This decision was inevitable, given the fifteen months of disagreements with Chancellor Kohl over the German monetary unification — fifteen months that had shaken his authority within the institution and that were beginning to threaten the mark's stability. As boss of the very independent Bundesbank, he had been forced to bend to the will of a politician.

When Pöhl was preparing, at the end of July 1991, to join the prestigious Oppenheim Commercial Bank of Cologne, negotiations on the Economic and Monetary Union were far from complete. They were finalized only a few months later, that December, during the European Council held in Maastricht (a small city on the Meuse, where the Netherlands borders Belgium and Germany). But the whole process was already established in outline and nothing could divert it from its course, a course that bore the indelible mark of only one man: Karl-Otto Pöhl. He had proposed it from day one, in a long article given to Frankfurt's financial daily, the *Frankfurter Allgemeine Zeitung*.[1] On the eve of the council of June 1988 in Hanover, the city of his birth and the place where the first drafts of the Economic and Monetary Union would be prepared, Pöhl was scheduled to announce his "vision of a European monetary space." When the financial adviser from the French embassy in Bonn forwarded to Paris his comments on the translation, he noted that it "does not introduce any new elements." The President of the Bundesbank only "spelled out and clarified" what he had been repeating for months. Once again, nobody seemed to be listening. In Paris as in London, everyone saw what he wanted to see; here a green light to go ahead, there a red light. François Mitterrand was delighted that the monetary union was being inaugurated; Margaret Thatcher heard Pöhl's remarks as a "probable" refusal to move forward and envisioned the formation of an Anglo-German alliance to ruin the Delors plan![2] But President Pöhl was not just a conductor on the train of the monetary union. He saw himself as its originator, the great architect. Thatcher's bizarre misapprehension would lead to the belief that the Bundesbank was hostile to, or even "plotting against"[3] the single currency.

Well-versed in politics, President Pöhl was a fine strategist. Like his colleagues at the Bundesbank, he fundamentally doubted that "the political environment would allow decisions and transfers of sovereignty on so large a scale"[4] as those that he deemed essential for the realization of an Economic and Monetary Union. But he remembered from the experience of the creation of the EMS, in 1979 — although he forgot it a few years later during the German unification — that the Central Bank cannot withstand the will of the politicians. Thus, he thought it would be best to get in front of it, the better to impose his conditions. While most of his council members dug in their heels at any mention of a monetary union, he was quick to describe it as "a far-reaching political goal," and "desirable." And even before the political leaders began to think it over, he wrote the scenario that he offered to them on a silver platter. Everything was included: the stages that should be followed to achieve it, the areas in which the politicians would have to relinquish their control, and the discipline they would have to impose. The whole package had to be accepted, or there would be no monetary union and the Bundesbank would preserve its unilateral control over monetary policy.

What did Pöhl actually say, that day? First, he gave a little history and recalled that the idea of defining a European monetary union was "contained" in the Werner report from 1970 (which the collapse of the Bretton Woods monetary system eliminated). "A monetary union assumes, on the domestic level, absolute and irreversible convertibility of currencies, the end of exchange rate fluctuation margin, irrevocable fixed parities and the total liberation of capital flows." On the other hand, he added, "that does not necessarily imply the harmonization of all policies; surviving differences in the tax systems, wage scales and other sectors would constitute advantages or disadvantages." In other words, the reconciliation of the interest rates does not require reconciliation of taxation on investment. At best, it "exerts a certain constraint towards harmonization." A single tax on investments for the whole community, in the form of a deduction at the source (which Pierre Bérégovoy tried to promote) is thus not essential.

Then, President Pöhl made a distinction, which he considered essential: *a monetary union is not a single currency.* The first supposes only that parities are irrevocably fixed; the second requires abandoning national currencies. They are not concomitant. To get from one to the other will still take time, even "if there is only one more small step to take." That "small step" was not to be made quickly: "There is a long way to go before we get to this final stage. Substituting a common currency for the national currencies would be the 'crowning' of the process of monetary integration." Pöhl immediately casts aside the idea that there might be a short cut in the form of "a parallel currency serving as an alternative, allowing the gradual establishment of a European monetary union." He thus rejected the idea that a European currency (called "common," in this case) could coexist with the national currencies, as favored by Bérégovoy and the British. Indeed, said Pöhl, "we would [still] not be able to avoid making the political decisions which are essential for the creation of a monetary union."

He also challenged the possibility that the ecu was playing this role, "because of the way it was designed," a design that the Bundesbank had been denouncing since Helmut Schmidt imposed it by creating the EMS. The ecu is defined by the weighted average of the parities of "the basket" of national currencies. However, "an ecu-basket would not have been able to exercise a great enough power of expulsion. . . . nor develop its own specific qualities." Thus, it would have to be given up, even its name. And, by way of warning, "a parallel European currency should have a level at least equal to that of the best of the national currencies" (insinuating the mark), which means that conditions would have to be met that would "already define the final phase." Consequently, "What is the point of making the costly detour to a parallel currency?" Here, the English were given notice, but Thatcher did not care in the slightest. She was not about to give in to the President of the Bundesbank, nor the reverse. She put a plan on the table for a "common currency," baptized the "strong ecu." But Great Britain remained isolated.

Then Pöhl came to his "vision" of the European Central Bank, or rather — and we will see that this nuance is of the greatest importance — to "a European system of central bank(s)." Immediately he added, addressing the scarcely veiled intention of the French, this is not essential to the monetary union. "One can also conceive of effective monetary cooperation between the national central banks if, at the same time, in other policy areas, convergence is sufficient." In any event, "a clear allocation of the functions" will have to be defined, and it would have to correspond to the objective laid down by the law on the Bundesbank, which is "to ensure monetary stability and therefore stable prices. . . A central bank system which would place a lower premium on this objective would not be acceptable." This system must, of course, be "independent of the national governments, as well as the European institutions," and "not to be authorized to finance public deficits by monetary creation."

Pöhl's article must be read to the end. For him, the creation of a European Central Bank does not mean the disappearance of the national central banks, and the primary among them, the Bundesbank. "A European Central bank system can hardly be organized but in a decentralized, federative fashion, and therefore according to the principle of subsidiarity — according to which only the bare minimum would be centralized and national jurisdictions would be preserved to the greatest possible extent. A European Central bank should thus resemble the Bundesbank system or the U.S. Federal Reserve more than the centralized structure of most European countries' central banks." Management of the banking structure should thus remain within the purview of the national central banks. But, in spirit, subsidiarity must also extend to the monetary policy itself, unlike what occurs in Frankfurt or in New York. The Bundesbank, the Bank of France . . . as a result, all of the national central banks will remain essential components of the future system.

Monetary stability obviously requires an adequate exchange rate policy. But with respect to third currencies, the dollar and the yen, "the stabilization of the parities cannot and must not be the essential goal of the monetary policy, especially in an inflationary environment." So there would be no exchange rate target, at least explicitly. Fluctuation would remain the rule. That does not exclude a certain cooperation, "including interventions on the exchange market." To handle that, "a European Central bank must be given and must have full control over at least part of the available national exchange reserves." The accord that established the EMS had already envisaged this, but at the time the Bundesbank had wanted "legislative regulation," which Schmidt did not want.

In the immediate future, it would be necessary "to strengthen the operating capacity of the EMS." However, that cannot lead the Bundesbank "to accept currencies of other members of the EMS as part of its reserves," "as it is being incited to do." That "would not strengthen the EMS, but would weaken it because the countries with soft currency would then escape the constraint of adjustment." Consequently, the Bundesbank's annual report from that time states that "the issuing house will limit itself to using the dollar as a reserve currency."[5] In addition, this same report recalled the important role played by the committee of the central bank governors in the hope that the latter would be able "in a professional, timely way, and without detrimental publicity, to proceed to the monetary readjustments necessary (inside the Community)." And it added: "Proposals on this matter, however, have been rejected by the Finance Ministers." The Germans have a good memory, when it suits them.

For the reality is, "The Deutsche mark has become the system's anchor. It has gradually acquired the role of principal currency of intervention and reference. It has become the European monetary system's standard of stability and has delivered a solid basis for the effective operation of the system. . . To remove the anchor without having something to replace it would be fatal not only for the Federal Republic, but in the same measure, for the other European countries."[6] The Bundesbank thus invested itself with a responsibility that ends up setting the Bundesbank's own objectives before European cooperation, in particular when it comes to market intervention. That excludes any automation of the "intramarginal" interventions, those intended to keep the parities within the limits of fluctuation. That also means that, having entered into the monetary union, the German monetary policy will still work exclusively toward the objective assigned by its statutes — that is "the stability of the mark."

Everything had been said. Pöhl's successors as head of the Bundesbank, in spite of having very different temperaments, and the members of the council (for the most part not very much inclined to give up mark) left everything as it was written. They didn't change one comma. Why should they? Isn't the Bundesbank the master of the game? Isn't its president omnipresent, alone against the politicians, making sure the negotiations do not go anywhere that he does not want? As for his homologues, Robin Leigh-Pemberton, Governor of the Bank of England, was very quickly thrown out of the ring when his plan for a strong ecu was rejected; Jacques de Larosière, Governor of the Bank of France, initially tried to defend the franc-mark parity, which depends on collaboration with the Bundesbank. He could not do anything that would compromise this objective. He advised his minister in the negotiations, but remained in the background. The other central banks either supported the German theses or had too weak a currency to have any influence.

The result is not surprising. The Delors report, made public in spring 1989 and approved two months later at the European Council of Madrid, is an exact copy of the theses stated one year prior by the President of the Bundesbank. Wasn't he, in any case, the principal writer? It's all there. The definition of the monetary union from the Werner Report; the fact that "the adoption of a single currency, while not being strictly necessary, could be regarded as a natural and desirable extension of the monetary union;" the distinction between moving toward a single currency and actually switching over, which was put off to a later (and unspecified) date; refutation of the British proposal of a parallel currency and of the French suggestion of joint management of the exchange reserves; the need for budgetary constraints that would permanently establish "an effective ceiling for deficits" — which precedes the future "stability pact" — and finally, the prohibition "of direct access to the central bank's credit and other forms of monetary financing," i.e. the "monetary floor."

"Because of the political structure of the Community and the advantage of incorporating the existing central banks into a new system," continues the Delors report, "the institutional organization would take the form of what could be called a European system of central banks (ESCB). . . [which] would include a central institution and the national central banks." The ensemble would, obviously, be "independent with regard to instructions from the national governments and the Community authorities." It would have "the stability of prices" as its objective. It would operate in accordance with the principle of "subsidiarity" within the following plan: "The council of the ESCB, composed of the governors of the national central banks and of members of the directory, will formulate and set the guidelines of the monetary policy, and the national central banks will conduct business in accordance with the decisions taken." Lastly, "The system will be responsible for managing the exchange rates and reserves."

While the Delors report was being drafted, the President of the Bundesbank and the President of the Commission shared roles. As Pöhl was locking down the draft of the future treaty, Delors was playing politics. His first political act was to propose breaking the process into three stages. The first stage would begin with the complete liberalization of the flows of capital, on July 1, 1990; it would be used to assist in negotiating the treaty, and to make it possible for all the currencies to join the EMS without hurting the fluctuation margins. The second would start when the treaty went into effect, scheduled for January 1, 1994. Its goal would be to increase economic convergence and to set up the European system of central banks (which was finally deferred to the third stage). In the third stage, the parities would be set irrevocably and the Community institutions would be given authority to handle all foreseeable monetary matters. It would be only "during the final stage [that] the national currencies would be replaced by a single community currency." So, three stages, but "a single process," said the report. Anyone embarking on the monetary union would also accept its conclusion, the single currency. France and Germany were satisfied, but for opposite reasons. The report notes the plan for a single currency. But, by binding the process to its final goal, President Delors was forcing the hand of the governments. He constrained them to endorse the timetable and the conditions stated by the President of the Bundesbank. On the one hand, the single currency would come up only at the end of the last stage, of which it would be the "crowning glory"; in addition, it was all or nothing. If you didn't want the single currency, you could not join the monetary union. This led to Thatcher's famous "No, no, no."

Delors' second political act was to organize a partnership with the least wealthy countries in the Community, whose support was essential to the adoption of the EMU. The report introduces, for their benefit, a link between the monetary union and regional inequalities. He argued that the monetary union would increase the risk of imbalances if the Community did not implement policies aiming to reduce the regional and structural disparities. With this in mind, he asked for a doubling of the structural funds, which were decided in principle in February 1988, effective before the second stage should begin. He thus laid the groundwork for a necessary increase in the Community's budgetary resources. This proposal was aimed at the beneficiary countries — Ireland, Portugal, Spain and Greece — whose support for the EMU was essential. But, to make it easier to pass, he extended the aid to areas of the richest countries should they be confronted with problems with employment or retraining. The argument is specious and contrary to the principle of subsidiarity; disparities exist, indeed, with or without the monetary union, and regional planning is not within the Community's domain. This led to the saying, among those who were against the EMU, that President Delors "paid [the beneficiary countries] for supporting his plan"[7] by offering them aid.

In Paris, Bérégovoy's initial reaction was hardly enthusiastic. He was opposed to a system of central banks that would be independent and leave the political leaders weaponless. Attempting to regulate everything by just one, single text was tantamount to declaring, today, what one's successors would be doing ten years down the road, which by then may need to be done differently. He feared that time was being wasted in endless negotiations instead of coming up with effective means at the European level to fight unemployment. Fundamentally, the French Finance Minister remained attached to his idea of a construction that would emphasize the ecu, more a common currency than a single currency. In a speech given in Frankfurt a few days before the fall of the Berlin Wall, he explained: "The bases of monetary Europe are parities that will be stable, then fixed and irrevocable; a monetary policy that is coordinated, then common, and finally single; a common exchange policy with respect to third currencies (principally the dollar); and coherent macro-economic policies."[8] In the immediate future, he sought to accelerate European growth by creating a financial partnership between France and Germany. In December 1998, he proposed to that end the organization of "a recycling of German surpluses," which would make them available to the countries whose balance of payments was overdrawn, such as France. But the initiative was not followed up.

Monetary integration had already taken another course. When Bérégovoy shared his reservations, based on the Delors report, with the President of the Republic, the President simply asked him whether he had any allies likely to support another solution. "France cannot isolate itself," added the President.[9] For Mitterrand, the conditions were not so important; the main thing was to move forward. "France must support the Delors report. You can always fine-tune one or two points." The Minister for Finance then set to work, proposing during negotiations the idea of "a European economic government" and setting, in the Treaty, the dates for moving to the third stage. The die was cast. In spite of Thatcher's sharp opposition, the Delors report was adopted without change in Madrid in June 1989.

With that, the Economic and Monetary Union was on track and moving. The very vocal debate that took place in the European Council made it possible to gauge the difference between the various positions. On the final objective, Mitterrand and Kohl confirmed their agreement. But the French President tried to speed up the monetary union, convinced by his advisers that it was the only way of loosening the vice grip of the Bundesbank, whose monetary policy was increasingly restrictive. The German Chancellor preferred a more deliberate pace, sensitive to the concerns of his electorate (investors) and to the Bundesbank leaders' advice to take it slowly. As for Thatcher, the debate in

Madrid sounded the beginning of her retreat by revealing irremediable conflicts within her Cabinet caused by the debate over Europe; this shortly led to the departure of Nigel Lawson, the Chancellor of the Exchequer.

Pöhl's work of locking things down was not yet finished. He wanted to show that his position was not personal, but involved his whole institution. The Council of the Bundesbank did that, just before the intergovernmental conference that was set for the end of the year. In a long resolution published on September 20, 1990, it talks of "its duty to call attention to the consequences of this process, and to point out the conditions that must be met in order for monetary stability to continue to be assured in the future."[10] It recalls that, in its opinion, they are "ineluctable, and not subject to compromise. The conditions were: a common monetary institution in the form of a European system of central banks; [that] the status of the ESCB and the rules concerning budgetary discipline must be fixed by a treaty ratified by the national parliaments and thus modifiable only with their agreement (and thus with that of the German Parliament); that the exchange mechanism of the EMS should have been in place for long enough, without a derogatory regimen; and the absence, during the second stage, of any institutional change which would restrict the room for maneuver of the national monetary policy." In other words, the European Central Bank could not exist before the third stage and the European Monetary Institute, planned for the second, would not have any monetary power. This last question, the only one that was discussed, eviscerated the second stage of the monetary union. Helmut Schlesinger, who was still only a vice-president of his institution, acknowledged himself that he did "not see very clearly why the second stage was needed."[11] Unless it was to create a means for delaying the deadlines by a few years; and to call for "the currency of those who are eternally wed," but that would only come later. " Only one thing is clear," he added, "the potential fiancés still have to agree on the conditions."

Pöhl could leave the Bundesbank in July 1991 without a concern. If, as he confessed himself, "he was preaching in the desert"[12] in connection with German unification, it was not the same for the Maastricht Treaty. The negotiators could only take up again, one after the other, the conditions formulated in 1988: the maintenance of price stability as the principal objective (Article 105); the prohibition on granting discovery to authorities, whether Community, national or local (Art. 104); the need for avoiding excessive public deficits (Art. 104 C); the creation of a European system of central banks — ESCB — composed of the European Central Bank and the national central banks (Art. 106); the independence of the national central banks, as well as the ESCB and ECB with regard to the national and Community decision-making bodies (Art. 107); and finally, the strict maintenance of national monetary control during the second stage (Art. 109 F).

However, the French Minister for the Economy and Finances obtained two concessions from the Bundesbank. First, Bérégovoy opposed the idea of limiting the monetary union to a "core" of five or six countries, as the Bundesbank wanted. "I will reject any provision which would exclude by principle such and such state, small or large,"[13] he declared in June 1990. He did not want the negotiation to hypothesize about each one's ability to meet the envisaged conditions, and insisted that the negotiation be extended to twelve. In the second place, he required that a timetable be set so that it would not be left to the monetary authorities to decide at what moment the states could be considered ready to move on to the third stage. He made that a condition of France's approval of the Treaty. But this timetable only establishes the date of moving to the third stage. That would be January 1, 1997, if a sufficient number of countries agrees or, in any event, on January 1, 1999 at the latest. The Treaty leaves blank the deadline for the generalized use of the European currency. Only the monetary union is programmed for before the year 2000. It will not be until the next century that all the Europeans will have the same currency symbols.

Above all, Pöhl attempted to organize the power within the ESCB. Bérégovoy let himself be convinced that "the Germans are ready to share power on an equal footing, [since] we will carry as much weight as they within the future directorate and within the council made up of the governors of the twelve national central banks."[14] But this analysis was shared neither in Bonn nor in Frankfurt. On the contrary, every provision was designed to give the power to the Bundesbank. How? The answer lies entirely in an institution baptized by President Pöhl with the barbaric name of the "European System of Central Banks," the ESCB; a system which includes the future European Central Bank and, at its side, the old but still valiant national central banks, whose death certificate was by no means sealed by the Treaty.

Let's stop for a moment to examine this new invention in monetary history. The ESCB was promoted as a federal system similar to the American Federal Reserve or the Bundesbank. Actually, it is quite different. In both the United States and in Germany, the central bank is a unified institution which, following the example of the Bank of England or the Bank of France, holds full monetary jurisdiction, both the decision-making power and the means of execution. The difference between the issuing houses, beyond the control of the banking system, lies only in the respective powers of the presidents of the ones and the governors of the others. This difference translates into democratic power shared between the members of the council in one case (which makes Pöhl, says David Marsh, "as much a hostage of the council as its master,"[15]) and the sovereign power of the governor in the other (at least until the status of the Bank of France was changed).

The ESCB is radically different. It does not escape through European construction, a mixture of federal and intergovernmental elements. Its council, like that of the Bundesbank, is made up of the governors and presidents of the national central banks and the president and the members of the directorate of the (future) European Central Bank. On the other hand, the national banks retain some monetary functions. They will be "the weapon hand" of the ESCB. They will act "on behalf" of the European Central Bank. The protocol appended to the Treaty explicitly provides that the national banks retain the possibility of carrying out the transactions necessary for managing the interest rates ("open market" transactions) and credit rates as decided by the ESCB Council (Art. 18). The treaty introduced "a possibility;" the Ministers of Finance and the governors have since transformed it into certainty. The national banks will thus keep the market. In the end, the ESCB has two faces: heads, it's European; tails, it's national.

One might for a moment have thought that this configuration, which weakens the role of the European Central Bank from day one, would never see the light of day. The Green Book on "the realization of the Economic and Monetary Union,"[16] written in spring 1995, had proposed that "a financial critical mass" be switched into euros, to be made up of the national debts when the "irrevocable" parities would be set. As of January 1, 1999, the European Central Bank would have had at its disposal a vast euro market and the national banks would have been quickly marginalized. The German authorities opposed it (the European Council of December 1995), conceding at most that any new public borrowing would be in euros, after entering the monetary union. Under pressure from the banks, they seemed to be moving. If they did not accept immediate conversion, that would mean that, for a (long?) time, a double debt market would coexist, one of credits in euros and one of credits in national currencies. Traders would thus retain the possibility, during the third stage, of arbitrage between the securities of the member states according to their quality. With the exchange rates fixed, the risk premium would disappear; it would be replaced by a differentiation of interest rates, according to the level of debt and the budgetary situation of the states. That would be a highly unstable situation and the European Central Bank would have scarcely any means of neutralizing it.

In the same way, the aggregate national exchange reserves would not be centralized. The assets would remain in the national banks, which would be able to perform any transaction authorized by the ECB. Within the ESCB, the national central banks thus retain considerable power. Then was Schmidt right when, in April 1989, he said of the Delors report: "Did it never occur to the governors that a centralized form of management should be considered? Or did they just decide to slide over all that, and only look at the question of how to get around the abolition of the powers inherited from bureaucratic autonomy?"[17] The Treaty doesn't leave much room for ambiguity. "Without prejudice to Community competences and agreements, the member states can negotiate in the international bodies and conclude international agreements" (Art. 109-5). Moreover, until the end of the whole process, and not only until the beginning of the third stage, the Finance Ministers, directors of the Treasury, and governors or presidents of the national central banks will preserve their place within the International Monetary Funds as well as in the club of industrialized countries called the G7. Hypocritically, the Treaty deferred the question of Community representation in the international monetary authorities to a decision, to be taken by majority vote, of the council of the ESCB (Art. 109-4). By no means did it envisage that the first would disappear in favor of the second.

Monetary power was not shared. The appearance of power can satisfy the vanity of certain leaders, but it was not the real power. France had been pursuing a mirage. It succeeded in only dressing in spangled blue the subordination of its monetary policy to power of the Bundesbank. Throughout the negotiations, the Frankfurt authorities ensured their future and preserved their power. The ESCB did not diminish it; it set the Community to guarantee it. Monetary sovereignty remained the privilege of the country whose currency was used to "anchor" the system. However, the Bundesbank did not imagine there could exist any other "anchor" with the European monetary union but the mark. They certainly could not accept that the anchor of the EMS was "the system itself," to quote Jean-Claude Trichet, then Director of the Treasury. While the national central banks retained significant power within the ESCB, since most of them had either a weak currency or a small country, the power remained hypothetical. For those that count, the control of power was an even greater a prize since each one had a voice, without demographic weighting. In the event of a difference of opinion, the majority and minority would have to learn how to coexist. But can one imagine that the Bundesbank, the system's "anchor," would find itself in the minority? In the event of dissension, would its council agree to give in as, in theory, the Treaty obliged it to do? It would be best to avoid such a situation by ensuring a solid majority within the ESCB.

The solution was simple. The council of the ESCB would be composed of the six members of the directorate of the European Central Bank, appointed by the European Council, and of the governors and presidents of the national central banks. If the monetary union were reduced to a "core," the treaty provides that the directory may be reduced to four members. In any case, the governors of the national banks would be the majority. The President of the Bundesbank would occupy a dominating position. Indeed, he would be able to count on the support of the governors of countries like Belgium and the Netherlands, whose national debt he had guaranteed for many years. To this end, these countries for several years pegged their currency to the mark and formed a *de facto* monetary union around Germany. In spite of high public debt, this anchor ensured them of interest rates close to the German rates, without stringent budgetary restraints.

However, the Bundesbank especially did not want to be involved in spite of itself with a responsibility to answer for the debts of any just state, and to have to defend the parity of the corresponding currency. It made sure that the Treaty expressly excludes any obligation of this type "except in the case of mutual financial guarantees" (Art. 104-B). And from Pöhl to Hans Tietmeyer, the successive presidents always decided against any "obligation of unlimited intervention" in favor of such and such currency. That was the cause of the hostility toward Italy's presence in the monetary union, a country whose debt is high and whose interest rates were, too, for a long time. One single exception was made to defend the franc. But that was imposed for diplomatic reasons by Chancellor Kohl. The Bundesbank yielded, against its instincts; but it criticized the obstacle to any readjustment within the EMS that this fixity of the franc-mark parity created.

This refusal to support the currencies that are not "pegged" to the mark gives rise to the German position on the "core." This would include five to six countries, Germany, Belgium, the Netherlands, Luxembourg, France and, if it wishes, Denmark (whose budgetary and monetary situation is comparable with the Netherlands). Following the extension of the Community to three new countries, Austria could join them, Sweden having finally decided to wait. Missing from this list are Great Britain, obviously, Italy — a co-founder of the Common Market, and Ireland, however much it may have declared itself a candidate for the monetary union. Pöhl had formulated this restriction shortly after the Delors report was published. Forced to accept negotiations with the Twelve, the Bundesbank had obtained, in return, the provision that access to the monetary union would depend on strict respect for four measures. Called the criteria of "economic convergence," they are low inflation, only a small variation from the lowest interest rate, exchange rate stability within the narrow margins of the EMS, and public deficit and debt limited to 3% and 60% of the GDP. These criteria do not exclude any country *a priori*. Even if not everyone can meet them at the same time, they can still look forward to moving to the third stage. However, in the spirit of the Bundesbank, these criteria play the same role of exclusion as the "core."

However, if they were applied strictly, it would raise some difficulties with regard to the public finances of several of the countries of the "core." When the limits for public deficit and debt were fixed, these countries were already well beyond the highest authorized levels: 130% debt for Belgium, more than 80% for the Netherlands and Denmark with, at the time, deficits far higher than 3% of the GDP. But at the price of a sustained effort of strict budgetary control and taking full advantage of the various possible interpretations of the statistical criteria (cleverly provided for in the Treaty), they had managed to redeem themselves. Now the recession made it questionable. But how could those countries be excluded, when they were already in a *de facto* monetary union with Germany? Was their excessive debt going to open the door of the monetary union to countries considered by Frankfurt and Bonn to be "undesirable"?

The German leaders went back to square one, that of "the core." The politicians pulled no punches. In a document on European integration from the CSU/CDU[18] parliamentary group, published in September 1994 with the backing of Chancellor Kohl, its writer, Karl Lamers, suggested "to reinforce the core already made up by the countries centered on integration and ready to cooperate. Currently, this core includes five or six countries," which are listed. A year later Théo Waigel,[19] German Minister for Finances, made the point again, affirming that "Italy, although it is a founding member of the European Community, will not be part of it." The criteria were thus to make the difference and the German leaders intended to be categorical: "There will be no compromise." How then to accept some and refuse the others? The answer lies in the *monetary criterion*, curiously obscure. Debate was centered within budgetary ratios, the only ones that could be interpreted as "trends." Actually, "being inside the narrow band of the EMS for more than two years" could be used as the discriminating factor and, for example, keep Italy out of the first group.

In the past, the Bundesbank had assumed the right to choose the countries taking part in the monetary union on several occasions, by accepting or refusing to support their currency. Two crises demonstrated this with disconcerting effect. The monetary crisis of September 1992 was, in this respect, exemplary. Historians will long discuss the measure of responsibility that rests with the German rate hike that took place in July. The Bundesbank's attitude during these decisive weeks was, in any case, anything but passive. Pöhl did not hesitate to support his successor by pointing out "the strange procedure"[20] followed by Great Britain when the pound joined the EMS. "One day," he says, "Mr. Major telephoned me to make this announcement, and he told me what exchange rate he had selected," whereas normally that is discussed within Ecofin, the Council of Ministers of Finance. The day of judgment had come. The pound sterling and the Italian lira were expelled from the EMS, in spite of the British and Italian governments' appeals to European solidarity, and the peseta and the escudo were forced to devaluate. A few months later, it was Ireland's turn to be dropped. Was the Bundesbank trying to derail the monetary union, or simply to make the financial market take over the job of "triage" that the German government was reluctant to carry out by full debate on the ratification of the Maastricht Treaty? The end result: Whereas all the countries were to have joined the EMS before the beginning of the second stage, at this date they were less than at the beginning of the first stage.

The same debate comes up, even more acutely, during the July 1993 crisis. Now it wasn't only the pound or the lira at stake, but the fate of the French franc. What was the Bundesbank trying to do? To break down any hint of independence on the part of French monetary policy, that was looking to lower interest rates? To wreck the Maastricht Treaty with the EMS? Or, to test the political will of the Bonn government vis-à-vis the government of Edouard Balladur? Edmond Alphandéry, the new Minister for Finance, was out of line when he had the impudence to transform a Franco-German economic council into a not very diplomatic "convocation;" indeed, that had irritated the German authorities. But their response was unambiguous. Chancellor Kohl let the Bundesbank know that they should defend the stability of the (official) franc-mark parity. He left it up to them to decide how. A drop in German rates was expected; the limits of fluctuation were expanding toward 15%. The central rate remained unchanged, but the franc was indeed lowered. The French government had to redouble its efforts to get back inside the narrow margin, without which there could be no thought of monetary union. Belgium and the Netherlands are undoubtedly on the winner's side in this game. But not Italy, who did not get back into the EMS until spring 1997, nor Spain and Portugal, not even Ireland, although the peseta, escudo and Irish pound remained in the EMS, admittedly far from their central rate. And from here on out, everyone could see that monetary stability depended less on government policies than on the goodwill of the Bundesbank.

This lack of solidarity is, obviously, at the heart of the debate on the relations between a monetary union reduced to a "core" and the currencies of those countries not participating. The President of the Bundesbank and the German Minister for Finance *jointly* asked the deputies, who were debating who was "in" and who was "out," "not to forget the lessons of the past."[21] If a new EMS was supposed to be formed after January 1, 1999, it could only resemble that which existed before 1987, when monetary adjustments did not cause the resolute hostility of one country or another. Monetary stability would have to be earned by "strict budgetary discipline." However, even for those who accept it, the support of the European Central Bank will be "automatic, but not unlimited."[22] For nobody in Frankfurt forgot Bérégovoy's refusal to let the mark be re-valued in autumn 1989 (before the wall came down), when the Bundesbank considered it necessary to the pursuit of its own monetary objectives. The German leaders took every precaution to ensure that such a situation could not happen again with the countries outside the monetary union. The Finance Ministers accepted in May 1996, at the Ecofin council in Verona, that by itself "the European Central Bank can take the initiative to change exchange rates by convening a ministerial meeting to that effect," a decision which had always been only within the power of the ministers. Intended to complete the unification of the European economic area, the monetary union could very well become a catalyst of division.

By describing his "vision of a European monetary space" in spring 1988, Pöhl had said that he did not believe the governments were willing to create the political conditions that he considered preliminary to any "monetary union." History proved him wrong on this point. The monetary union, he had explained, did not imply that the governments must give up their sovereignty *if they are not ready to do so*. The existence of irrevocable fixed "parities" could be satisfied perfectly well simply by a strong coordination of the national monetary policies. Knowing he was being listened to, Pöhl wanted to be realistic. He could impose his design of a "European central bank system," but he could not anticipate the politicians' decisions. Having his doubts, he chose to leave open the alternative by making the ESCB a semi-European, semi-national system. Either the governments would take the plunge and create a political union in Europe, and the existence of a European monetary arm would be appropriate in the fullest possible sense, or they would retreat; he felt it was essential that the national central banks retain their control over the monetary policy.

A few months before the 1999 deadline, nothing seems to have slowed the forced march toward the monetary union. But debates over what form it should take persist. One step forward, one step back. The future bank notes might have a euro side and a national side, the mark, the franc, the guilder. We are told that that would make them easier to use, but that would also make it possible to continue to define national money supplies and balances of payment. The bond market? If the conversion of the national debts into euros is not the general rule, the national markets will explode. And what about the budgetary policy, corseted by a "stability pact" whose purpose was not to increase discipline, but to preserve its national character? The Maastricht Treaty did not decide anything. Under Pöhl's direction, it gave birth to a monetary Janus, which leaves it up to the politicians to decide on which side the coin will fall.

Notes

1. Karl-Otto Pöhl, "La vision d'un espace monetaire européen," *Frankfurter Allgemeine Zeitung,* May 28, 1988.
2. Margaret Thatcher, *op. cit.,* p. 571.
3. See for example Bernard Connoly, *La Sale Guerre de la monnaie,* Paris, Albin Michel, 1996.
4. *Ibid,* as well as the following citations.
5. Annual report of the Bundesbank, Frankfurt, 1988.
6. Karl-Otto Pöhl, speech given in London to the Association of Foreign Banks on February 1, 1988.
7. Cf. Bernard Connoly, *op. cit.,* p. 199.
8. Lecture given at the Franco-German Chamber of Commerce, Frankfurt, November 6, 1989.
9. Remarks made at Bercy in the author's presence.
10. Bundesbank resolution on the Economic and Monetary Union in Europe, September 20, 1990, published by *Handelsblatt* on the same date.
11. Helmut Schlesinger, lecture given May 6, 1991 at the Economic Institute of Hamburg.
12. Quoted by David Marsh, *op. cit.,* p. 46.
13. Speech at the colloquium held in Bercy on the second stage of the EMU, June 21, 1990.
14. Interview in the newspaper *La Montagne,* September 18, 1992.
15. David Marsh, *op. cit.,* p. 80.
16. The European Commission, *Green Book on the Realization of the Economic and Monetary Union,* Brussels, June 1995.
17. Minutes of the April 25, 1989 meeting of the Committee for the Monetary Union of Europe, co-chaired by Valery Giscard d'Estaing and Helmut Schmidt.
18. Report of the CSU/CDU parliamentary group, *Réflexions sur la politique européenne,* Bonn, September 1994.
19. Statement made to the Bundestag finance committee, September 20, 1995.
20. Speech by K.-O. Pöhl at a conference held in Deauville on October 2, 1992.
21. Remarks reported in *Le Monde,* December 1, 1995.
22. Decision of the Ecofin Council in Verona, April 1996.

Chapter 8

The Euro in Search of a Home

Ten years and six months. That is how long it took to get to January 1, 1999, after the Economic and Monetary Union was launched in Hanover. The former President of the Bundesbank wasn't lying when he predicted that "the road would be long." And no German leader ever planned to go faster. When the various French leaders requested moving up the deadline, they invariably gave the same answer: "The criteria and the timetable were set in Maastricht. They are still valid, without restriction."[1] Besides, how could the timetable be changed without renegotiating the Treaty, which would require a new ratification — a risky proposition to say the least? Paris ultimately agreed, and the French and German Ministers of Finance used *The New York Times* to tell the financial markets that "The monetary union will be made at the specified time."[2] They were right to say "monetary union." To reach the promised land of the single currency, set for 2002, would still take three more years. All in all, since the franc was last devalued in January 1987, the advent of a European currency required fifteen years of monetary stability.

Could this decisive stage for European integration be reached without first, or at the very least simultaneously, having established a "European political union?" After the fall of the Berlin Wall, the Germans stopped raising this question so insistently. Without giving them more credit than they are due, we must admit that the heads of the Bundesbank were not the last ones to try for a political union. Karl-Otto Pöhl had insisted on it from the very start, without being heeded, while shortly after the Maastricht Treaty was signed, Helmut Schlesinger said, "We still lack a structure of political union, which, in my view, is of capital importance for the lasting success of the monetary union."[3] Given this German insistence, Jacques Attali, one never short of ideas, even imagined a day when France might "propose some political advances in exchange for less financial rigor,"[4] although he had formerly been against the idea that political union should precede monetary union. But that's not what they thought in Frankfurt. There could be no "bargaining." The political union was no more negotiable than the requirements of rigor and monetary stability. Jacques Delors, who began his mandate as the head of the Commission by setting aside the political union in order to avoid holding up the single market and then the monetary union, ended up admitting that "There will be no monetary union without a European political power. It is absolutely vital."[5]

Only Helmut Schmidt doubted its utility and feared that it would only cause "more mistrust" of Germany.[6] Let's review the former chancellor's arguments. He thought, first of all, that a political union even went "against the evidence. Since, according to Maastricht, the European Central Bank will be completely independent of politics, the common currency absolutely does not require a supreme political authority." In the second place, he considered that "premature implementation of the political union would almost necessarily expose us to enormous demands for tax, and financial and social equalization." In other words, the less political the union is, the more likely the success of the monetary union will be. But he was underestimating the main point: the need for a legitimate power that could enforce compliance with the common rule. And this rule goes by a name that resonates with every German: stability.

If the question of the political union could be eluded during the negotiation of the Treaty, it was because those questions relating to the structure of the monetary power were quickly resolved. Contrary to what some had feared, the organization of these powers did not cause the interminable discussions on voting procedures that had for years held up the plans for political union. Here, there would be neither a right of veto, nor scholarly calculation of weighted votes to take account of the countries' relative sizes. From the beginning, the "one man, one vote" principle had prevailed. In the future structure, the President of the Bundesbank would have the same weight (theoretically) as the President of the Luxembourg Monetary Institute. But why should he worry? He knew that his real influence would be much greater. Wasn't that already the case within the committee of the central bank governors, which meets in Basle?

President Delors' tactical skill also played a part. He was able to make "the success of the monetary union contingent on" solidarity with the "regions" that were lagging behind. The principle of doubling the structural funds, adopted in February 1988, settled Schmidt's question about demand for financial and tax equalization before it was asked. Admittedly, that required increasing the budgetary resources of the Community, the "Delors I" package. But separating the question of financing the structural funds from the debate on the monetary union only better circumscribed it. The risk of creating a budgetary power strong enough to counterbalance the monetary power of the ECBS was thus evaded. Then, why call for a political union if the monetary union carries it out so well by default?

As he did for the Single European Act, Delors made the prospect of an economic and monetary union attractive. There would be "more growth, more jobs, less inflation." The cost of transactions, it was explained, represented a loss, which varied according to the nature of the transaction, but whose cumulative effects were considerable. Thus, the Commission explained, if a tourist set off to make a tour of Europe with a bank note of 100 francs or 100 marks, and changed it at each border without spending it, he would get home with half. Thus with ecus in his pocket, he would be richer than with francs or marks. The same applied to companies, banks and states. And, as in 1985, the Commission entrusted to a group of experts the responsibility of quantifying the cost of monetary non-Europe, and the profit that the union was expected to bring to private individuals and for the economy as a whole.[7]

The savings on transaction costs was supposed to have the same effect as those generated by the harmonization of technical standards. It was supposed to lower the cost of money, which would increase investment, and therefore growth, and reduce inflation. Solicited again, the experts delivered their verdict. "The gain in cumulative growth could, in the long run, reach 5% of the GDP, employment could increase by 1.5% and inflation could be reduced by 6%." On the whole, "a cautious estimate would put the total of the transaction costs at approximately 0.5% of the GDP (that is, over 100 billion francs per year for the whole Community), an amount which would be reduced to about 0.25% of the GDP with regard to the border costs for trade in goods." In other words, the nonexistence of monetary Europe would cost twice as much as that of commercial Europe.

Unfortunately, the result of these erudite calculations does not come from the effects induced by the savings in transaction costs. It comes from assumptions as to "systemic changes, which will lead to changes of economic policy and then to behavior changes within the economy."[8] On their own, indeed, transaction cost savings have hardly any effect. The individual loss that they represent is not a loss for society. The cost of exchanging money is no different in nature from the cost of the meal that our tourist, going from capital to capital with his banknote, would consume at each stopover. The exchange brings a profit to the financial establishments; it provides employment for the people who stand at the counters, thus giving them a livelihood. It does not matter whether this employment would be more useful elsewhere. Since in an exchange "nothing is lost, nothing is created," the overall level of employment remains practically unchanged.

At the conference (already mentioned) in Hamburg in June 1991, Schlesinger gave these calculations the back of his hand. "I don't know to what extent these studies overestimate the benefits of the Monetary Union and underestimate the risks, but it seems to me that they do." Financial expenses would continue to exist between countries, the unification of the markets would be slow and, besides, it would not be done in the near term. Private individuals would have to wait for the single currency before they could benefit from the transaction savings. The single currency, not the monetary union — that means at least three more years. But the Commission's calculations rely on the first and assume that the process has been completed. Not over the second, which is a simple system of fixed exchanges.

Schlesinger explained his reasons for challenging the Commission's figures. "The rate of exchange can be quite useful for a country that does not succeed in developing its economy at the same rate as others. If the tool of devaluing the national currencies no longer exists, imbalances result in growing unemployment and a need for state transfers. True, if the prices of the factors of production, in particular wages, were sufficiently flexible, one might manage to avoid that. But can we count on that? Even in the government sector, we can't bank on wage reductions." Thus, the situation can only worsen if the applicant countries cannot support perfect rigidity of the exchange rate. The results of the "core" countries' long stability are unambiguous: growth did not exceed 2% on average from 1988 to 1996 (1.5% since 1991) and unemployment, after a hiatus in 1897-1989, rose again to reach a record level of 12%. That is the highest since the crisis of the 1930s, which it would be shameful to repeat.

For that matter, can the condition of the European economies be attributed exclusively to the will to maintain monetary stability at all costs which prevailed during the fifteen last years, including right after the unification of Germany? Pierre-Alain Muet[9] has shown that while the American and European economies experienced the same recessions, one at the beginning of the 1980s, the other at the beginning of the 1990s, the American economy rebounded each time and achieved several years of strong growth. The European economies, meanwhile, fell into the doldrums. One rolled back its unemployment rate while the others, at best, managed to slow down its rate of increase for one or two years. For Muet, these differences in economic results in the aftermath of recessions has little to do with the intrinsic performance of one economy or another, since they are condemned by globalization to make the same efforts toward productivity. Rather, they stem from very different economic policies implemented on the two sides of the Atlantic, especially the monetary policy. The Federal Reserve sharply lowered interest rates and kept them at null in real terms for a fairly long period, while in Europe rates had to follow the slow and gradual policy of the Bundesbank, and for the most part remained positive. It is true that the United States manifests a "benign neglect" with regard to the dollar, while Germany seeks to limit any significant rise of the dollar against the mark in order to satisfy investors, and to prevent any additional decline in order not to handicap the industrialists.

The difference also relates to the budgetary policy of expansion of demand in the United States and restriction in Europe. With its dynamic policy, the American government succeeded in containing the budget deficit, whereas the European governments' policy of reducing deficits by restraining growth caused the deficits to explode. High deficits, combined with positive real interest rates, sent debt soaring. And financing it, because the burden had increased, resulted in still further compressing demand, especially public investment. The European economies thus suffered from a poor combination of monetary and budgetary policies. Add to this the fact that in France, a very long period of wage austerity and the financing of social benefits combined to further weaken purchasing power and, finally, household consumption.

This first answer is not enough. How could so many different governments within the Community be led to implement the same economic policy, and to stay with it for so long, in spite of criticisms and opposition? The reasons are obviously European. "Europe," writes Muet, "suffered, and suffers today, from an inadequacy between its economic integration and its (lack of) political integration."[10] Since the Treaty of Rome was signed in 1957, intra-Community trade developed twice as fast as that with countries outside of Europe. The Community countries are now conducting about two-thirds of their trade among themselves (and far more, for the "little" countries) compared to one-third in 1958. But, despite this increasing interdependence, the economic and monetary policies of the states have remained national.[11] Without political union, the monetary union has no chance of bringing Europe "more growth, more jobs and less inflation."

Two failures weighed on the behavior of economic policies in the Eighties — the German revival of 1979-1980 and the French revival of 1981-1982. When the EMS was set up, dis-equilibriums between the balances of payments within the Community had led the governments to ask Germany to serve as the "engine" to drive growth forward. But this revival ran head-on into the oil crisis and came at the very moment when the U.S. Federal Reserve reversed its monetary policy. Given the risk of inflationary pressures, the Bundesbank sharply raised its interest rates to cool the German economy, destroying the ruling coalition in the process. Chancellor Schmidt resigned. His successor took note of what had happened. France, after the Left's electoral victory in 1981, then tried to get out of the recession on its own, by jump-starting its economy in spite of heavy inflation inherited from the 1970s. The trade balance, already showing a deficit, plunged into the red and brought down the franc with its continuation. Three times in a row, Pierre Mauroy's government had to devaluate and make budget cutbacks. François Mitterrand drew his conclusions and, after considerable thought, chose to go with the European anchoring — which was not unlike the German anchoring.

This double failure sealed the fate of the European economy for more than a decade. Germany concluded that it would never again be the engine of a revival; France had to admit that it could not act alone as a counterweight. The EMS became asymmetrical: From then on, the countries in deficit would have to make all the effort to re-adjust on

their own. Any spirit of political cooperation was abandoned. Governments other than Bonn had no choice but to align their national policies with the German policy. Even Great Britain, under pressure from
the Finance Ministers in defiance of their Prime Minister, gradually
gave up the pursuit of a completely independent policy from 1987 on.
The monetary crisis of September 1992 certainly gave back to Great
Britain and Italy their monetary autonomy, but it also consecrated the
primacy of national interests over the definition of European objectives.

The cooperation that the political leaders had boated about so
much had became a mirage. Within the EMS, convergence was carried
out by monetary alignment on Germany. It was a hard cross to bear for
the French governments. Eric Aeschimann and Pascal Riché have bril-
liantly shown how Pierre Bérégovoy, Edouard Balladur and Jacques
Chirac in turn all saw their desire to reduce interest rates crash to
pieces on the monetary wall of Frankfurt.[12] The first was forced to raise
the rates, and his only satisfaction was to close the gap between French
and German rates; the others benefited from the rate reduction decided
in Germany, but they had to resign themselves to patience. Every time
they tried to accelerate the downward movement, they had to move
back a little later to safeguard the franc.

With this loss of monetary autonomy, the European currencies
were inhaled by the mark within the EMS vis-à-vis the declining dollar.
The European economies gradually lost their ability to compete. The
Commission of the European Communities[13] calculated that between
the beginning of 1987 and the end of 1992, the cumulative losses of competitiveness were 20% compared to the United States and 1.3% compared to Japan. Two-thirds of the loss was due to the nominal varia-
tions of the exchange rates, depreciation in the case of America and appreciation in the others. This formidable monetary pressure created a
continuous loss of market share that neither gains in productivity nor
lower wages could stop. In thirty years, the European economies' share
of world trade (except for intra-Community relations) dropped from
25 to approximately 20%.

Flexibility in employment and wage deflation are the direct consequences of this monetary constraint. What the economies lose in
monetary competitiveness, the firms are supposed to make up in terms
of productivity and wage costs. The loss of monetary independence
and the crippling of the labor market are two sides of one-and-the-
same phenomenon. The economic policies had by no means lost their

effectiveness, as has often been said. Rather, they were completely re-oriented due to the absence of European political union. They were no longer striving for full employment, but, on the contrary, weakening employment in order to become more competitive. Microeconomics had supplanted macroeconomic policy in the governmental arsenal, and pumping up the supply side had taken the place of the traditional bolstering of demand. For fifteen years, the OECD made this the "core" of its recommendations to the European countries, under the label of "structural adjustments."

From the early 1980s, economists like Professor Edmond Malinvaud had imagined that budgetary policies could compensate for the recessionary effects of this supply-side policy, by supporting business activity. The high level of interest rates very quickly condemned this solution. In a few years, debt exploded under the combined effect of accumulated deficits and interest rates higher than growth rates. The governments then had to reduce budget deficits to stabilize the debt, although, in fact, they did not manage to do so entirely. Interest charges represented barely 2% of the state budget in 1973; twelve years later, they were over 15%. This exponential growth gradually demolished other expenditure, especially capital expenditure. The situation deteriorated considerably with the recession of 1993. To keep the reduced tax receipts from causing an uncontrollable expansion of deficits, the governments had to reduce expenditure at a risk of preventing recovery. That would have become an urgent obligation, with or without the requirements imposed by the Maastricht Treaty to reduce the public deficits to 3% of the GDP.

To break this deadlock, Professors Drèze and Malinvaud[14] proposed circumventing the national budgetary constraints by a combination of major works financed by Europe, and a policy of strengthening supply at the national level through broad reductions on the social taxes on low wages. Delors picked up this idea in his White Book on "growth, competitiveness, and employment" with a proposed campaign to enhance Europe's infrastructures, in particular highways, railways and telecommunications.[15] Projects likely to turn a profit were selected to be financed by loans. But the Finance Ministers always refused the essential community funding to alleviate investors' and funders' concerns in the wake of the Eurotunnel bankruptcy. The Maastricht Treaty provided the creation of the European Investment Fund for this purpose, but by refusing to incur any debt on behalf of the Union, they obstinately deprived themselves of the only instrument of economic revival. When Lionel Jospin's government took up this proposal in June 1997, they ran into the same resistance by the German leaders, who opposed any measure that would increase expenditure by the Community or the states. That left only the policy of "structural adjustments" in terms of the flexibility of the labor market, whose inefficiency in creating jobs has been well proven.

Progress toward the monetary union thus suffered from the lack of a political union, which had been discussed since the beginnings of the project. Reacting to the Delors report, Bérégovoy had suggested an "economic government" to serve as a counterweight to the European central banking system. This idea was given a cool reception in Bonn and Frankfurt, as well as in Paris. The idea had shocked as much as it displeased, in Germany because it raised the stakes to the level of the European Parliament, in Paris because it was likely to open a breach in the French opposition to German requests for increasing the powers of the aforesaid Parliament. Also, the debate was very quickly cut short. With less than 2% of the GDP, the European Union's budget did not permit it to conduct a European economic policy. However, nobody planned to increase the budget. It was very quickly pointed out that there was a Council of (national) Finance Ministers, called Ecofin, which could act as the embryo of an "economic government." It was therefore decided to institute "stronger monitoring" of the member states' economic performances; this opened the way for the Germans to propose a "stability pact."

The Treaty of Maastricht being ratified, the Bundesbank leadership was the first to mount the barricades. Otmar Issing, its chief economist, criticized "its serious political lacunae;" Hans Tietmeyer recalled that the monetary union required that "the political union be created at the same time." But nobody took the risk of going into details. In September 1995, Theo Waigel, the German Minister for Finance, started the debate again by requiring a "stability pact" to take effect after entering into the monetary union. The idea was already implicit in the Treaty, but Waigel went further. He tightened the budgetary criteria; he tried to lower the suggested threshold from 3% to less than 1%. In addition, while speaking in this context of a "monetary* Schengen,"[16] that would link only certain countries (of which "Italy would not be a part"), he locked up "the core" and sought to give it a legal form to further set it apart from the other countries. Paris said that they would stick with the Maastricht Treaty, which prohibits "excessive deficits" and provides for sanctions in the event of prolonged backsliding (Article 104-C). But the Juppé government ended up giving in to German demands, leaving his successor no choice but to go along.

Such a "pact" by no means represents a step toward a European political union. On the contrary, it makes it more difficult. Together with Jean Arthuis, the two Finance Ministers provided the framework. "While safeguarding national sovereignty over the definition of budgetary policy and conduct, (it) will guarantee that the interested states will actively and without interruption pursue a healthy budget policy," defined as aiming for "a balanced budget or, in the medium term, a surplus."[17] In an interview with the BBC given six months before, Tietmeyer, the President of the Bundesbank, had stated it as clearly as can be: "I think that in addition to the Maastricht Treaty, we need tools, including sanctions, for countries which do not sufficiently adhere to the budgetary discipline, which means that national deficits must be under control and that we will probably have to define some rules relating to the financing of these deficits."[18] To that end, he concluded, "The monetary union is a kind of political union that goes beyond the monetary plane." The newspaper Les Echos was one of the few to take note of this matter and to denounce it as "taking control of the member states' budget policies."

In insisting on the link between monetary union and political union, the German leaders were reminding their partners who had lost sight of monetary realities that currency is always instituted by a political authority and is not the "natural" product of the market. It exists only because it has "the force of law," which is invested in it by a legitimate authority having sovereign power. Thus, there cannot be a single currency without a European authority being recognized as the guarantor of its value, thus ensuring its protection and control. By insisting on the question of political union, the German leaders were, in fact, posing another question. What authority would guarantee to the German public that the European currency would be as strong as the mark? What authority could impose respect for budgetary discipline on countries that could not do it themselves?

While President Chirac was visiting in Bonn, October 25, 1995, Kohl stated that it was necessary to give "the monetary union a politi-

---

* Reference to the Schengen Agreement to lift all border controls between 14 countries of the EU, which went into force on Feb. 1, 1994.

cal home." What was he suggesting when he said "home"? The European Council, the Commission, or a government that would be accountable to the European Parliament? He was careful not to reveal his thoughts. One month later, Waigel formulated his own. "It would be unacceptable for the European Council to have jurisdiction to decide procedure in the event of excessive deficits of the member states of the Monetary Union. It would open the door to arbitrary policies." The Council brings together the heads of State and government, the only ones invested with democratic legitimacy; if that is challenged, then who will establish sanctions? The Commission controlled by the Court of Justice? That would mean renouncing any chance of a political union.

It is not the call for greater discipline that is most astonishing in the Waigel proposal. No one is required to do anything at the European level that goes against what they are doing at the national level. But what must have struck to the heart those people most devoted to Europe is the fact that *it negates any European policy at all.* One would have thought that before giving up national policies in favor of a European policy, the ministers would seek to establish that policy's principles and to guarantee that it would not cause monetary instability and inflation. They were expected to debate how the European Union should be equipped in order to effect economic policy. However, that debate never took place. No reflection was undertaken on what a European policy could be that might be something more than a reinforcement of strengthened coordination of national policies. However, as long as one labels simple intergovernmental cooperation with the name "European economic policy," then even when "Community matters" are being discussed, the national will take precedence over the European, and the "economic government" will remain a meaningless concept. Which the national ministers won't mind at all!

Delors had envisaged giving the Commission a means of action, while the harmonization of the VAT was being debated. His proposal to centralize VAT tax receipts at the Community level would have given it a powerful lever by which it could impose financial equalization between the states. But could the national governments turn over to the European institutions such a large amount of money, without knowing how it would be spent? They were afraid, and rightly, to lose control over a tax that represents approximately one-third of the total of the tax and welfare receipts in every country, and to have to cut down on expenditure. The Commission proposal was putting the cart before the horse. It was rejected, in spite of several attempts. And the harmonization of the VAT was never finally resolved.

The Green Book on "the realization of the Economic and Monetary Union" proposed to convert into euros "a financial critical mass" made up of the credits inherited from the member states' debt. This could have given the idea another chance. Indeed, it opened the way for raising the management of national debt to the European level, which constitutes an exemplary governmental prerogative. Precautions would have to be taken to prevent one country from making the others support the budgetary cost of its debt. But it would suffice to provide for a transfer of the tax receipts intended to finance interests charges in proportion to each state's share of debts.

This Europeanization of the national debts would have two advantages. It would confer on Europe real economic power by financing the amortization of the national debt, a power that would be all the greater since the average gross debt of the European Union approaches 80% of the GDP. By the same token, it would create a true "European signature," indispensable in unifying the euro market and making it broad enough to be "liquid." Only under this condition could the European Central Bank conduct its monetary policy without having to depend on the national central banks. The prospect of a "European economic government" would appear to have begun to take concrete form. There is also a weak side to this proposal. Managing the public debt cannot become a European responsibility unless, simultaneously, the European Parliament is given the right to debate it. The authors of the "Glorious Revolution" in England understood this in 1685, when they created simultaneously the first Parliament to vote on what tax would be necessary to meet payments on the debt, and, with the Bank of England, the first central bank, to guarantee its value. Three centuries later, the lesson is still valid.

Would the budget difficulties confronting all the countries lead the governments to reopen this question before the deadline of January 1, 1999? It couldn't be ruled out. Waigel, searching for an expedient that would mask the deterioration of German deficits, now had to compromise the doctrine he had promoted so staunchly throughout the years; he suggested the idea of a revaluation of the Bundesbank's gold inventories (and dollar reserves). Changing the accounting method for gold[19] and dollars is not in itself condemnable, but the reversal of the appreciation that thus redounded to the federal budget is in formal contradiction with Article 104 of the Maastricht Treaty. That article "prohibits the ECB and the central banks of the member states from allowing uncovered balances or any other type of appropriations to the institutions or bodies of the Community, to the national or local administrations." The Commission and several Finance Ministers immediately responded by reminding Chancellor Kohl's Minister of the meaning of "rigor."

However, the Commission created an important opening when it pronounced, as in conformity with the treaty for the Bundesbank, to revalue its gold inventories to buy back public receivables. But then, why not extend the reasoning to currency reserves? Indeed, conversion to the euro would render superfluous the foreign-exchange reserves held in European currencies by the national central banks; it was assumed that pooling the reserves in dollars would be sufficient to finance interventions on the exchange market by the future European Bank. Rather than sterilizing these reserves, the solution would be to use them to repurchase part of the national debt. This would result in a reduction of the interest charges that weighed heavily on the budget deficits. Degearing would thus support growth.

That would have been a fair reward for the past. For years, the German leaders had been making Europe pay for the "strength" of the mark with high interest rates that plunged the economies into stagnation and unemployment, and induced public deficit and debt. Today, the European economies need a monetary revival that lower interest rates alone cannot provide. This result can be achieved by using the gold and currency reserves for debt relief of the states. *But the German government cannot claim the right to carry out such a transaction alone, almost on the sly. A European accord is essential.* Regardless of whether the future European Bank will be independent, Waigel, even if he had to retreat before the opposition of the Bundesbank, furnished the proof that determining the monetary policy remains the prerogative only of the government. That must also be valid in Brussels.

A "European economic government" will never be born from coordination, however much "strengthened," of *national* economic policies. It requires the Community to have levers that the European budget cannot provide when national governments (with Germany in the lead) propose to reduce it rather than to increase it. As has often been the case in the history of European states, the solution will be found in the problems raised by the management of the public debt. After "one market — one currency," "*one currency — one debt*" should be Europe's creed. No one can doubt the need for a European (economic) government. But there will be one only on that day when part of the states' budget responsibility is transferred to the Community. Debt management is the only part that is, today, conceivable. The stakes entailed in such a transfer are as simple as they are decisive: whether to give "a political home" to the economic and monetary union.

Looking at the Economic and Monetary Union a year after the euro went into effect, these debates seem to be a thing of the past. The criteria of convergence have done their job and the accession of a center-left government in Rome, led by Romano Prodi, made it possible to rein in Italy's public finances enough to allow it to qualify. Thus on May 2, 1998, the European Council was able to fix the list of eleven candidates for the euro. Only Greece was judged to be not ready, while Great Britain, Denmark and Sweden, although they met the criteria (except for SME membership, for two of them), declined to join at this time. The financial markets gave the necessary boost, driving the parity between the dollar and the European currencies into a zone more consistent with the "fundamentals;" on January 1, 1999, the euro was in the neighborhood of 1.18 dollars, but by spring it was closer to one euro to one dollar, and then settled in at a more sustainable rate close to 1.10 dollars.

Still, the debates that accompanied the advent of the euro are still valid. No on e has found a solution, to this day, except for some of the member countries. The committee made up of the finance ministers of the 11 euro-zone countries is a pale shadow of the economic government called for by Bérégovoy. It cannot decide anything without the approval of the council of the 15 finance ministers, Ecofin. And the refusal of the finance ministers of the G7 countries (France, Germany, Italy) to give up their seats for the nominal president of the euro-eleven has further delayed — until Great Britain takes up the euro? — that which the treaty was unable to achieve: the replacement of national representatives by European representatives within the international monetary authorities. Finally, while the market is, perforce, practically unified (the pricing of investments in euros having been finally achieved in most countries), the management of public debt has remained a national problem and the Union remains constrained from borrowing. As for tax harmonization and rationalizing banking con-trols, there was no progress by the end of 1999. European and at the same time national, the Economic and Monetary Union remains, more than ever, the monetary Janus invented by Pöhl.

Notes

1. For example Werner Hoyer, German Minister for European Affairs, in *Le Monde*, September 12, 1996.
2. Jean Arthuis and Theo Waigel, "L'Union monétaire se fera à l'heure dite," *New York Times*, September 20, 1996, reprinted in *Le Monde* September 22 and 23, 1996.
3. Interview in *Der Spiegel*, February 17, 1992.
4. Jacques Attali, *Libération*, October 4, 1995.
5. Jacques Delors, *L'Expansion*, April 28 to May 14, 1995.
6. Helmut Schmidt, *Die Zeit*, September 29, 1995.
7. Michael Emerson *et al.*, *Marché unique, monnaie unique*, foreword to Jacques Delors and Henning Christophersen, *Commission des Communautées européennes*, Paris, Economica, 1990.
8. *Ibid*, p. 18.
9. Pierre-Alain Muet, *Le Chômage persistant en Europe*, Paris, FNSP, 1994.
10. *Ibid*, p. 14.
11. I developed this point at length in *Chômage demande traitement de choc*, Balland, Paris, 1994.
12. Eric Aeschimann and Pascal Riché, *op. cit.*
13. "Evaluation de la compétitivité aux États-Unis, au Japon et dans la Communauté," *Economie européenne*, N° 54, 1993.
14. Jacques Drèze, Edmond Malinvaud, *Croissance et emploi, la perspective d'une initiative européenne*, Brussels, June 1993.
15. *Commission des communautés européenne, Croissance, compétitivité, emploi*, Brussels, December 1993.
16. Theo Waigel, statement to *Focus* magazine, September 15, 1995.
17. Jean Arthuis and Theo Waigel, "L'Union monétaire se fera à l'heure dite," *Art. cit.*
18. Remarks reported by *Les Echos*, March 10, 1995.
19. The Bank of France estimates its gold reserves on the basis of the average price over last three months on the world markets, cf. The Bank of France's annual report to the President of the Republic.

THE POLITICAL QUARREL

Chapter 9

The Missing Citizen

Is it true, or is it false? It is characteristic of myths to be unverifiable. The ink was hardly dry on the Maastricht Treaty defining European citizenship when legends surfaced about its birth. Citizenship was not originally intended to be introduced into the treaty on political union. The proposal, they say, was made only at a very advanced stage in the negotiations, by Felipe Gonzalez, then Prime Minister for the Spanish government.[1] Anxious about the course of events and cognizant of the risks that inevitable disappointment would surely produce among the public, he suggested that the Treaty "should say something" about citizenship.

The negotiators paid it lip service: "Citizenship in the Union is hereby instituted. Any person having the nationality of a member state is a citizen of the Union."[2] The idea of a distinct citizenship was dismissed almost as soon as it was mentioned, due to the obligatory collateral nationality. To give it the appearance of innovation anyway, they hastily pasted together a sturdy "chapter" incorporating all the elements scattered in the various treaties, such as: the right to circulate among member countries and to reside abroad, the right of petition. The only innovations were the introduction of voting rights and recognition of eligibility in the local and European elections for any citizen of the Union wherever he may reside, and the right to call upon the recently instituted mediator. The result was in keeping with the ambition: "null or negligible effects on those who are its object," wrote the Commission.[3] The political goal was achieved nonetheless: the citizens were propelled to the front of the European stage.

It was high time. Gonzalez was right. Growing unemployment and the "closed door" negotiations had generated public mistrust toward the Community governments and institutions. Ungrateful or more likely ignorant of this unexpected solicitude, the citizens seized the opportunity of the debates over the ratification of the Maastricht Treaty to express their dissatisfaction at being the forgotten element in Europe. In Denmark, the Treaty was rejected during a first referendum and in France it barely made it through. National as well as European political leaders were quick to admit their error and to promise that the time of negotiating behind closed doors was over; that in the future the citizens would be fully associated with European construction; that Europe had to deal with their concerns and respond to them concretely; that it was to be done for them and with them. As a demonstration of their good faith, they all promised that the upcoming intergovernmental conference (the IGC) set for 1996, with an agenda to revise the treaties, would show concrete proof. But promises only take in those who are willing to be taken in.

"The citizens of the Union," as the Maastricht Treaty calls them, might have believed, if they read the preparatory reports for the IGC, that a real change had been made. Every single report makes that claim, with greater or lesser emphasis, in the preamble to its proposals. In the one that defines the operation of the Treaty of the European Union, the Commission sets a peremptory tone. "The first goal of the future Intergovernmental Conference is clearly defined: to make Europe the business of the citizens."[4] Consequently, "The ambition of the Treaty, *a Europe closer to the people*, is not for the Commission an empty phrase, but an absolute requirement, a constant criterion of its initiatives." In short, "The Commission will be listening to the men and the women (of Europe)." The "think tank" created for the event, called the Westendorp Group (named after its president), on one side, and the European Parliament and European Council on the other, were not to be outdone.[5] All spoke of a "Europe closer to the citizens." The conclusion was obvious: at the end of the meeting held in Turin on March 29, 1996, the Council asked the IGC "to found its work on the basis that the citizens are the heart of European construction. The Union," it added, "must imperatively meet their needs and their concerns in a concrete way."[6]

But between words and actions, there is diplomacy, and it is not in the nature of diplomats to be concerned with the public. Their focus is the sovereign state, sole holder of international legitimacy. Once more, they negotiated without taking the trouble either to address, or to publicize the proposals that were on the table. As with the preceding treaties — the ECSC, Euratom, the Treaty of Rome, the Single European Act, the Maastricht Treaty — the diplomats did the public's thinking for them; they defined the best way of meeting their needs and, to start things off, selected those that deserved to be inscribed in a treaty. "The end result," wrote Emma Bonino, a European Commissioner, "is that the governments of the member states, as if they had learned nothing from Maastricht, continued to negotiate among themselves *in camera*, and gave very little room for the public or their representatives to speak."[7] The sad thing was that the Commission did the same; it, too, failed to take the lesson and open up a public debate. Once more, the public had to wait until the heads of state completed their labors — at the council of Amsterdam on June 16 and 17, 1997 — to finally be informed. In fact, it took a few months more, since the law was signed only on October 2 after the approval of the "draft" that was adopted in Amsterdam. By then, it was much too late to have any impact on the debates and to influence the negotiations.

There is, however, something eminently correct about this situation. If "the citizens of the Union" are left on the fringes of Europe, it is not entirely due to political cynicism, but because their presence contradicts with the nature of European construction. Political will is not enough to make a citizen; in the traditional concept of law, there is no citizenship without state. All the lawyers agree on this point. The constitutions born of the American and French revolutions founded a form of government based on the legitimacy of the assent of the people. They define civil rights with respect to the state, i.e. the rights that limit its power. In the absence of a European state, how could one define a European citizen? And if you could, then why not equip the Community and then the European Union with a Constitution? To those who wondered about this shortcoming, Professor Jean-Louis Quermonne addressed the only valid answer. If it turned out that way, it is "not through the fault of the European Parliament: on two occasions,[8] the Parliament sought to provide it with [a constitution]. Rather, it is because 'the constituent power' belongs to the member states and is exercised via diplomacy."[9]

The concept of citizenship runs counter to the specific nature of European construction: *an association between sovereign states that agree to delegate to supranational institutions a part of their rights.* This association is founded on treaties that commit only the signatory states and apply only to them. As was stated by Fernand Herman, who was a rapporteur of the constitutional Commission of the European Parliament, they "do not directly commit the citizens of these states." The Maastricht Treaty takes great care not to employ the term "European citizen." It speaks of "citizens of the European Union."[10] The term is incorrect in any case, since the European Union, created in Maastricht to give a single framework to the three "pillars" instituted on that occasion, is not a legal entity. [11]

"Any person having the nationality of a member state is a citizen of the Union." In Article 8, the Treaty avoids any definition of the constitutional type. European citizenship is not a result of rights that the treaties accord directly to nationals of the member states, independent of their membership in one or the other of them, but results from their very quality of belonging to these states. Only he who is first a citizen of his own country, who is a "national," can be a citizen of the Union. One would have thought that the introduction of a European citizenship was intended to create a common identity, making it possible to go beyond nationality. It has the opposite effect: it solidifies the nationalities. Union citizenship is added to national citizenship, it does not replace it. Furthermore, the Westendorp Group, which convened the Ministers for European Affairs of all the member states, unanimously concluded that "the Treaty indicate even more clearly that Union citizenship does not replace national citizenship."[12]

Since European citizenship is a concept without any legal basis, why introduce it into the Treaty? Professor J. Weiler, co-director of the Academy of European Law in Florence, hesitates between two explanations, one as provocative as the other. Either it is the appeal of "an Americanized Europe on the model of Saatchi & Saatchi," the big Madison Avenue advertising company; or it is the "inability to conceive of citizenship in terms other than those which derive from the culture of the state and the nation." We might suggest a third: the negotiators' refusal to think of European construction in any terms other than those of a treaty. As long as they are locked into that mindset, citizenship can only be window-dressing intended to make the Maastricht Treaty more attractive and "closer to the citizen," without conceding anything. The formulation of the Treaty thus marks the end of the road for the efforts started by Gonzalez. Seldom has a misunderstanding been greater.

This failure is not the fault of the citizens, but of the process of building European. The gap between the initial intention and its realization is vast. For the people as for the political leader, who is to some extent the public's spokesman, citizenship has to do with rights and obligations with respect to the state. It supposes that the founding laws list the basic rights, such as economic and welfare rights, following the example Declaration of the Rights of Man, the European Convention on Human Rights and the preamble to certain constitutions. For diplomats, the situation is quite different. Citizenship is incorporated in the concepts of state and nation. At treaty level, it is not expressed as individual rights, but as freedoms and the security that the states collectively afford the public. These manifest in the form of freedom of movement between the states (a right recognized from the start by the Treaty of Rome); in the security of goods, which is enhanced by the existence of a European legal space; and in the security of the states where foreign policy converges with common security, including ultimately a common defense. Diplomats consider that, from their point of view, the claim of citizenship was fully satisfied with the introduction into the treaty of the so-called second and third "pillars," corresponding to these security objectives. That is an entirely different "state" concept of citizenship, diametrically opposite to that which is the source of the philosophy of human rights.

The debate on citizenship is not mere judicial quibbling. It is a fundamental debate over the European identity. From one perspective, it is exclusively a state matter, of which states are the initiators, as well as the delimiting factor; from the other, it is a complete reversal of the logic founded on *the recognition of rights common to all the nationals of the member states*, defining a citizenry and a collective identity. The one inevitably leaves the public by the wayside; the other puts it at the heart of the political process. If Europe really wants to get closer to the public, as everyone keeps saying, then as Manuel Oreja (European Commissioner in charge of the preparation of the IGC) noted, it is necessary "to change the starting point: it is no longer primarily a matter of compromise between the member states that will have to characterize the negotiations, but the concern for proposing to every European a true pact of citizenship."[13] That has not been done, but it should be done now.

Citizenship had not stood out as a specific necessity before the Maastricht Treaty, because the basic rights of the Community's nationals were recognized by means other than treaties. This was the work of the Court of Justice of the European Communities, and was implemented in stages through the Court's decisions. In 1962, it first recognized the individual's right to cite the provisions of the treaties before a national court in order to claim the rights that are covered therein (the Van Gend judgment, in Loos). In its wisdom, the Court deduced that the Community legislation was superior to the national law of the member states. The Court thus spawned an *autonomous* Community legal order. In the second stage, the Court took the basic rights recognized at the state level, but not included in the texts of the treaties, and used them as the basis of Community legislation. It proposed, with reason, that these rights were *necessary* to the realization of the purposes of the treaties and that, consequently, they could not be ignored.

In particular, the Court of Justice drew upon the principles common to member states' constitutions and used them to compile the general principles of the Community's legal order. Since every member state had agreed to the European Convention on Human Rights, it retained those provisions and integrated them into its pronouncements. Thus, when the European Union joined the European Convention, some heralded it as a step forward, but others saw it as "primarily symbolic and not inducing any real progress."[14] In fact, some lawyers thought it might be best to go one step further. For example, José Luis da Cruz Vilaça, former President of the European Community's highest court, suggested that since the constitutional status of the Community was based on the international treaties between sovereign states, it should follow the example of the Court of Justice, which had itself created what it called "a constitutional charter of a Community of law."

The problem actually is less legal than political. Just when we are striving for a Europe that is closer to the public, it seems shocking that the European treaties do not directly protect any basic rights. They make European rights dependent on the rights given at the national level, even if it does integrate them into a Community order that can be directly applied. The rights guaranteed at the European level express values shared by all the members, and in this sense they define a common identity for all the European people. Claiming them as *European rights* would give them greater force. Moreover, the treaties do not give the public any guarantee against encroachments by the Community institutions, as they would have the right to expect. The principle of subsidiarity was introduced in an attempt to bridge this gap, but it has no real effect. On the one hand, it does not address the public except at the institutions, and on the other hand, it relates to only those domains shared between the Community and the member states, not to those where the Community institutions act in full competence.

European citizenship must be founded on a European legislative act that outlines the basic rights. A very broad consensus exists today on this point. Citizens will not feel closer to Europe until Europe confers upon them a comprehensive set of rights and freedoms, which must go beyond those that derive from freedom of movement and the rights added by the Maastricht Treaty. The fact that a citizen enjoys rights recognized by the states does not transform the citizen of the Union into a subject with rights on his own. It would be better to create a direct source of legal standards addressing individuals and elevating the basic rights to the European level, so that they would no longer depend on any state's national law or on a Convention that is outside the Community. It would not be difficult to define these rights; they are contained in the Declaration of the Rights of Man and of the Citizen, included in the European Convention on Human Rights: protection of human dignity and private life; equality before the law; freedom of conscience and of worship; freedom of thought, information, meeting and association; the right of ownership; civil freedoms; and the right of asylum. As basic rights, Europe must say loud and clear that *these are the basis of the values common to all the citizens of the European Union,* and that *they apply to any person residing on the territory of the Union.*

The Commission, the Parliament and most of the jurists were ready to add to this base the Treaty's provisions on equal rights in matters of welfare protection and gender equality. Similarly, they wanted to add a clear rejection of racism, xenophobia, sexism and any form of discrimination. Finally, there was a fairly broad consensus that a clause should be added to protect the public against any abuse of power by the European institutions (for example, confidentiality of personal data, the right of sasine). In addition, it is hard to imagine a European citizenship that would not grant everyone equal freedom to live in the country of their choice. However, this freedom is currently limited for reasons of law and order (which makes some sense), but also for lack of personal resources, which is far more contestable — the three directives of 1990, which relate respectively to students, retirees and other nationals, make their right to stay in a country other than the one in which they originated subject to various restrictive conditions.

We should go further, in any event. The European Socialists are proposing that in addition to the fundamental rights, we should affirm the rights to various aspects of social welfare: health, housing, employment, education, etc. These rights are different in nature from personal freedoms. They assume that adequate economic and social policies have been established which do not belong within a statement of rights. But the debate over public services shows that we need to define the universal character of these rights if we want to ensure equal access for all. Since Community jurisdiction is based on law, it is imperative that the law is extended to all the fields that must be taken into account by Community action. This is why the parliamentary spokesmen of the German social democrats say, "These rights must be cast in stone, officially, at the European level."[15] The heads of state, at the meeting in Amsterdam concluding the IGC, obviously did not hear them.

It is not enough to declare some rights. We must also define the ways and means by which they can be applied. What good would it be to proclaim the basic rights of the public if the public had no guarantee that it could force the authorities to respect those rights, and obtain compensation for damages in the event of violation? The laws must provide a mechanism for appeal. Some already exist, in cancellation and deficiency, which should be improved and supplemented by a constraining right — for example, by obligatory remediation and reparations. What happens if a state fails to observe these rights? The Westendorp Group debated this question at length while considering the enlargement of the Union. They considered the possibility of imposing sanctions as severe as "the suspension of the rights that appertain to membership, for any state guilty of serious and repeated violations, and even the possibility of expulsion."[16] This proposal is in conformity with the idea of a Europe designed as an association of states agreeing to adhere to democratic principles; it is incompatible with a Europe that proposes to ensure all its citizens the enjoyment of the basic rights. To expel a state that is in violation would mean recognizing the European institutions' inability to guarantee to all who live in Europe the principles that they proclaim. *It would be an acknowledgment of impotence.*

This debate touches on a major question for European construction: the European authorities' *right to interfere* in "the internal affairs" of a state. The permanent state of war in Northern Ireland certainly abrogates basic freedoms, and it demonstrates the limit of what Europe is ready to do to enforce respect for the values it promotes. No doubt it would have acted more boldly if Great Britain were not a member of the Community. Europe never even imagined that it could serve a role in mediating and striving for a political solution and the disarmament of the armed groups; that role was, finally, taken up by American and Canadian figures. Europe's muteness on the conflicts between Greece, Turkey and Macedonia is another illustration. The member states always avoided interfering in each other's problems of internal security. They ended up thinking that it was their duty to intervene in Bosnia and Kosovo, but not in Northern Ireland.

Bringing Europe closer to the public would also require simplifying the texts of the Treaty. On this point, too, there is unanimous agreement. The texts' complexity has become a challenge to democracy. European citizens are generally unaware that there is not one Community but three — ECSC, Euratom and the economic Community — each governed by different treaties that have never been combined. The Maastricht Treaty added two new "pillars," one for "foreign policy and mutual security," and one for "Justice and domestic affairs;" and it created a Union to oversee the unit. But this Union, which covers a Community domain and two domains that remain intergovernmental, is not a legal entity. Therefore, it can neither conclude treaties nor be a party to them, even though it is in charge of foreign policy. Moreover, does the European citizen know that there is not one but several treaties, plus protocols and statements that have proliferated over the course of time? With the addition of the Maastricht Treaty, the provisions governing the work of the European institutions are scattered in *seventeen* equivalent treaties or acts, which are only semiofficially coordinated. In itself, the Treaty establishing the European Community contains an appendix with 17 protocols and 27 declarations. As Herman wrote, "the Maastricht Treaty did not impose any order on this jumble, but made it still more confused."[17]

A study conducted at the request of the European Parliament, in the context of the preparation of the future Treaty of Amsterdam, established that the texts of the treaties or equivalent acts encompass 920 articles. Of this total, 389 could be abolished, and 215 would form a secondary legislation. The fundamental laws comprise only 316 articles, which is quite a lot already. This simple rationalization would not bring about any amendment to the basic institutions. It would only make the treaties more readable, which would be a big help. The request for readability is unanimous. In its report on the operation of the Treaty on the European Union, the Commission stated that "the time has come to simplify [the treaty] by rewriting the whole thing, to make it more readable." It added: "This is required for both technical and political transparency." The Westendorp Group, the European Parliament, the Council, and again the Commission all called for the same measures in their preparations for the IGC. Simplification, transparency, legibility — they kept coming up. The conference was completed in Amsterdam and nothing changed. What was everyone waiting for? Why didn't they take action? What are they waiting for, now?

In addition to the political goal, this simplification would also serve a legal objective: to establish a hierarchy among the Community standards, i.e. a formal set of priorities as to which standard prevails over another. Besides, Statement No. 16, annexed to the Maastricht Treaty, expressly provided that "the IGC convoked for 1996 will examine the possibility of establishing a suitable hierarchy between the various categories of standards." This hierarchy is essential for the safety of those who are being judged. Indeed, it ensures that secondary standards conform to the higher standards, and that secondary provisions can apply only within the limits authorized by the first. However, this lack of hierarchy is "the direct consequence of the procedures and the instruments chosen by all the Community treaties for exercising Community authority."[18] This has to do with the fact that "no norms have been adapted and differentiated according to the nature and the level of the selected action: legislative acts, regulations, etc.," and the fact that it is impossible to classify Community acts according to their function and their goals. Moreover, the Commission continues to create "innominate acts" (i.e. resolutions, conclusions, declarations, communications that are not codified) whose status is not defined, but that are supposed to involve legal effects. As a result, writes Professor Tizzano, "there is confusion and uncertainty around any question of defining the production of Community norms."[19]

The situation is even worse since the production of norms goes on at a furious rate. Between 1985 and 1991, the annual average of Community standards went from 25 directives to 106, and 600 regulations increased to nearly 4,000. When the Single European Act went into effect, there were 24,445 regulations and 1,675 directives. Add to that 678 communications from the Commission in force, and 185 communications of the Council and the Commission. The Community's output has since slowed, but it remains impressive. In 1995, the Commission produced 600 proposals, recommendations or draft acts, and 275 communications, memoranda and reports; the Council adopted 39 directives, 242 regulations and 175 decisions![20] The Council of State estimates that today in France, one of every two laws comes from Community legislation. Is the public familiar with them? And yet, "everyone should be aware of the law," if it is of European origin.

How can Europe respond to this need to define the rights it intends to guarantee, while making the statement of its institutional principles more manageable? The need was proclaimed throughout planning stages of the IGC, but at the last minute, it was forgotten. It is true that the difficulty is great and the divergences profound. In the individual countries, these questions are handled by the Constitution, which is the institutional expression of citizenship. Although many favor the idea of a European constitution, nobody has any illusions; it is less topical now than a few years ago. Moreover, never has there been so much discussion of the public and so little about constitutions than during the preparation of the IGC. Even the European Parliament, which used to be pushing for a constitution, has not seen it feasible to re-open this debate.

Moreover, while the idea may be tempting, it encounters many political obstacles. For a country like Great Britain, which does not have a written constitution and has never felt the need for one, the idea of a European constitution is neither plausible nor appealing. But beyond the British case, the concept of the constitution, traditionally associated with that of the state, feeds the fears of those who are afraid that the European Union will irremediably supplant the nation states. Moreover, there is no consensus now, and there may not be any in the foreseeable future, as to what form (federal or otherwise) the European State should take. The constitutional approach thus seems impracticable. But the status quo is impossible.

The problem before us can be stated simply: Europe cannot do without popular legitimacy if she wants to bring the citizens along. *However, it must accept the idea that it will have to find a different approach than the constitution of a state.* Europe probably can best find the answer to its current dilemma by returning to its own sources. Europe's entire history testifies to the impossibility of any single solution. Neither religious faith nor arms have managed to impose it. Indeed, any such solution would imply the negation of European diversity and the characteristics that have survived all the tests of time, and all of man's attempts to do away with them. The "complexity" valued by Edgar Morin is the wealth of Europe. It is its strength. Europe can establish its legitimacy only by accepting that. Contrary to a constitution that standardizes, what is needed is a way to organize this "complexity." Complexity need not signify confusion. To organize Europe requires, on the contrary, an effort at legibility and transparency that makes it understandable in order to make it possible for everyone to feel comfortable there. There can be no feeling of common membership in the same ensemble unless it leaves room for the recognition of differences. Erasmus called that tolerance. It has always been the sticking point in European unity.

To take up this challenge, Europe must go back to its sources and, more precisely, to the great philosophical debates of philosophy of rights and law. If citizenship implies the existence of a monolithic state, then Europe must give it up. But if we are looking for a concept of citizenship based on something other than a culture of the state and the nation, then there is room for hope. The solution, obviously, is *to found it on common values, of which human rights recognized by all the member states constitute the backdrop.* If the European Union ever gained legal standing, and became a signatory of the European Convention of Human Rights, that still would not be enough. This law leaves many gaps in the enumeration of rights — it omits social welfare rights — and it does not protect these rights against action by the institutions. At best it constitutes a "safety net," as many authors have said.

The European Council of Amsterdam, which, on June 16, and 17, 1997, closed the Inter-Governmental Conference, did not fulfill any of the promises made to the public after Maastricht, nor did it respond to any of their concerns. The new Treaty is satisfied with general assertions of rights and principles which once again relate to the states and not to the public. There is no reference to equal rights and the rejection of racism, xenophobia, sexism and any form of discrimination, however unanimously that was considered to be necessary. The national leaders left it up to the Council — that is, to themselves (or more likely to their successors, since no date was set), "to unanimously take the measures necessary to fight discrimination." There is nothing new on social rights, beyond what is contained in the social charter which British Prime Minister Tony Blair accepted in the Treaty. And, finally, there is nothing on the right of Union citizens to be protected from the abuse of power by the European institutions.

But what could one expect from a text that remains at the level of a treaty between states? "The Union," it is said, "is founded on the principles of freedom, democracy, respect for human rights and fundamental freedoms, as well as the state of law — principles that are common to the member states." The diplomats remain diplomats; they only express the rights of the states. Before we'll see those rights affirmed in a way that would found a European citizenship, we will have to wait for another Gonzalez to speak on behalf of all the citizens of Europe.

Notes

1. See John H. Weiler's narrative, "L'Importance fondamental de la citoyenneté européenne," in *La Conférence inter-gouvernementale sur l'Union européenne*, Paris, ed. Clément Juglar, 1996, p. 130.
2. Article 8 of the Treaty establishing the European Community.
3. The European Commission, "Report on the operation of the Treaty on the European Union, May 10, 1995," published by the Centre européen de Sciences Po, *La Conférence inter-gouvernementale, enjeux et documents*, Paris, Presses de Sciences Po, 1996.
4. *Ibid.*
5. The various reports are published in *La Conférence inter-gouvernementale, enjeux et documents, op. cit.*
6. The European Council of Turin, "*Conclusions of the Presidency*, March 29, 1996," *ibid.*, p. 363.
7. Emma Bonino, "Faire face à la réalité," in *L'UE a-t-elle le soutien de ses citoyens?*, Brussels, The Philip Morris Institute, April 1997.
8. February 14, 1984, following the adoption of the Spinelli plan, and the February 10, 1994 resolution regarding the constitution of the European Union.
9. Jean-Louis Quermone, *La Conférence inter-gouvernementale, enjeux et documents*, Introduction, *op. cit.*, p. 7.
10. Fernand Herman, "Pour une constitution européenne," *op. cit.*, p. 41.
11. In its Title I, relating to the introduction of "a European Union," the text speaks only about "nationals of the member states." The term "citizen of the Union" was introduced only in the provisions relating to the European Community (which is a legal entity) included within the Treaty of Rome by the Maastricht Treaty.
12. Working group report, *La Conférence inter-gouvernementale, enjeux et documents, op. cit.*, p. 262.
13. Manuel Oreja, "Quarante ans de cooperation européenne à un tournant," in *La Conférence inter-gouvernementale sur l'Union européenne, op. cit.*, p. 19.
14. José Luis da Cruz Vilaça, "La Constitution de l'Europe: mission inachevée," in *L'Europe a-t-elle besoin d'une constitution?* Brussels, The Philip Morris Institute, June 1996.
15. Heidemarie Wieczorek-Zeul and Jürgen Meyer, "Plaidoyer pour une chartedes droits fondamentaux européens," in in *L'Europe a-t-elle besoin d'une constitution? op. cit.*, p. 63.
16. Report of the think tank,' *op. cit.*, p. 258.
17. Fernand Herman, "Pour une constitution européenne," *op. cit.*, p. 44.
A. Tizzano, "La hiérarchie des normes communautaires ," in *La conférence inter-gouvernementale de l'UE, op. cit.*, p. 77.
18. *Ibid*, p. 79.

19. Figures quoted by Maurice Croisat and Jean-Louis Quermone, *L'Europe et le Fédéralisme*, Paris, Montchrestien, 1996, p. 95.

Chapter 10

Power to All the States

To address the challenges of expansion and the public's mistrust, the Commission assigned two goals to the Inter-Governmental Conference in its 1995 report: effectiveness and democracy. "Democracy is in the very nature of the Union," it explained, "and its future depends on its effectiveness."[1] On one hand, it was necessary "to bring Europe closer to the citizens;" on the other, "first to reform, then to expand." Parliament, the Council — all the various participants agreed to these objectives. But neither was achieved in Amsterdam. There was a little stronger majority vote for the European Councils, a little more legislative power for the European Parliament. There was a little less of the intergovernmental and a little more of the Community. It was, on the whole, a failure. After the customary self-congratulations, the Belgian, Italian and French governments ended up admitting that "the Treaty of Amsterdam does not meet the need."[2]

Given a choice between two contradictory plans, the *status quo* finally carried the day (some had thought that "impossible"[3]). Just as they did with the Single European Act and the Maastricht Treaty, the heads of state and government avoided choosing between France's and Germany's opposing concepts of democracy. While both sides called it democracy, they meant entirely different things. For the French, no matter what government is in place, democracy is embodied in the legitimacy vested in the agents who represent the states. For the Germans, conversely, it resides in a fully empowered Parliament, which is the expression of the people's will. What could be more democratic, says one side, than a Council of Ministers voting by majority? What could be more democratic, the other answers, than a Parliament holding legislative power? State democracy against parliamentary democracy — the institutional misunderstanding was complete. And it remains so.

The Treaty of Amsterdam would have been an opportunity to clear this up and get out of the deadlock. However, that would have required one party or the other to change its position — that one give up building Europe on the power of the states, or that the other reconsider its federalistic approach. That in turn would call into question the obligation defined in the Treaty (Article B) to maintain the institutional system, which the Treaty calls the *acquis communautaire** [roughly, "community provisions;" see below], made up of the Councils (the European Council and the councils of ministers) where the states' representatives meet, the Commission that embodies the European Community, and the European Parliament, which expresses the power of the people but whose powers are carefully circumscribed. Nobody wanted to open this particular can of worms. People in power are rarely willing to relinquish it. The heads of state preferred to leave the details to a new intergovernmental conference, to be scheduled after the year 2000.

The result was exactly what had been denounced throughout the entire preparation of the Inter-Governmental Conference: a tangled proliferation of procedures, "accompanied by a complication bordering on the insupportable."[4] The Commission, in a forthcoming assessment, would again criticize this phenomenon which, for the public, closes off the operation of the Union with an "extremely hermetic"[5] seal. Neither effectiveness nor democracy came out victorious with the treaty adopted in Amsterdam. The few decisions that were made are not likely to alleviate fears of institutional paralysis, expressed throughout the preparatory stages. It would even seem like progress if, contrary to the usual, they do not lead to new complications! In the immediate future, rather than start another theoretical debate between those who believe in a Europe of nations and the apostles of federalism, we must explore the vagaries of the institutions. That is a voyage that will pro-

*Defined in the *Glossary of Community Expressions* as, "All the regulations, decisions, etc., adopted under the European Treaties, and all the decisions taken by the European councils of ministers, the European Commission, the European Court of Justice, [etc.,] . . . since the European Communities were established."

gressively attempt to decipher the overall architecture, the maze of jurisdictions, and finally, the confusion of powers.

We owe the new architecture of the European institutions to the Maastricht Treaty. As so often happens, when one component needs fixing, the whole ensemble is made more complex. It all started with the decision to add a treaty called the "European Union" to the treaty called the "European Community." This was nothing more than the old Treaty of Rome, amended by the Single European Act and then again in Maastricht. The Treaty of the European Union was intended to create "a single institutional framework, with equal power in all three "pillars" and charged with ensuring the coherence and continuity of the actions taken by the Union in its various components."[6] But this unity is a facade. The reality is a nested stack of institutions resembling a Russian matryoshka doll more than a rational architecture.

Before Maastricht, the Community was composed of the three Communities — Coal and Steel (the ECSC), Euratom and the Economic Community — which all address the same institutions (the Councils, the Commission and the Parliament) but which are governed by three different treaties. They form the first "pillar," which in practice constitutes the *acquis communautaire*, a blend of intergovernmental and Community powers. In Maastricht, two other "pillars" were added, one devoted to "Foreign Policy and Mutual Security" and one on "Justice and Domestic Affairs." These two "pillars" deal exclusively with intergovernmental cooperation and they operate according to procedures that are entirely different from those of the *acquis communautaire*. There is no unity, and the Commission is still struggling to make the three pillars more "consistent."

The creation of two new "pillars" did not address the need to create new areas of cooperation; they existed before Maastricht. European political cooperation (EPC) was initiated in 1969 and focused on foreign policy; the commitment to cooperate on legal and police matters was inaugurated in 1971. The purpose of the two new pillars is to institutionalize these. The existence of these forms of cooperation, albeit intergovernmental, clearly shows the desire of the member states to release themselves from community action. They want common, but not Community, programs. The difference is that the cooperation does not involve a transfer of sovereignty. That has several consequences. The governments, through the European Council, remain completely sovereign. In contrast to the fields where the Community holds sway, the Commission only has a shared right to take initiatives — a right which is furthermore limited with regard to justice and domestic affairs, and is only associated with the work of the Council. The European Parliament only is consulted; it can formulate questions and recommendations, but it does not have a power of joint decision even for matters touching on the rights of people and public freedoms. The decisions, with some exceptions, are unanimously made by the member states. Finally, the projects in these fields are outside the control of the European Court of Justice.

These policies are also conducted according to specific procedures. Their chief characteristic is a useless complexity that generally leads to impotence, or to the masking of impotence. The agreed projects are still financed out of national budgets, and are thus subject to their constraints, except if the Council unanimously decides to have it covered by the Community budget. In addition, decision-making relies on multiple structures — the Council, the Permanent Representatives Committee, labor organizations — plus the group of foreign policy advisers, a coordinating committee, and advisory groups for justice and internal affairs. This is not a structure conducive to quick action! Under these conditions, it is not astonishing that the Commission and the Parliament are, at the very best, reserved about the two new pillars. After 18 months of experience, the Commission considered the cooperation on foreign policy "disappointing" and cooperation on justice "ineffective." It estimated that "the operation of the supposed single institutional framework to ensure the harmony between the various 'pillars' of the treaty was not satisfactory."[7] Since then, nothing has given it any reason to reconsider this judgment.

For the Commission, the search for effectiveness and democracy is summarized in one word: *communitization*. Its objective is to incorporate (to the extent that this is possible) foreign policy and justice into the scope of the *acquis communautaire*. That means, on one hand, accepting a certain transfer of sovereignty in favor of the Commission and, on the other hand, adopting the procedures that obtain in the Community domain. Will that be enough to guarantee effectiveness and democracy? It's doubtful. The Commission's own assessment of the Maastricht Treaty hardly encourages optimism. Admittedly, it is "pleased that the democratic legitimacy of the Union was strengthened. The Parliament's approval of the members of the Commission constitutes a very promising first step in the right direction. The increase in the European Parliament's legislative powers is also welcome." But, it soon deplores the twenty procedures in force, when three would have sufficed. This criticism is aimed at the *acquis communautaire* and it is to be feared that adding two pillars to it will only entail the pure and simple addition of existing intergovernmental procedures, and not of their simplification.

Cooperation between states does not actually require European institutions. The secular framework of diplomatic relations is enough. The more one attempts to fit it into the Community mold, the more one is driven to specify what parts will prompt the European Council, and the Council of Ministers (without consulting the Parliament or, on the contrary, only upon such consultation) to subdivide according to whether the decision must be made unanimously or by qualified majority, whether it relates to the definition of general guidelines or joint projects. Moreover, everyone who contributes to the decision-making process within the states considers it normal to participate in the European decisions since, in a way, they remain national decisions. But, for their part, the permanent representatives attached to the European institutions cannot imagine that any discussions could take place without them, since their role is precisely to represent the national states. In short, the procedures can only proliferate and become more cumbersome. However, we have to avoid any improper procedures. This was clear with the Yugoslav affair and with the Schengen accords, signed in 1986 and only implemented in the Amsterdam Treaty. In fact, the procedures alone are in question. What is missing, Leibniz said to the Abbot de Saint-Pierre, "is the will." The will to overcome the difference in positions between member states remains cruelly absent.

The *acquis communautaire* limits Europe's scope. "Maintaining" it as stipulated by the Treaty is an impediment to development. Contrary to the statements of the Commission and many European leaders, it is anything but an opening to the future. The opposition that the Commission likes to stress between "two different operating modes, Community and intergovernmental," is only a pretence. It persuades the public, which is unfamiliar with the subtleties of European construction, that the Community "domain" would be free from the intergovernmental, and thus that it would be removed from detritus of the national interests. A sweet and comprehensible dream, but light-years from reality. Anyway, the Commission can only mention it; it cannot criticize it. It is charged with the mission of guaranteeing the Treaties:

the Maastricht Treaty "strengthens and consecrates the central position of the European Council."[8] However, how can we qualify a body made up of the heads of state (who derive their legitimacy from national elections, embody the member states, and are ultimately agents of their countries' national interests in all the decisions they make), if not as an intergovernmental institution?

The national states are not only present in the Community domain through the Council, i.e. the political leaders, heads of state and ministers. The intermediary of the national civil servants represents them in a more insidious way. They are omnipresent at every stage, from the preparation of the decisions to their implementation. Everything starts with COREPER (The Committee of Permanent Representatives of Foreign Ministers), who coordinates the day-to-day activities of the various councils on behalf of the Ministers. All together, there are 20 different councils, acting for ministers in different areas: general affairs, economy and finance, employment, the environment, etc.. COREPER is a major player — it makes 80% of the decisions. The technocratic character of this authority has been denounced many times. But its existence only shows how prevalent the power of the state is in the daily life of Europe. And nothing can be done without the diplomats and the national civil servants, since most of the decisions concern the councils of ministers, not the Commission.

Once the decisions have been made, the national civil servants are still there, and in a completely official capacity. In the language of Brussels, that is called "committee-ology, the "science" of committees. The expression dates back to the European Council of July 13, 1987, which institutionalized and standardized the practices, but the practices themselves are older. They originated with the management committees that the Treaty of Rome provided in 1958, to allow the national governments to make sure that the powers conferred on the Commission would be exercised in close communication with the national administrations. To some extent, they are national oversight committees. Alongside the management boards, consultative committees appeared in 1962. They are charged with formulating opinions on the preparation of the laws (and there are more than 75 of them). There are also regulation committees, which are required on Council regulations and whose recommendations the Commission is obliged to follow. Lastly, committees known as safeguard clauses can be created upon the request by any member state; they allow the Commission to take urgent, directly applicable measures before being confirmed by the Council.

Before the European Parliament's powers were reinforced, these practices caused a fierce conflict with the Council following the Maastricht Treaty.[9] Given the procedure of joint decision-making, which associates the European Council with the Parliament, Parliament demanded to have the same rights as the Council, a claim which the Council always vigorously opposed. A Resolution was adopted on this matter. Parliament, in the absence of agreement with the Council, made its decisions on a case-by-case basis. The introduction of joint decisions has, in fact, allowed the European Parliament to question all of committee-ology, and, in particular, to oppose the introduction of any committees other than advisory ones.

The vote on a law on voice telephony was used as a pretext. After its final rejection by Parliament, on December 20, 1994, a *modus vivendi* had to be found. Without acknowledging Parliament's claim to parallelism, it constrained the Council to keep Parliament informed. In its assessment of the Treaty, the Commission did not consider it useful to reconsider this agreement, although the agreement had assumed that it would. In addition, it stated that these committee-ology procedures "have the advantage of strongly involving the national administrations that will be responsible for implementing the executive acts." Jacques Santer, like Jacques Delors before him, justified this position by explaining that "the Commission needs the opinion of national experts; and the experts, who will have to implement the Community decisions later on, need to be involved in the process." But the whole question is "whether it is legitimate and effective for the Commission's executive powers to be turned over to representatives of the states and the Council (itself representing the states)."[10] Or, finally, doesn't that take away the little sovereignty that had been conceded to the Community level? Delors himself denounced the national civil servants for "leading battles of delayed action in order to win back part of what had been ceded by a compromise at the ministerial level, which had originated in bureaucratic excesses!"[11]

It is impossible to avoid involving the national administrations, and thus the national civil servants, in implementing the European directives and regulations. No one imagines creating a European administration from scratch and superimposing it on the member states. That would result in competition and conflict between administrations. The national administrations implement the Community decisions, like the

German Länder, which carry out the federal legislation. But, unlike them, they also take part in developing them. They are the spokesmen for both the national and the Community interests, playing one against the other to establish their autonomy and to consolidate their bureaucratic powers. Since each decision is the result of a compromise, there is a risk that standards that have been set for all of Europe might be reinterpreted and re-nationalized at the time of implementation. The Commission has to make sure that the national administrations will actually adhere to the principles that were jointly adopted, since the principle that "Committee-ology reconciles the national administrations' involvement and the uniform application of the Community law,"[12] means that the Court of Justice is, in the final analysis, charged with enforcement. But, as the European Parliament has stressed, that would require reducing the number of Committees and limiting them to an advisory role, while conferring general responsibility for the acts of implementation upon the Commission under Parliamentary supervision. There is no other way to combine effectiveness with democracy. We have a long way to go.

On a second level, let us take the public through the maze of jurisdictions, a journey that holds another set of surprises. It would have been simple to distinguish three types of competence: Community areas, areas which require intergovernmental cooperation, and finally, strictly national areas that were never intended to merge with the European domain. With each group, it would have been easy to imagine establishing a single procedure. But the slogan of Europe seems to be, "Why make it simple, if you can make it complicated?" Europe is building itself layer upon layer with interwoven policies: the common market, agricultural policies, European political cooperation (which, after Maastricht, became the "foreign policy and mutual security"), monetary policy, structural policy, education, health, environment, justice and internal affairs, just to name the principal ones. But the list is long, so long that in response to the expansionist tendency exhibited by Brussels, encouraged by the direct powers given to the Commission by the Single European Act, a strict delimitation of jurisdictions was recommended. But this idea never came to fruition. For his part, the former President of the Commission preferred to introduce the concept of subsidiarity into the Treaty — a principle bound to have great success, but which led to the total confusion of jurisdictions.

Subsidiarity, as the public was led to believe during the debate on the Maastricht Treaty, would redefine jurisdictions by allotting "to each level what it can do best." At a conference on this topic given by the European Institute of Public Administration, Delors even proposed "a table that would give some structure to the debate on the allocation of functions and the transfers of sovereignty." From this point of view, he saw subsidiarity as "not only a limit on the intervention of a higher authority with respect to a person or a community which is able to act on its own behalf," but "also an obligation for this authority to act with respect to this person or this community, to offer the means of fulfill-ment." In short, the Union should actively "carry out the tasks which can be undertaken more effectively together than by the member states working separately."[13]

The reality was very different, once again. Article 3B of the Treaty of the European Community, which defines subsidiarity, starts with a first subparagraph proclaiming, "The Community acts within the limits of competence that are conferred and the objectives which are assigned by this Treaty." The second subparagraph then clarifies it, saying: "In the domains which do not come under its exclusive responsibility, the Community does not intervene, in accordance with the principle of subsidiarity, unless and insofar as the objectives of the action being considered cannot adequately be carried out by the member states." In other words, subsidiarity is not a general principle; it is possible only where the Treaties do not grant the Commission exclusive competence.

In the domains where it has full authority, Community action can neither be limited nor blocked by considerations of subsidiarity, since the states have given up some of their sovereignty. The President of the Commission even calls subsidiarity "a fig leaf to hide the lack of politi-cal will to implement the commitments already subscribed," a principle "evoked in order to obstruct common policies expressly desired by the authors of the Treaty."[14] Delors considers subsidiarity only in terms of implementing the directives, which can be left up to the member states "in order to break with an often ineffective centralism." As much as possible, "the laws should stay focused on the essential" and leave the practical details aside. Where the Treaties have accorded the Commu-nity full jurisdiction, the Commission does not have to justify taking initiative; that is its right. "The assignment of jurisdictions is a policy decision, which doesn't need any help from the judge." He can intervene in this case only to make sure that "the concrete procedures do not vio-late subsidiarity."[15]

Paradoxically, although there are domains defined as giving the Commission "exclusive jurisdiction," there is no corollary of a domain where the Commission has no jurisdiction. Nothing prevents it from grabbing control, as long as it is not acting in "exclusive competence." It must only show that Community action would be more effective than that of the member states or the "regional authorities." Thus, we are far from a traditional federal system. Subsidiarity does not acknowledge borders and by no means curbs the expansionism of Brussels. It only obliges the Commission to prove that Community action is superior to national action. Thus, anytime there is no reason to adopt a different standard from one country to another, the Commission may be seen as having a right to intervene. But are we sure that, both for protecting workers from asbestos exposure and for standardizing the number of fire extinguishers per company, subsidiarity justifies writing European directives? Between simple cooperation between states and the "exclusive domain" of the Commission, a new domain surfaces where jurisdiction is debated between the Commission and the states. This domain has, obviously, given birth to many specific procedures and has involved a re-examination of Community legislation with regard to this principle of division.

Those who see the principle of subsidiarity as a means of strictly delimiting jurisdictions between the European and national levels are sadly mistaken. It is by nature an instrument for regulating the ever-increasing transfer of control to the Community, an instrument the Commission thinks is necessary as "a permanent counterweight to the spillover mechanisms that tend, in a complex world, to centralize power too much."[16] This effect led the European economic integration to be described as a dynamic process, which has "the endogenous property of improving over time." Consequently, there can be no limit on Community competence. Any step ahead justifies another, like a cyclist who must pedal continuously to stay in balance. Thus, the Single European Act led to the liberalization of the flows of capital. The latter revealed the need for a reconciliation of tax policies, an arena that was, however, outside of Community jurisdiction. Then, it made the establishment of a common monetary policy inevitable, and thus was born the EMU. The EMU led to the creation of the Cohesion Funds, which came on top of the Structural Funds to bring the various economies closer together. Lastly, the prospect of a single currency created the need for a greater coordination of economic policies. In other words, the spillover effect acts as an accelerator of integration, while "subsidiarity" is used as brake on Brussels' expansionism. What the Commission allows to be limited here, it takes back over there.

This interplay between the brake and the accelerator increases the proliferation of procedures. On one hand, the existence of an exclusive Community "competence" does not keep the Commission out of those decisions to be made by the member states. Admittedly, the Commission holds a monopoly over submitting proposals and, by withdrawing one, it can disrupt the decision-making process at any time. But the member states (through the councils) preserve the monopoly of the decision, which they may or may not share with the European Parliament, depending on the circumstances and the variable procedures. Additionally, the gears of integration impel the Commission to extend its scope, even if it has to justify it. There is no field that might not, one day, come under the Community's sole jurisdiction, including foreign policy, defense, justice and domestic affairs. For the Commission, their transfer to Community control is a question of time, not of principle. In contrast to political federalism, which is based on a strict constitutional delimitation of jurisdictions between the various institutional levels, the construction of Europe rests on a kind of functional federalism that is constantly siphoning off new jurisdictions toward the supranational level. One can see why the public is skeptical that this is serving its interests and why it seeks, vainly, to protect itself from the Community institutions' tendency to infinitely extend their purview.

The final surprise in our exploration of the European institutions is learning just how confused are the parameters of power. From the start, the system was based on an independent "high authority" without the veneer of democracy, and on an Assembly of national parliamentarians without Europe-wide legitimacy. Contrary to democratic principles, the legislative and executive powers were joined together in the same hands instead of being separated. And not the hands that embody Community actions, but those of the states, the European Council of the heads of state and the (national) Council of Ministers. This orientation, far from being condemned, was "confirmed and even accentuated by practice in recent years." The Commission even finds it "natural that the representation of the states was strengthened." In addition, it proposed to go further than Maastricht and "to engage the national parliaments more directly and more visibly in the control and the orientation of the national choices applying to the Union" (a proposal that the Westendorp Group embraced).

The debate on the role of the national parliaments is to some extent the result of the confusion of powers, and subsidiarity in particular. In domains where the Treaty does not grant the Community "exclusive competence," the national parliaments have the right to exert their control on legislation that they deem worthy to remain at the national level. But that would seem to require that the principle of a European legislation is subject to them, directly or through COSAC, the authority that brings together members of the national Parliaments, before the Commission sets any a procedure in motion — which is obviously not the case.

But this debate also reveals how confused the thinking has become on this subject. We should not be shocked by the fact that national parliaments cannot contest the European Parliament's voting on Community legislation. The right to negotiate was conferred by the Treaties on the national governments, not the national parliaments. Some say the parliaments should have the right to amend directives, but that would inevitably lead to the paralysis, then to the disintegration of European construction. As for the control that Parliaments wield over their national governments, that is totally legitimate. However, that has less to do with European procedures than with national constitutional practices. And it is hard to see how the Treaties could intervene on that level.

A certain number of countries with longstanding parliamentary traditions have taken the necessary measures. Since 1974, Great Britain has had a special subcommittee for European legislation, which discusses every proposition that is to be used as a basis for future European laws. The Netherlands has done the same since 1986. The most advanced country is Denmark. When the country joined the European Community, Denmark's parliament, the Folketing, adopted a provision that obliges the government to obtain a parliamentary mandate before negotiating anything at the European level. When the result is different from the initial mandate, the minister is required to return before the Folketing to obtain its agreement before he can commit his country to the negotiated law. In the other countries, the national parliaments' control over the government's European legislation only came up when the Maastricht Treaty was being ratified. Thus, "a European Article" was introduced into the German fundamental law, which provides for the intervention of the Bundestag and Bundesrat prior to "the government's participation in the legislative acts of the European Union."

In France, increasing the rights of Parliament goes against the Constitution of the Fifth Republic. Admittedly, at the time of the debate on the Maastricht Treaty, the French Parliament obtained the right to advance information. But the conduct of diplomacy is the precinct of the head of state, who is not accountable to the assemblies. In addition, the constitution marginalizes the role of Parliament by restricting its control over the government and by strictly limiting the scope of the law. Most of the matters that concern regulation are discussed at the administrative level, not in Parliament. Within Europe, France is an unusual case, an ongoing source of misunderstandings with its partners who have a parliamentary tradition.

Even though a European Assembly, thereafter called the European Parliament, was created right from the start, and even though it was legitimated by its election by universal vote since 1979, it had no legislative power until the Maastricht Treaty. The Parliament had to extract this power bit by bit, even though that is its reason for existing: the budgetary process in the 1970s, the introduction of the processes of "cooperation" and "assent" in the Single European Act and, finally, the recognition of a "joint decision-making" power in Maastricht, in 1991. Still, it should be noted that, as its name indicates it, joint decision is shared with the Council. In the event of dissension, that implies a complex "conciliation" process that can last more than a year. Moreover, this process is strictly limited to fields concerning the domestic market and measures relating to the fields of education, culture, health, the environment and consumer protection. However, the introduction of "joint decision-making" allowed a general rewriting that broadened the scope of the other procedures, "assent," "cooperation" and, finally, "obligatory advisory notice." In addition, the European Parliament now has the power to give an opinion on the choice of the President of the Commission and to approve his nomination.

Not only do the legislative procedures keep multiplying, they vary according to whether the Council must decide unanimously or by qualified majority. It is understandable that the Commission is critical of how the Union operates. The Maastricht Treaty "made it even more complicated," the evaluation reads, "by adding new structures which amend and supplement those already existing, and by leaving ambiguous certain provisions of the preceding Treaties that it neither revisited nor formally repealed."[17] While preparing for the IGC, the Commission, the Westendorp Group and the European Parliament all were pleading for the procedures to be simplified. They proposed reducing them to three: joint decision, assent and consultation. The procedure of cooperation would be abolished. The object of the three others would be spelled out. Assent would be limited to legislation affecting the institutions, the amendment of the treaties, expansion, adjustment of its own resources, and to international agreements; the consultation procedure would be reserved for areas of intergovernmental cooperation, in particular foreign policy and mutual security; finally, the procedure of joint decision would be simplified and applied in all the other areas.

The heads of state and government did not take up any of these proposals. The Council of Amsterdam did not commit to any redistribution of power, only to minor adjustments to the institutional design of European construction. A few more areas were given over to vote by qualified majority, a few more areas were ascribed to joint decision by Parliament (from 11 to 34), and there was a slight tilt from intergovernmental toward Community for matters of justice and domestic affairs. Nothing was done to reduce and simplify the procedures. The Franco-German compromise did a wonderful job of safeguarding the institutional equilibrium. However, this equilibrium, such as it is, merely represents the point where two contradictory schools of logic cross, a point that cannot be maintained for long.

It was implied that the vote by qualified majority was being extended to all cases, but in fact it was applied to only 10 fields out of the 47 where decisions had been made unanimously. This extension marginally redistributed power between the member states, but it did not transfer any additional power to the European authorities (the Commission and Parliament). On the contrary, it weakened the Commission. To achieve a unanimous vote, the Commission would use its monopoly of proposal to withdraw a text and to present it again, amended in order to arrive at a compromise acceptable to all. Admittedly, the reform put an end to obstruction by one country, which Margaret Thatcher liked to practice. But by forcing them to seek agreement, the unanimous vote protected a country from having the others impose upon it a law that the government, duly elected by the voters, had opposed at the national level. Can one imagine what would have become of the French government if, shortly after the elections of June 1997, it had been placed in the minority on the budgetary "stability pact" that it had denounced in front of the voters, without being able to force its partners to supplement it with an "employment pact?" The extension of the vote in the majority is thus likely to appear, not like a democratic progress but, on the contrary, as a destruction of national legitimacy, and one day may create a true crisis of public distrust for Europe.

The rejection of the French proposal to reduce the number of European commissioners undoubtedly saved the Commission. Everyone recognized that adding commissioners every time there was a new member state would quickly lead to its paralysis. However, limiting it would no longer have allowed for every country to be represented. The small countries, already affected by the granting of vote by majority, would see their influence decreased even further; so they were strongly against the idea. Ultimately, it was decided to keep the number of commissioners fixed at 20 as a long as the Union has no more than twenty members, thus delaying until 2003 or 2004 the reform of the Commission. This will give everyone time to reflect on the Commission's role in the European institutions. One can, indeed, question the validity of the argument for a restricted Commission, that "more coherent is more effective," (the only argument which animated the French diplomats). One can see in this proposal their old mistrust for any institution making supranational claims. As the former Belgian Minister Fernand Herman said, the European Commission and the Parliament remain "France's two *bêtes noires*; that has not changed for almost thirty years."[18] In other words, effectiveness would, in fact, have strengthened the (intergovernmental) power of the states and not of that of the Community institutions!

The Council of Amsterdam's failure to break the status quo led to an inversion of the main priorities: to expand, before being reformed. But everyone was aware well that the debate was only being put off. Given that the procedures are complex "to the point of being unacceptable," institutional reform is inevitable. The CDU-CSU parliamentary group outlined one possibility that made a great splash in autumn 1994. Ignoring France's hidden agenda, it proposed "taking as a starting point the federal model, with which Germany has a certain amount of experience, and moving toward a new concept of institutional review, gradually conferring upon the Parliament the character of a legislative body with rights equal to the Council. This body would assume (in addition to other tasks mainly relating to the intergovernmental arena) the role of second Chamber — that is, a Chamber of the States, with the Commission acting as a European government."[19] The debate was cut short and the proposal remained nothing more than a draft. It was rejected because it called for starting with a "core" of five or six countries, ready to increase their cooperation and go forward from there.

The merit of the German proposal was, and remains, that it started the institutional debate. Its shortcoming is that it dodges the question of the States' power in the functioning of the European Union. If the greatest confusion reigns in the European institutions, it is not only because of the proliferation of the procedures, but because the same national leaders must play both national and European roles. They are members of the European councils only because they are heads of state or government, or ministers in their own countries. National political leaders, elected on the basis of national objectives are thus placed at the heart of European decision-making. Without saying so explicitly, the German proposal shifted national leaders' centers of gravity by allocating them to a "second Chamber" that would have only a legislative power shared with the European Parliament.

The role of the States in Europe's institutions is clearly at the heart of every question relating to the reform. Marginalizing the Council is not the only way to reduce its influence. The introduction and the progressive reinforcement of domains under the Community's purview would be another approach. And under pressure from Germany, in particular, the claim to regional representation continues to gain ground. The first regional antennas appeared in Brussels in 1985, and soon led to the development of interregional associations, the inclusion in the Maastricht Treaty of a regional committee with the possibility of direct regional representation within the Council of Ministers and in the working groups (Article 146). The regional prerogatives remain limited, but a breach was opened and some of the larger regions (Catalonia, Lombardy, Flanders) are driving through. Dropping their claims of autonomy and boosted by a high level of development, these regions are now playing Europe against the nation states. As long as the latter control Europe, they have little chance of attaining their objective. But they will be no less a factor tomorrow.

The failure of Amsterdam only delayed the inevitable reform. In the long term, the status quo is not tenable. The tangle of procedures gradually makes Europe ungovernable and incomprehensible. The states' central position in the institutional set-up, which seemed for a time to be the guarantee of a well-controlled integration, now appears harmful to the very idea of Europe. The next few years will be decisive and the positions that the French government takes will be of prime importance. France's will to keep the states' power at the heart of European construction (affirmed time and again since General de Gaulle), while still promoting an integrated Europe, obliges France more than the others to redefine what a Europe would look like that would truly fulfill itself without obliterating the States. Would we want it?

One cannot hope to get out of this institutional misunderstanding without getting past the Manicheism that underlies it. Neither the propped up defense of state sovereignty nor the incantatory evocation of federalism offers a credible prospect to Europe. The interdependence of the economies condemns the first, the weight of the national identities the second. Europe must invent institutions that go beyond its internal divisions without taking away its diversity. The question is whether to achieve this by weaving together the power of the states and Europe or, on the contrary, by separating the fields of jurisdictions and procedures to apply in each domain. The first solution, which until now had been the preferred route, has caused such distress and rejection that it hardly leaves the answer in doubt. The objectives of effectiveness and democracy, established in 1996 at the intergovernmental conference, will not be achieved tomorrow unless the lines of responsibility are clearly specified.

Right now, Europe seems to be facing a new challenge: coming up with a *European defense identity*. Certainly, that Great Britain goes along with this concept and has agreed to fuse the Europe's armed representative (The Western European Union) into the institutions of the European Union have freed up the possibilities for European foreign relations and security policy. But the first steps taken seem to have moved in the opposite direction from that which had prevailed in the monetary and judiciary sectors. Community integration is being abandoned in favor of a return to intergovernmental channels.

Since the French-British summit at St. Malo in December, 1998, nothing has changed this view. Following the publication of his "white book on the future of Europe and its institutions," the British premier could have addressed the European Council. But he preferred a bilateral meeting between the leaders of the two countries in Europe that have a nuclear military arsenal, to announce that the Union should have "a capability of autonomous action, based on credible military forces," that would allow Europe to use either its own forces or NATO's, depending on the circumstances. A few months later, another bilateral meeting (between the French and the Germans, the summit in Toulouse) gave these two a chance to get together before this decision would be acted upon by the 15, at the European Council held in Cologne in June, 1999.

Until NATO's military intervention in Kosovo, Europe had been absent throughout the conflict. Not only did it take a decision from the U.S. President to get the European countries to swing into action, but even more tellingly, the French, German, British and Italian governments coordinated their efforts without, at any time, thinking it might be useful to involve the European Union. The European Community played no role until it was time to think about aid to Kosovo, and how to pay for it. In other words, when the focus shifted from military to economic challenges. After the Franco-German divisions' successes during the break-up of Yugoslavia, the governments concerned could only congratulate themselves on their cooperation — and claim that community involvement was in no way necessary.

The final episode, as of fall, 1999, was the establishment of the great "foreign affairs and security policy" called for in the Treaty of Amsterdam. Its head was only just appointed (in the person of the former secretary general of NATO and former Spanish Minister for Foreign Affairs, Javier Solana) when France diverted the debate from military questions to the traditional institutional questions. First, France proposed incorporating it into a permanent committee of 15 ambassadors, who would serve as the eyes of the States. Then, in a joint letter dated October 13, 1999 addressed to the sitting president of the European Council (Paavo Lipponen, of Finland) the French president and the German chancellor proposed, on the eve of his debut on October 18, that "The heads of state and of government support and defend in their entirety [Solana's] powers and the exercise of his functions," and suggested that he introduce, on a regular basis, European Council deliberations on matters of foreign relations and security, and that he "play his role fully in the European Union's political dialogue with third-party states, and within the international organizations."

This vision of the role of the person heading up the foreign affairs and security policy of Europe goes well beyond the desire to augment "the visibility, the efficiency, the consistency and the continuity" of the policy. It makes him the alter-ego of the president of the European Commission and takes questions of foreign policy and defense away from the Commission and the European Parliament. The French-German suggestion places these topics solely under the discretion of the intergovernmental sector, as France has been pushing for since de Gaulle's time.

Such an orientation marks a blow to the evolution of European construction conceived as a progressive integration within a community framework along the lines of that which the Treaty of Amsterdam accomplished in the judicial pillar. While the construction of a double European space, one monetary and one judicial, might lead you to believe in an gradual and irresistible enlargement of the scope of the *acquis communautaires*, the heads of state and government are trying to create a European Union that would walk on two antinomical legs, one a heading towards greater integration, the other pulling in the opposite direction, toward the reaffirmation of the permanence of states. The Executive, that is, the Commission, and the European Parliament, would thus be shorn of two of the most essential attributes of sovereignty: foreign policy, and defense.

Notes

1. The European Commission, "Report on the operation of the Treaty on the European Union, May 1995," *op. cit.*, p. 112.
2. Joint Declaration of the Belgian, Italian and French governments, September 17, 1997.
3. Club of Florence, *Europe, L'impossible statu quo*, Paris, Stock, 1996.
4. *Ibid.*, p. 113.
5. *Ibid.*, p. 138.
6. The Council of the European Union, "Report on the operation of the Treaty on the European Union, April 1995," *op. cit.*, p. 41.
7. The European Commission, "Report on the operation of the Treaty," *op. cit.*, p. 114.
8. *Ibid.*, p. 124.
9. Jean-Domenica Nuttens, "La 'comitologie' et la conférence intergouvernementale," *Revue du marché commun de l'Union européenne*, April 1996, pp. 314 sq.
10. *Ibid.*, p. 325.
11. Jacques Delors, *Europe, L'impossible statu quo*, Foreword, *op. cit.*, p. VI.
12. *Ibid.*, p. 326.
13. Jacques Delors, "Le Principe de subsidiarité," Institut Européen d'administration publique, Maastricht, March 21, 1991, in *Le Nouveau Concert européen, op. cit.*, p. 165.
14. *Ibid.*, p. 170.
15. *Ibid.*, p. 166.
16. Jacques Delors, "La Dynamique de la construction européenne," Conference at the Center for European Studies, Brussels, November 30, 1989, in *Le Nouveau Concert européen, op. cit.*, p. 158.
17. *Ibid.*, p. 150.
18. Fernand Herman, "Pour une constitution européenne," *op. cit.*, p. 49.
19. CSU-CDU Parliamentary groups, *Réflexions sur la politique européenne, doc. cit.*

Chapter 11

The Search for the Holy Grail

This is the tale of an impossible quest, the pursuit of an unachievable goal, the inexorable drive toward martyrdom. It is the account of the failure of a great ambition for Europe: political union. And, incidentally, the failure of the European Council of Amsterdam, which was supposed to reform Europe's institutions before expanding to include new countries. It is the genesis of a myth, a combat of titans that had set two concepts of Europe against each other since the first steps of European construction. The Community was pitted against national sovereignty, the future against the past, innovation against roots. It is also the story of actors, and of struggles between actors: elected officials against diplomats, European activists against national activists, the Commission against the Council — and with the Parliament waiting in ambush. In short, it is the chronicle of Europe.

This story begins in June 1950 with Robert Schuman, the French Minister for Foreign Affairs. On the eve of the Conference of Paris (which laid the foundation for the ECSC Treaty), aware that the prospect of losing national sovereignty was none too popular, he flung an interdict right onto the negotiating table. He refused to discuss the supranational character of the "High Authority," which was intended to manage the "coal-steel pool." Without this initiative, Europe probably would never have seen the light of day. Baptized "the Commission" in the Treaty of Rome, it embodied Europe even before that had taken shape. It was to be its heart and its guarantor. By its very existence, it creates a frontier: where the Commission has authority, that is Europe;

where this authority is disputed, there the nation states remain.

The creation of the ECSC was more than a success; it was retribution for the failure of the Congress of the Hague in 1948. Forgetting that that would have been acquired at the price of contracting to a specific economic field — the customs union — far from any political claim, the European federalists believed they could outsmart the nation states. They had their chance in 1952, with the European Defense Community. The Assembly of the ECSC, chaired by the Belgian Minister Paul-Henri Spaak, was charged with working out the architecture of the "political Community." The plan, adopted by the Assembly with near-unanimity in March 1953, advanced three propositions. They proposed to place the legislative power in the hands of a Parliament to be made up of two houses, one of them elected by universal vote; to make the High Authority an executive council answerable to the Parliament; and finally, to reduce the power of the Council of Ministers to that of "assent" on major issues. Thus, the battle was drawn between the three poles of the institutional triangle. It still remains a battle today.

How could they get this plan adopted? The Spaak plan reshuffled the ECSC's cards. It introduced two fundamental amendments, whose shadow still hangs over the reform of the institutions. The High Authority lost the initiative, which the Parliament gained, and the power of the Council of Ministers was transferred to this same Parliament. This double inversion obviously reduced the Assembly's potential allies, which could count on neither the European leaders of the High Authority, nor on the national governments. The Assembly thought it could get around that roadblock by addressing the national parliaments directly. But their constitutional practice did not allow them to take up international agreements that did not emanate from their own government. The French Parliament's rejection of the plan, in August 1954, put an end to this attempt. The governments, too, decided not to go with it. The political union was stillborn; it still has not recovered.

The national governments drew two conclusions from this failure. The first was to take another look at grounding integration on the economy; the second was to entrust its fulfillment to "governmental delegates" and "experts" who would make sure that States' rights would prevail. While they were negotiating the Treaty of Rome, the diplomats took in hand the construction of Europe. And they have never relinquished it. A committee was formed and Spaak, the guarantor of the European will, was made President. Dominated by diplomats, the committee immediately withdrew the legislative power from the Assembly and gave it to the representatives of the States; that is, to a Council of (national) Ministers sitting at the center of the web. The existence of a supranational power, which originated with the ECSC, was preserved through the institution of a European Commission — intended to succeed the High Authority — but it was only given power to initiate legislative proposals, not to make decisions. The Council could take a decision on Commission proposals, by "qualified" majority vote, weighted to prevent any one country being able to block the decision. However, if the Council deviated from the Commission proposal, it would require a unanimous vote. Lastly, the Court of Justice was given the right of interpreting and implementing the Treaties, and the Community legislation was recognized as having "primacy" over national laws.

The institutional triangle was in place. It never moved again. Seeking to preserve the supranational nature of the Commission and forced to introduce an intergovernmental dimension, the Spaak committee linked the two and invented the "Community method." It created a subtle balance between the two antagonistic forces, the supranational and the national. And the Assembly paid for it. On this occasion, the States and the diplomats took the power into their own hands, and brushed aside the assemblies and elected officials. From now on, Europe would be crafted through the diplomatic negotiation of treaties, not by debate in any constituent assembly. The design of the political union results from this. What else could it reflect for a diplomat, if not foreign policy? And how can the development of a European foreign policy be reconciled with the preservation of national sovereignty (without which national diplomacy has no more role), except through the method of intergovernmental cooperation? Why be concerned with the public since they are "contained" in the States? The Council against the Commission, the Council and the Commission against the Parliament, the Community method against intergovernmental cooperation, the public against States — all the ingredients of the future European institutional debates are there, right up to the final failure of the Treaty of Amsterdam.

It is characteristic of any equilibrium to be subjected to various conflicting pressures. General de Gaulle was the first to give it a try. In November 1959, he proposed to establish a "political cooperation," a dialogue between the Six on foreign policy, and broached the idea of a permanent secretariat of the Foreign Ministers. This formula was rejected out of hand by the other governments, which saw it, within reason, as jeopardizing the "Community method." The General did not give up easily. During a press conference on September 5, 1960, he clarified his thought: "Having said that building Europe (in other words, uniting it) is an essential goal for us, we now need to proceed, not according to dreams, but according to realities. Now, what are the realities of Europe, what are the pillars on which Europe can be built? In truth, they are the States." Thus it was necessary "to ensure the regular cooperation of the States . . . and the periodic deliberation of an assembly made up of delegates from the national parliaments."[1] On February 10 and 11, 1961, in the Salon de l'Horloge at the Quay d'Orsay, he convened in Paris the first summit in the history of the Community and restated the idea of a political Europe. A few months later, a second summit took place in Bad Godesberg, and Christian Fouchet was given the mission of preparing the text of a Treaty which "gives form to the desire for a political union."

Displayed on November 2, 1961, the first Fouchet plan proposed to create a political union that would deal with foreign policy, defense science, culture and the protection of human rights. It would be equipped with a Council of the Heads of State and Government, which would meet three times a year, and would be assisted by a "policy Commission" made up of high-ranking civil servants of the member States, sitting in Paris. This plan, thirty years before Maastricht, cleverly set the "political union" outside the competence of the Community, which it was careful not to touch. It was weak in two ways. On the one hand, the Fouchet plan reinforced the intergovernmental pillar so much that it would be unacceptable to most European countries; on the other, it linked "the organization of Europe to a reform of NATO,"[2] which was unacceptable to the Netherlands government. Under these conditions, the plan could only fail, despite the General's support. But the French diplomats carefully kept it in their drawers, presenting it again in one form or another each time the question of a political "Europe" came up.

Does the failure of this attempt to tilt European construction toward a State-led Europe give the impression that it would be possible to strengthen the community nature of the existing institutions? The President of the Commission, Walter Hallstein, worked out a whole set of proposals toward that end. This was a crucial moment in the history of the Community. The decision to amalgamate the three executives of the ECSC, Euratom and the EEC on January 1, 1965, gave the Commission a prestige that it wanted to exploit. In parallel, the date was approaching when a certain number of fields would become liable to vote by qualified majority, including agricultural policy. Lastly, insufficient revenue from the import levies on agricultural produce made it necessary to find additional resources for the financing of this same agricultural policy. This time, the balance leaned too much toward the Community side. But the Commission's mistake was in trying to deal with financing, budgetary autonomy of the Community and an extension of the European Parliament's powers, all at one time. This was an "explosive cocktail which, more again, was going to provoke crises in the Community."[3] In addition, the President of the Commission thought he could force the Council's hand by presenting his proposals to the European Parliament before he submitted them to the States.

Having failed to separate the financial regulation (which was of direct interest to French farmers) from the institutional aspect, General de Gaulle decided to curtail any French participation at the Community meetings. This was the "empty chair policy," which lasted from July 1965 to January 1966. Re-elected, after having to go through a second round with François Mitterrand and Jean Lecanuet, General de Gaulle tried to get the five other Member States to re-consider the majority vote. But they were opposed to any amendment of the Treaties. They accepted only a "statement of dissension" on the procedure to be followed in the event of divergence: when the decision was to be made by the majority and when very important interests were at stake, the discussion must continue until the moment when a unanimous agreement could be reached. Such was the content of "the Luxembourg compromise," signed on January 30, 1966. The principle of majority vote was not threatened, but the "shock" was such that the Council did renounce this voting procedure for many years.

This two-fold failure was not only negative. The initial institutional balance emerged stronger, definitively metamorphosed into an *acquis communautaire*. Any later reform would have to take it into consideration. It would find in the two contradictory attempts a very ready format, which the future plans for political union would draw upon at their leisure. But the main outcome was undoubtedly the abandonment, for two decades, of any judicial reform. "The great plans to reinforce Europe, at the beginning of the Seventies," notes Professor Jean de Ruyt, "initially the economic and monetary union, then the

European Union, never succeeded in getting past the stage of declarations of intent by the heads of government. They were careful not to introduce the least constraint of an institutional nature and deferred the institutional phase to a later phase which, almost always, failed to arrive."[4] The option of amending the treaties was thus closed, until the Single European Act in 1986.

Then pragmatism carried the day, as is witnessed by the revival and the expansion of European construction at the Hague summit in 1969. Failing to arrive at an agreement on implementing a political union, the heads of state and government entrusted to their foreign ministers the task of "studying the best way to make progress in the field of political unification from the point of view of its enlargement." The political affairs directors of the Ministries for Foreign Affairs, chaired by Etienne Davignon, produced a report in which they proposed to develop the cooperation between the Member States. For that, it is necessary " 'to take advantage' of the existence of the Community structure, to sit in its shadow but without merging with it, and to wait until the irresistible dynamics of the development of the Community obliges the States, large and small, to draw the natural conclusions."[5] The diplomats hardly had to show any imagination at all. They were satisfied to re-use the Fouchet plan, but by not giving it a legal status, they avoided writing the intergovernmental cooperation into a treaty, as several States still refused to do. At the same time, despite French reservations, the heads of state and government accepted what de Gaulle had refused. They gave the European Parliament control over the Community budget, and charged the Foreign Ministers with studying the possibility of having it elected by universal suffrage.

Diplomacy was the very heart of the problem. Jean Monnet, the head of the committee for the United States of Europe, was omnipresent. He enthusiastically welcomed President Pompidou's and Chancellor Willy Brandt's revival of Europe, which was given a new dimension by the accession of Great Britain, Denmark and Ireland. Even before that took effect, on January 1, 1973, the (now nine) member states decided at the Summit of Paris, October 19 and 20, 1972, "to transform all the relations of the Member States into a European Union, before the end of the current decade and in conformity with the already subscribed Treaties." It was to include an economic and monetary union, and new policies regarding regional, social, energy, industrial and technological matters.

After several months, wrote Monnet, "it appeared that nothing had advanced. The decision-making mechanism was blocked at the level of the ministers who, joined together as a council, were defending their national administrations. It was beginning to look as though the power to decide European things was exclusively a national prerogative."[6] To free Europe, Monnet proposed that the heads of state and government should, themselves, constitute a "provisional European government," (a name which very quickly would be changed to the "European Council"). This body, which had no legal basis, was formally instituted at the conclusion of "the summit" of the Nine on December 10, 1974, when the new French President, Valéry Giscard d'Estaing, stated, "The summit is dead, long live the European Council."[7] This was an interesting, to say the least, attempt to circumvent "national prerogative" by "an act of faith in intergovernmental cooperation,"[8] to use Professor de Ruyt's felicitous formula.

In spite of Monnet's efforts, the partisans of federal Europe held back. Charged with preparing a plan for a European Union, Belgian Prime Minister Léo Tindemans echoed the report that he had presented to the Council in November 1976: "Intergovernmental cooperation will not solve Europe's problems. These practices emphasize the differences in power and interests between our States and do not serve our mutual needs."[9] But at the same time he was strengthening intergovernmental cooperation, d'Estaing had raised the French veto on the increased powers of the European Parliament and on its election by universal vote, which had been proposed in a separate legislative act signed in Brussels in September 1976. A little more State, a little more Europe. In contrast to the Fouchet plan or the Hallstein proposals, these developments became acceptable because their concomitance left the balance of powers unchanged. The Commission understood this very well, having, since 1978, asserted an increase in its powers of control in exchange for allowing the extension of votes by qualified majority within the Council.

Tindemans' judgment was partly contradicted by the facts. Since the revival of the Hague, European construction had progressed more through intergovernmental cooperation than institutionally. Sometimes progress was made outside of the European Council, as was the case with internal security. The ministers took the initiative to act in concert against drugs, terrorism and clandestine immigration. More often, business was conducted within the Council, as with the monetary question. When the heads of state sat down in 1978 to create the European Monetary System, a simple agreement was enough and no one felt it was necessary to clarify the details in a treaty. But with a Community based on law, to expand European cooperation without any legal basis would be questionable. It was inevitable that plans for institutional reform would surface again.

In November 1981, the Foreign Ministers of the Italy and the Federal Republic of Germany jointly presented a draft "European Act" intended principally to integrate the various forms of cooperation, both in terms of policies and police efforts, and the intended new policies on culture, human rights, technology, etc. in the common Community framework. Aware of the difficulties that would attend any effort to amend the treaties (Denmark had already signaled its opposition to the entire exercise), Messrs. Genscher and Colombo proposed an Act. That is more constraining than a simple declaration, but it does not require ratification. Still, it took more than a year and a half of discussions for the Council to arrive at a text that was acceptable to all. June 19, 1983, the Council of Stuttgart adopted a "solemn declaration on the European Union." It formulated the principle, which gradually became essential, of "the unicity of the conclave where the ministers act as Council and discuss questions of cooperation."[10] The statement was heavy on the side of objectives (which would be found again in the Single European Act and the Maastricht Treaty), but light as to the means of implementation. The time had come to amend the treaties. But the Council could only do that after the meeting at Fontainebleau in June 1984, once the question of Margaret Thatcher's "bill"[11] was resolved.

The European Parliament did not have any such handicap. Recently elected by universal vote, it was convinced of the need for institutional reform, due to the conflict with the Council over the first budget. The Italian deputy, Altiero Spinelli, took the initiative. He had formerly participated in the deliberations of the ECSC Assembly, and with a group of nine members of the Parliament who were in the habit of meeting in Strasbourg at the "Crocodile" restaurant. In July 1981, the Parliament approved the creation of an institutional commission, charged with "drafting amendments to the existing Treaties." On the basis of Spinelli's report, the Parliament adopted a resolution in September 1983 and named four lawyers to transform it into a treaty. This was adopted on February 14, 1984, with 237 votes for, 31 against, and 43 abstentions. Taking the *acquis communautaire* as its basis, the Parliament's outline distinguished the Union's exclusive jurisdiction, exercised by the Community, from the "competing" and "subsidiary" national jurisdictions. The latter were defined by the fact that "the Union only carries out tasks that can be fulfilled more effectively jointly than by the Member States working separately" (Art. 12). This represented political cooperation, at least for the time being, in the domain of the "intergovernmental" cooperation.

As in 1952, Parliament's true innovation related to the decision-making procedures. The plan removed from the Council, and thus from the governments (even the national parliaments), any ability to block an initiative. Unanimity was no longer required for any type of decision. However, for a ten-year period, Member States would retain the ability to defer a vote by invoking "national vital interests," which were to be justified and published. The legislative power was divided equally between the Parliament and the Council. Lastly, the Commission, dispossessed of its "monopoly of initiative," was automatically converted to a "power of execution."

On the whole, the Spinelli report upset the balance of the *acquis communautaire*. The Council and the Commission gave up the driver's seat and the Parliament took it over. Like the Assembly of 1952, the European Parliament thought it could circumvent the national governments by establishing a direct dialogue with the national parliaments. But, since the same causes generally produce the same effects, the Spinelli plan endured the same fate as that of Spaak. Aside from the Italian Parliament, no one wanted to accept this invitation, and some purely and simply ignored it. The governments, which the European Parliament had wanted to circumvent, ignored it, too. This ostracism left the European deputies powerless. But their audacity had had at least one benefit, of "lifting the heavy taboo that, since the constitutional crisis of 1966, inhibited any initiative aiming to adapt the Treaty of Rome to the Community's development."[12]

Is the history of European construction only a long, repetitive story? Just as they did following the ECSC Assembly, the Heads of State and Government responded to the European Parliament by creating two ad hoc committees, composed of "representatives of the Heads of State and Government of the Member States," in the style of the Spaak committee. The first, known as the "Adonnino Committee," had a mandate to prepare "a Citizen's Europe," i.e. an accompaniment to the freedom of movement of the people. The second, chaired by the former Irish minister James Dooge, was tasked with deliberating institutional affairs. Maurice Faure, who had already participated in the Spaak committee, was the rapporteur. Quite naturally, it concentrated on the topics that had been debated for thirty years.

The report proposed to create "a true political entity — that is, a European Union." It would have three overall objectives: to complete a unified internal market and create a common currency; to "promote common values of civilization" (in terms of social welfare, the environment and the legal structure), and finally, to seek "an external identity" by developing political cooperation (foreign policy and defense), in particular to include the institution of a permanent secretariat, "distinct from the Council and the Commission." In addition, the report indicated how the institutions were to be improved. This included establishing a rule of majority vote, with no exception; reinforcing the autonomy of the Commission and its powers of execution; extending Parliament's powers by creating a procedure of "joint decision" and reinforcing its control over Union policies; and finally, consolidating the Court of Justice's areas of control. In conclusion, the report proposed "the convocation of a conference of the representatives of the governments that would negotiate a plan for a European Union based on the *acquis communautaire*, the present document, and the solemn declaration of Stuttgart, and taking as its starting point the spirit and the substance of the draft treaty approved by the European Parliament."[13]

There was nothing there that had not been endlessly repeated for three decades. But for at least three countries, Great Britain, Denmark and Greece, it too was much. Their representatives had been saying so, throughout the entire process, and the many "footnotes" through which each one had the opportunity to comment on the text of the report left no doubt about the attitude their governments would adopt. By preferring a "coherent" report rather than one that could be unanimously approved, the Dooge Committee did not make the Council's task any easier. Jacques Delors' tour of European capitals, before he took over the leadership of the Commission on January 1, 1985, had quickly convinced him that the Council was heading for failure. Whereas Faure regarded his text as "ambitious,"[14] the new President of the Commission saw it only as a minimally improved version of the Fouchet plan. In particular, the insistence on the political secretariat, an idea that France brought up regularly, threatened the Commission and the equilibrium of the institutional triangle that the report claimed to preserve.

Delors therefore set aside the overall plan and retained only one of the Dooge Committee's objectives: to complete the internal market by January 1, 1992. However, during the intergovernmental conference, at the meeting in Luxembourg, he did reintroduce a certain number of proposals from the Dooge Committee. The existence of the European Council was given juridical validity. It became the executive of the Community. The extension of the majority vote, for measures which "have the purpose of establishing and conducting the internal market" (Art. 100 A), was unanimously accepted, whereas the same proposal had been refused when it was applied globally. Conversely, in those domains where vote by qualified majority became the rule, the Parliament's backing would now be required, in the form of a procedure of "cooperation." Moreover, a procedure known as an "assent" was established for agreements of accession and association.

The Commission's powers were reinforced. Thus, each institution's powers were enhanced in respect of the balance of their mutual relations. In addition, two new chapters were introduced, on the environment and research, and the principle of economic and social cohesion in favor of the poor areas was inscribed in the treaty. These innovations ensured that Great Britain would receive aid to offset its financial contribution; this was a result of the settlement of the budgetary dispute. Lastly, the President of the Commission insisted that the treaty on political cooperation, which institutionalized the empirical practice resulting from the Davignon Report, should not be a separate document, instead inserted in a "special section," in order to "hold onto the idea of European Union for the future." Thus was born the Single European Act, signed in Luxembourg on February 17, 1986.[15]

The negotiators were the first to be astonished by their agreement. "Everything was set for a complete failure, which did not occur," commented Mitterrand on his return to Paris. But he considered "the compromise" that the new Treaty represented in "very much this side of what I would call the vital minimum for Europe."[16] The institutional and political topics, which were more important to the French, had advanced very little. Either the Single European Act ratified what already existed — on the one hand, the central role of the European Council, the only authority where Community and foreign policy matters could be discussed, and on the other hand, political cooperation —

or else it went back to the letter of the Treaty of Rome, the vote by qualified majority. France had had to accept an extension of the (still limited) powers of the Parliament and, especially, had not been able to form a political secretariat that would have served as the Parliament's spokesman for foreign policy. In spite of its name, the Single European Act, the Treaty maintained two separate entities, "the European Communities" and "political cooperation." These prefigured the "pillars" of the future Maastricht Treaty, which defined as their objective "to contribute jointly to make concrete progress toward the European Union" (Article One). But the European Union as such did not exist.

Progress was slow. Everyone wanted "political union," but no one could agree on a definition. Thirty years of debates had not reconciled the viewpoints. There could be no political union (and thus no European Union), for the Benelux countries as well as for the Commission, until the Community procedures would apply in the same way to the different policy areas, including foreign policy. France, on the contrary, reduced the political union to cooperation in foreign policy, and intended to keep everything else strictly within the intergovernmental context, with distinct and non-Community procedures that the Treaty attempted to specify in fine detail. Moreover, the first group considered that a political union would imply real legislative power for the European Parliament, whereas the French viewed such with caution and strongly preferred majority votes within the councils of ministers, whom it felt should remain the masters of the legislature. Even the status of the European Council remained ambiguous. Admittedly, it constituted a single authority where Community questions should be discussed, such as those concerning cooperation between Member States. But, composed of the heads of state and government, it embodied the "national prerogative" that Monnet denounced.

Could the progress that was missed during the negotiation of the Single European Act be made up later on? In spite of an exceptional political situation, the fall of the Berlin Wall, the answer was unfortunately negative. The Maastricht Treaty did not bring any real political progress; in fact, it may even have been a step backward. Admittedly, that which used to be only a goal had, through the magic of words, become reality. The European Union is therein decreed, "instituted" by Article A of the new treaty. But the proclaimed oneness of the institutional structure (Article C) remained factitious. The opposition between Community and intergovernmental was only reinforced by the

structure of the "pillars." Once again, only economic and monetary integration progressed. Even the appearance of a third pillar was not
new. It was simply the legal documentation of an intergovernmental
cooperation that began in the very early 1970s and whose principal act,
the Schengen Accord, was not integrated into the Treaty at that time.
As for the institutional questions themselves, apart from the powers of
joint decision granted to the European Parliament, the heads of state
avoided failure only by making the ploy of convoking a new intergovernmental conference in 1996. Nothing in the Treaty expressed the
"more Europe" that the German unification in spring 1990 made so urgent. The public was right to remember Maastricht only in terms of
what was going to affect their daily life — that is, the single currency
and its criteria of convergence.

Far from being a new departure, Maastricht marked the end of a
cycle. Since the ECSC Treaty, European construction was built on the
basis of an institutional triangle, whose point of equilibrium has been
carefully preserved. Neither crises nor plans for reform have succeeded
in shaking the initial status quo. Any extension of the powers of either
institution has always been compensated by an extension of both. The
States, the Commission and Parliament each consolidated its position.
This allowed limited, but real, progress. But these powers are in conflict — the "intergovernmental" can only be made stronger at the ex-
pense of the "Community" and the Parliament can gain legislative
power only by reducing that of the councils and the Commission. The
moment would inevitably come when the balance would be broken.
Maastricht made it clear that the breaking point was near. The debate's focus on the Treaty on the Economic and Monetary Union allowed the Council to believe it would have another chance; still, they
had to seize that as an opportunity to re-think the institutional bases
on which Europe was being built. The status quo condemned Europe
to failure. The Council of Amsterdam, concluding the intergovernmental conference, could only report that fact.

The reasons for this failure lie in the incompatible concepts of political Europe that have been clashing for a half-century. Great Britain
and Denmark challenge the very idea of a political Europe; they do not
want to confer legislative powers on the Parliament, or give Europe an
international role. For other countries without a state tradition, like
the Benelux countries, but also, to some extent Germany (which until
the fall of the Berlin Wall had been deprived of its international sover-

eignty), the political union is identified with the construction of a European political entity founded on the European Parliament. However, the European Parliament had been isolated since the 1950s, its legislative power passed to the Councils of the Ministers of the Member States. In spite of being elected by universal vote, it never succeeded in acquiring sufficient legitimacy to found the authority of an executive power.

For her part, France always stood up for a political Europe, but not one that was based on the Parliament. According to Hubert Védrine, France wanted "a powerful European Council, but it had misgivings as to any increase in the powers of the European Parliament which would make it equal to the Council of Ministers"[17] (i.e. the national governments). He went on to borrow the words of Giulio Andreotti, the Italian Prime Minister, who qualified the creation of the European Parliament as "demagogic." For a Frenchman, for whom nothing is political unless it is for and by the State, the political union merges with the international expression of Europe, whose power it expresses. Consequently, it is identified with foreign policy, the exclusive domain of diplomats and not a political forum for public debates. Hence the French leaders' recurrent proposal of a President of Europe who would be elected by universal vote, transposing the institutions of the 5th Republic to the European stage. But France is still completely isolated in that view; its partners' democratic visions anchor them to the Parliament.

So institutional reform and foreign policy were inextricably linked. For a long time, the French had refused purely and simply to grant the least legislative power to the European Parliament; this had, as a corollary, the view that foreign policy is an inter-State matter. General de Gaulle, at the Paris Summit, set the terms when he baptized the foreign policy he wished for Europe as an instance of "European political cooperation." His goal was to bring the various national positions into alignment, to adopt a joint position if possible, even to undertake joint action. True to de Gaulle's nature, this cooperation would also be a means of uncoupling the European countries from the United States. To oppose American hegemony, to stretch the bonds that tie the European countries to NATO (which it wanted to have reformed), France required that Europe speak with one voice (without, however, giving up the autonomy that France's seat on the United Nation's Permanent Security Council represents). So many reasons which, conversely, made (and still makes) France's partners wary vis-à-vis French proposals, and more attached to the security provided by their membership in NATO and the American military presence in Europe.

Védrine (who was diplomatic advisor to President Mitterrand and then General Secretary of the Presidency of the Republic, before becoming Foreign Minister), summarized the French problem perfectly. The need for cooperation results from the notion that "there are fewer and fewer international problems that a State can solve on its own, even if each is still in a position to determine its own policy vis-à-vis its bilateral relations with certain other States, or to take certain international actions." This situation forces us to negotiate constantly with our "main partners [whom we must] simultaneously support on one subject while opposing them on another, while seeking their support on a third."[18] It obliges France to play many chess games and to choose the most suitable forums to exert its influence and to prolong this dream of still being a world power: whether political autonomy, bilateral action, the Security Council or the European Council. For a country like France, writes a foreign observer, "European political cooperation" seems like "the continuation of a national policy."[19] Or, maybe it is a means of keeping alive for a little longer prolonging the life of a national policy that no longer has the means to fulfill its ambitions. That requires political cooperation to remain in the hands of the States. General de Gaulle was the first to understand that. And his successors followed suit.

Officially created in October 1970 in Luxembourg by a document with no legal standing, "European political cooperation" developed since then without much change. Ensconcing it in the institutional framework of the Single European Act, and then the Maastricht Treaty, did nothing to enhance the procedures. They continue to rely only on cooperation between States, outside of the Commission and the control of the Court of Justice. No field of common interest, which would justify a Community approach, has been defined. The Foreign Ministers, to which the heads of state and government (hypocritically) entrusted this task, could not come up with any. The task groups keep multiplying — there are some twenty of them — which shows that subjects of common interest are not lacking. They have to do with diplomacy in relation to issues worldwide, and the influence that a State such as France wishes to exercise. The Middle East, South Africa, preparation for the Helsinki security conference, non-proliferation, Rwanda — logically, managing Europe's security would have to constitute a Community field. But the divergences of position with regard to NATO as well as the WEU were always a sticking point. For the same reasons, it took until 1990 for a task group to consider relations with the United States.

The Yugoslav crisis made it painfully clear that Europe was unable to arrive at a common goal, even when the fate of the continent was at stake. Right in the midst of negotiations of the Maastricht Treaty (the pillar of "foreign policy and mutual security"), Germany decided to go it alone and granted recognition to the republics born from the break-up of Yugoslavia. Right though to the end, Europe remained incapable of overcoming its dissentions and putting an end to conflict. At no time did it assume the least responsibility on an autonomous footing. The humanitarian aid was provided under UN control; the Dayton peace accords were negotiated under the aegis of the United States; the peacekeeping force, which involved all the European countries, was placed under NATO command with no particular responsibility being given collectively to the WEU. "The history of the Union's diplomatic engagement in the Yugoslav crisis," wrote Nicole Gnesotto,[20] "is that of a progressive dispossession and a constant disillusion." The composition of the "Contact Group," made up of Germany, the United States, France, Great Britain and Russia, even showed "an evolution toward an ad hoc diplomatic management where the Nation States take the lead over any other collective authority. It is a return to the concerted action of the most powerful nations in the management of Europe." Europe thus sealed its own defeat at the crucial moment when the United States had shown that they had no intention to intervene systematically in European crises, in the absence of the Soviet danger.

The former President of the Commission, assessing the performance of the political dimension of the Maastricht Treaty, told the very anti-European *Sunday Times* in 1995 that he had "never believed in the concept of a common foreign policy; it's too ambitious and unmanageable due to the diversity of the Member States."[21] Throughout the negotiation of the Treaty, Delors had let his doubts be known, insisting that "precautions must be taken to avoid going ahead by forced march, which could lead only to an internal crisis or impotence,"[22] since there had been no progress toward defining the interests that should be defended and promoted at the European level. Without such a definition, the institutions and the procedures remained useless. However, that was the solution that France continued to prefer. It was still calling for a common European foreign policy, as it had done for thirty years in one form or another, and campaigning for the abandonment of unanimity in the decisions (although, in fact, France was the first to refuse to give up a national foreign policy).

Védrine explained this attitude that had such dramatic consequences for the future. "France," he wrote, "is a member of all the highest circles and leadership cliques that rule the world, whatever they may be called. If it is opposed to having the G7 set itself up as the world's directorate, it is because the Seven are dominated by the United States. And France has a *national interest* in not having its relative weight diluted."[23] It is a strange statement that seems to come from another age, and yet a perfect reflection of the "impossibility of renouncing the sovereignty of the Nation State, even though it had been an empty shell for years,"[24] denounced by our partners. For the reality is that the States no longer mint their own currency, their legislation is subordinate to European law, military interventions is carried out under the command of NATO or the UN, and border control is no longer a national matter. How, then, can we still speak of sovereignty? By participating in the "directorate of the world" and thinking that that means the directing of Europe, one may preserve the appearance of sovereignty. But Germany, now that it has become more powerful, has the same pretension. Europe was organized this way after the Second World War, to get beyond national interests. French diplomacy's nostalgia for its power and its glory is taking us straight backward.

Since the beginning, Europe has only progressed economically. Foreign policy is no exception. With the Treaty of Rome, international trade policy became a Community competence. While the Commission acts on the basis of mandate of the Council, it only negotiates, on behalf of the whole of the Community countries, within GATT (General Agreement on Tariffs and Trade) and now the WTO (World Trade Organization). By participating in development efforts (the Lome Convention) it also participates in the management of a certain number of Third World countries. But, up until now, in spite of the prospect of the creation of a single currency, the States did not allow their national representation in the international bodies to be taken over by the European Community, nor have they given up having the four "strongest" of them participate within the G7 (Germany, France, Great Britain, Italy).

This causes many inconsistencies, which were denounced during the preparations for the IGC. Creating "a unity of policy planning and quick response mechanisms" associated with the Council (as was decided in Amsterdam) will not be enough to overcome them.

The economy was also used as a channel for European cooperation relating to internal security, the third pillar of the Maastricht Treaty on the European Union. This was not based on any plan for organizing a unified European legal space, aiming to ensure the same protection of people and goods throughout the Union. It resulted directly in response to the problems inherent in the freedom of movement proclaimed by the Treaty of Rome. Soon after, in fact in 1971, a plan for cooperation was set up. First there was the "Pompidou Group," then in 1975 "the Group of Trevi," (named for the Roman fountain near the building where the ministers met). These meetings aimed to define a common approach to the possibility that freedom of movement could generate "a security deficit." The ministries for the Interior thus gradually developed their own European policy, outside of both the normal diplomatic channels and the Community institutions. Handling frontier questions between a small number of States often amounted to a "generalized bilateralism," which defined a European security space.

This space first resulted in the Schengen agreements signed in June 1985 between the Benelux countries, France and Germany, even before negotiations opened on the Single European Act. These agreements compensated for the weakening of border controls between European countries by reinforcing controls between those and third countries. This prevented a person who would be denied entry to one Member State from taking advantage of differences in legislation to enter via another State. A common approach was deemed necessary, in particular with regard to political asylum.

The terrorist threat and increasing international criminality, especially ties to drug traffic, were used as justifications. Actually, the real reason for European police and legal cooperation was very different. "It was founded on a less legitimate and more political perceived threat, that the borders were permeable to a massive immigration coming from the South, and later also from the East."[25] The security dimension, which dominated the approach of the police authorities, given the lack of any proclamation of basic rights at the European level, led to what Didier Bigo calls "a transfer of illegitimacy between drug traffic, terrorism, criminality, clandestine immigration, immigration and political refugees; in other words, as if the criminal character of the first gradually faded into the others."[26]

During the Maastricht negotiations, many Member States, including France, wished to keep the policies regulating the police force and justice with an intergovernmental framework. The reasons are complex. Negotiations for the Schengen Treaty had been difficult, and had ended only in June 1990, without all the Member States signing. The German unification posed new problems; it changed the relationship with the Central European countries, which required amendments and resulted in delaying is effective date to December 1993. Moreover, while the Schengen agreements got by without defining the terms of reference used, especially the distinction between "internal," "external" and "foreign" borders, the Treaty could not do the same. And these questions are not only theoretical. The answer is far from obvious when it comes to maritime borders (for example, the North Sea), and air space even more, and would require practical installations in the ports and the airports, which the States were not ready to pay for.

However, taking into account the overlap between internal security and justice policies with the single market, it very quickly became imperative that they be managed at the Community level. To this end, the Schengen agreements were integrated into the Treaty of Amsterdam in the form of a protocol. However, specific provisions were retained for Ireland and Great Britain, who wished to retain control of their maritime borders, and for Denmark, for constitutional reasons. A five-year deadline was set, at the end of which the agreements would become fully effective. Lastly, if at that time these provisions were considered to be sufficient, the States could decide whether some of these matters should be decided by qualified majority rather than unanimously. And, the Treaty of Amsterdam would have to be ratified by the fifteen Member States beforehand. That has not happened.

Can the European political union move ahead, based only on the economy? The Maastricht Treaty left the question hanging, and the failure of the Council of Amsterdam leaves it on the table. Admittedly, some progress has been made. But it remains narrowly circumscribed at the State level. Nothing is being done without the States or apart from the States. They remain the point obligatory gateway through which every aspect of European construction must pass. Over the course of time, they have become the principal obstacle to the creation of a political space. The economic and monetary union cannot drive Europe's political union. More precisely, if it is, then this political union will be diametrically opposed to the model of a society that our political leaders are touting, a model based on the assertion of the basic rights of man and citizen. Europe will be reduced to a market society where inequality and power are the only forms of government. To quote Paul Valéry, it would be the defeat of the "European spirit."

Notes

1. Charles de Gaulle, *Mémoires d'espoir, Le Renouveau*, Plon, Paris, 1970, p. 206.
2. Cited in George-Henri Soutou, *L'Alliance incertaine, op. cit.*, p. 160.
3. Jean de Ruyt, *op. cit.*, 1987, p. 11.
4. *Ibid.*, p. 15.
5. *Ibid.*, p. 220.
6. Jean Monnet, *Mémoires*, *op. cit.*, p. 590-591.
7. *Ibid.*, p. 604.
8. Jean de Ruyt, *op. cit.*, p. 17.
9. *Ibid.* p. 19.
10. *Ibid.*, p. 35.
11. This refers to the reduction of the British contribution, justified by the fact that Great Britain benefited little from the common agricultural policy because of the weakness of its agriculture and the insignificance of agricultural imports coming from the Commonwealth.
12. Jean de Ruyt, *op. cit.*, p. 45.
13. Text published in Jean de Ruyt, *op. cit.*
14. Pierre Favier, Michel Martin-Roland, *op. cit.*, volume 2, p. 211.
15. Only nine Member States signed it that day; Denmark, Italy and Greece signed on February 28 in the Hague, just after the Danish referendum.
16. Cited by Pierre Favier and Michel Martin-Roland, *op. cit.*, volume 2, p. 218.
17. Hubert Védrine, *op. cit.*, p. 468.
18. *Ibid.*, p. 754.
19. Simon Nuttall, European political co-operation, Oxford, Oxford University Press, 1992, p. 309.
20. Nicole Gnesotto, "La Défense europeénne au carrefour de la Bosnie et de la CIG," *Politique étrangère*, Paris, Spring 1996, p. 116.
21. Interview in the *Sunday Times*, October 1, 1995.
22. Jacques Delors, "Speech before the Institute for International Strategic Studies, London, March 7, 1991," in *Le Concert européen, op. cit.*, p. 304.
23. Hubert Védrine, *op. cit.*, p. 570.
24. *Réflexion sur la politique européenne*, CSU-CDU, *doc. cit.*
25. Didier Bigo, *L'Europe des polices et la Sécurité intérieure*, Brussels, Ed. Complex, p. 25.
26. *Ibid.*, p. 27.

Wanting Europe

Can we construct Europe without wanting Europe, without wishing for a society reconciling the unity of its humanistic and democratic values with the diversity of its cultures? Can we give birth to this Europe if the desire for Europe does not supplant the defense of national interests? The fall of the Berlin Wall raised hopes and created a sense of urgency. The failure of Amsterdam brought us back to Earth. The Nation States won that round and are going forward in a stronger position, although the victory may be Pyrrhic. They hardly had to lift a finger to defend their sovereignty. Europe did not challenge them on that. On the verge of adopting the single currency, Europe arrived at this last rendezvous with the 20th century in a state of resignation. Decisions that will define the future were deferred to an improbable, new intergovernmental conference, after the year 2000.

The failure of the Council of Amsterdam leaves the public disabled. This revised version of the Treaties was supposed to put them at the heart of European construction, but a miracle of diplomacy managed to keep them at bay once again. Amsterdam was supposed to be a new point of departure, but the momentum created by the preparations was crushed by the egoism of the States. Europe ensures the public neither the peace nor the prosperity promised by all those who want to see Europe serve as an example to the entire world. Mass unemployment and the insecurity at the borders undermine their confidence. Besides, are they only citizens? As Europeans, they enjoy only the rights of the market. For civil, political and social liberty, in other words, for Liberty, please address yourself to the States. "Anyone who has the nationality of a Member State is a citizen of the Union." But can anyone want Europe without wanting a common identity of rights, a common freedom?

Wanting Europe. It was palpable throughout Central Europe in the wake of the fall of the Berlin Wall and the velvet revolutions that swept away the communist regimes. For the millions of men and women who became free, it was no more, or less, than a "return to Europe." The iron curtain had forced them to turn toward the East. But they never belonged to it. Their history, their culture and their memory are the same as ours, as our future is theirs: quite simply, Europe. The Europe of the Enlightenment, freedom and democracy is ineluctably linked to the Europe of capitalism, colonialism and cruelty. In this struggle toward freedom and progress, Central Europe always did its share, perhaps even more than its share. The East was always over there (it is still), where the Russian territory begins, and Turkish and Asian territories. Once again, history and geography coincide. For Prague, Warsaw and Budapest, a return to Europe means a "return to normal."

But what they wanted was not the same as the governments of the European Convention countries, who took the position of the eternal fiancée: that our countries are not ready. Before saying yes and preparing the contract, they said that Europe, "such as it is today," needed to consolidate its institutions and to strengthen its own union. Amsterdam was supposed to do that. Europe, "such as it seems," is still waiting. After such a long and painful separation, the Poles, Czechs, Hungarians, Lithuanians and others expected a warm and enthusiastic reception. François Mitterrand's initial reaction was to ask them to be patient, for twenty or thirty years. It's not just that they weren't expected and we weren't ready for them. At the very least, their desire is not shared.

The re-emerging want recognition and security, while their Western cousins respond with economics. They expect Europe to give them a guarantee of "no going back" to the past from which they have just managed to extricate themselves; the Community inspects their baggage and asks where every single item came from — where was this made? For how much? They want to be protected from the big neighbors between whom geography has placed them, and who, over the centuries, have too often used them as a buffer zone. The Community tells them to open their own markets and to trade their low wages for investments. What can they do but turn to the United States for the security that Europe is not providing? Accession to NATO will be an act of democratic recognition and security. Because of Moscow's hostility to NATO expansion, few will be chosen. But, for the beneficiary countries, accession to NATO will precede by several years accession to the European Union. The others, who remain on the threshold of NATO, may well stay on Europe's doorstep, too. In both cases, Europe loses.

By using the economy as grounds for refusing to admit the Eastern democracies, Europe missed the opportunity to reform itself and become the Union that it "appears to be." It was unable to affirm itself as a community based on the rights of man and the citizen, whereas two centuries after the French Revolution all of Europe claims to be such. It was not able to seize the historic moment, to match the physical abolition of its division with the reunification of its values. Europe owed it to itself to say yes, from the first day. Yes to political accession, to mutual security, to common citizenship. Yes, too, with regard to the diversity which makes it clear that "Europe will be always a checkerboard of languages and cultures in daily life, politics and the economy."[1] Yes to this pluralistic Europe, the "complex" which, through the centuries, never wanted "to conform to an imposed hegemonic model."[2] Yes to freedom.

The unification of its two halves offered Europe a chance to make a new start. Obviously, the historical scope of the event was not enough to make them take the chance. No one was requiring them to give up the Nation State, especially when several of them had just gained their full sovereignty. But its return was accompanied by a desire for a common destiny that the Western half did not want to share. Instead of exclusively defining Europe by the accession of the States duly noted by treaties, we could have visualized a community of individuals founded on the assertion of the rights and liberties of the individual — and not of the peoples, which always ends up relating to States. Then a dream could have become a future. Instead, the threat of regression hangs over a Europe that missed its chance.

The suddenness of the opening of the Berlin Wall and the collapse of Communism cannot excuse the scant eagerness of the States to make the leap to the European Union. German unification took one year, during which the future of Europe hung in the balance. President Mitterrand's proposal of a "European confederation" shows that he was acutely aware of the need "for finding a substitute structure to come after the empires, to come after the Europe of tribes and the Europe of war."[3] And he was not the only one. But Mitterrand saw it only in terms of the French diplomatic tradition, or maybe in that part of the Gallic heritage that he had embraced, a confederation of Nation States. Getting Germany to recognize that its borders could not be changed helped to close the wounds of the past. To integrate the re-emerging democracies into a great Community entity, not only to recognize the dismemberment of the ex-GDR, would have given Europe a future.

Europe preferred to persevere in a losing battle. Six years after Maastricht, the European Council of Amsterdam once again put off the realization of the political union, i.e. the effective European Union, to a later date. Since according to today's logic it will take fifteen to twenty years for the other States to join, the Heads of State figured that there was no urgency to transform the economic union into a political entity. Neither was there any need to conceive of an independent European security policy, to conform to the ambitions boasted in the Maastricht Treaty. And finally, there was no reason not to open the negotiations for enlargement now, since it had been decided that the Community institutions would not be reformed until the Council had as many members as the Commission. With a Commission of twenty, the institutional reform can quietly wait until the next millennium!

Europe will not get itself out of this situation until somebody puts an end to the current state of affairs. We have to re-think the whole process, in order to base it on the enlargement of the Community and not rest on the legal basis of political Europe. The failure of Amsterdam is the failure of an approach that posited the economy as the means to achieve political union, "an obligatory point of passage," as Mitterrand said during the negotiation of the Economic and Monetary Union. If nothing changes, this failure presages the failure of the expansion, which would make the full integration of the candidate States wait during a long transition period. A delay that would be very much in their interest, the experts say, since it would give them a chance to adapt their economy to the constraints of the single market. A delay that equally defers the moment of the effective enlargement of the

Community, and therefore the reform of its institutions.

Longing for Europe in the East. Longing for union in the West. You can't have one without the other. While the former may not have been (completely) dulled, the latter still needs to be manifested in some other way than through verbal declarations that are immediately contradicted in action. Wanting Europe, wanting a European identity — by failing in Amsterdam, the States also failed to make progress toward European construction. It is up to the public to take over. Let the political leaders show them the way by behaving like Europeans. How should they do that?

First, it should be affirmed that European citizenship rests on a set of fundamental rights that would constitute a *European Bill of Rights*. To cement the legitimacy that Europe needs, this Charter should, as the German social democrats propose, "establish a linkage between the public's basic rights and the European institutions' legislative functions, in order to protect the public against any violation of these rights by the "European" bureaucratic machinery.[4] It should be drafted by the European Parliament, which represents the citizens of the Union. However, to attain the force of law, it will have to be directly approved by the public, in the form of a European referendum that would be voted on throughout Europe on the same day(s). Respect for European cultural diversity implies that it not be considered adopted unless it obtains a majority in each State, so that rights and obligations are not imposed on the citizens of any nation. This Charter of fundamental rights could not be reduced, but additions could be made, which should be approved by the same process of a European referendum.

Simplifying the Treaties, to make them readable and to delete obsolete articles, poses a different problem. Since we are bypassing this opportunity to transform them into a constitutional form, this task belongs primarily to the Commission. Guardian of the Treaties, it is up to the Commission to do the revision that everyone considers essential. As the Maastricht Treaty envisaged, during this revision the Community's legal standards should be arranged hierarchically. We should also seize the opportunity to clarify and distinguish how these standards can be revised. Probably, several acts should be written.

The most important would take the form of a *Founding Act*[5] unifying and defining the European institutions, specifying their mutual relations, which matters the States had transferred to the competence of the Union, the nature of European legal transactions, etc.. This Act would be distinct from the European Charter of Rights. It would have the status of a treaty and could be amended only by a new treaty between the Member States, which would probably have to be a unanimous decision. Taking into account the complexity of the ratification process, this Act should contain only the essential provisions, those truly founding the European Union and its operation. It is particularly essential that the matters which can be addressed at the Union level be stated there in order to guarantee the public that the Commission would not take it upon itself to extend its areas of competence. Lastly, this text should spell out a process for revising any provisions resulting from the Treaties (if not specified elsewhere). The definition of specific policies — agriculture, competition, monetary union, environment, research, etc. — would be remanded to other, legislative texts.

The Founding Act should pose a simple principle: that *Community areas of competence have European legitimacy — that intergovernmental projects are national responsibilities.* In the domains ascribed to the Community, the European Commission and Parliament alone would be qualified. The Commission should take its lead from the Parliament and be accountable to it. The Member States would no longer participate in the Community decision-making process, but they should still be associated with it via (advisory) committees in order to ensure that the national administrations properly implement the Community laws.

In the intergovernmental domains, the decisions would remain in the hands of the European Council and the councils of (national) ministers as they are today. However, the national parliaments should control the decisions taken at the European level by governments that are uniquely answerable to them. The European Parliament and the Commission would get out of the intergovernmental decision-making process just as the Heads of State and the national governments would remove themselves from the Community process. However, just as the administrations would still be associated with the implementation of Community decisions, the Commission should have the mandate to ensure effective integration of intergovernmental decisions and Community policies.

A second document, a kind of *organic law* of the Union, would pull together the Articles relative to Community policies—of which the European competence will have been established by the Founding Act.

The Commission would see to the revision and reorganization of this section of the treaties, under the supervision of the European Court of Justice and the European Parliament. The Parliament would have to approve the new text by a solemn vote, under the conditions defined by the Founding Act. The Community policies would thus lose their treaty status and would enter the normal legislative framework. However, these provisions would still constitute a higher standard than the acts that are passed to implement them. Only the European Parliament could revise them.

Today as yesterday, any new foundation for the enterprise of European construction must solve the problem of procedures. The recent failures teach us that none of the three institutions alone, Council, Commission, or Parliament, can carry out a reform that would shift the balance of power. The *acquis communautaire* exists to combine their efforts, but it will not be enough to ensure the success of this new foundation. Restricted to its legislative function, the European Parliament did not acquire a sufficient legitimacy for its authority to be accepted out of hand. That is the challenge of carrying out a reform whose principal objective is to transfer sovereignty from Nation States to a European non-State (already achieved, in practice). The stakes are high enough without adding any further dispossession of the Nation States. At this stage, the powers of the European Parliament should be strictly limited to the nomination and control of the Commission and to the policies that right now are fully within their domain of action. There will be no more *spillover*, nor *subsidiarity*, to drag national areas of jurisdiction toward the Community, since the Parliament could expand its scope, and hence the Commission's, only by amendment of the Founding Act.

Then the European Community could consider a different approach to its enlargement. Any country wishing to become a candidate should take the initiative to endorse the European fundamental acts according to a procedure that would be outlined therein. Presumably, this would include a public referendum endorsing the Charter of fundamental rights, by which the citizens public would express its belief in the common values of Europe, and ratification of the Founding Act defining the institutions. This step would be the equivalent of accepting the rules and the laws of the Union. Until a State took those steps, it could not present its candidature for the European Union. On the other hand, endorsement of the fundamental texts would make it a full member of the European Union and its institutions. It would open the way for negotiating the time span necessary to transcribe and implement the ensemble of directives into national law, which could be accompanied by specific clauses to protect vulnerable sectors from a frontal competition with the European market. With this procedure in place, Europe would start the new century unified, while allowing the Central European economies the time they need to adapt.

Europe is at a crossroads in its history. The failure of Amsterdam made it painfully clear that "the status quo is impossible." Certainly the Member States can choose to persist in managing Europe by tangling it in the conflict of national interests. But they must realize that, by doing this, they will eventually cause it to implode. That is where their pusillanimity is leading. Only the market, which the liberals so love, would derive any benefit. The Nation States would not withstand it. Europe would not come into being, but the States would cease to exist. Nobody can imagine that such decomposition can occur without major political jolts and the explosion of inter-State conflicts, which would bring us back to the darkest hours of the century just ended. No one, of course, wants that. But Europe requires infinitely more: that we do everything possible to eliminate this risk. It expects the national political leaders to make a start, which is also a leap into the future.

The time has come to sort out these misunderstandings. The post-war period is over. Undoubtedly, the concern that Germany still causes, on her own territory as well as for her partners, will take a long time to ease. But the fear of Germany cannot be the basis of the European plan anymore, and keeping it under control can no longer be a pretext for keeping the States at the center of European areas of jurisdiction. Conversely, Europe cannot be left in the hands of the judges (of the European Court of Justice) and central bankers (of the future European Central Banking System). These are two requirements that actually make up a single exigency. If judges and bankers make the law in Europe, it is because the States made it so by not wishing to (visibly) give away their powers, in order to control their neighbors. It is because policy-making was banned in Europe so it could be monopolized by the States.

As in the first days of the post-war period, Germany and Europe again have dependent roles. How we look at one influences how we see the other, and vice versa. Forty years ago, Europe was built based on the relationship with Germany. Now it is time to found it on Europe — all together, on equal footing. Europe will come to be only if the governments have the will to make their actions conform with their ambitions; if they get beyond the Treaties between States and base the enterprise on the citizens if they make Europe a political space on its own. Then Europe could be what it appears to be. Is it too much to hope that this Europe we wish for can dissipate the mists of Amsterdam?

Notes

1. Ralf Dahrendorf, *Réflexions sur la revolution en Europe*, Paris, Seuil, 1991, p. 138
2. *Ibid.*, p. 138.
3. Pierre Favier and Michel Martin-Roland, *op. cit.*, p. 225.
4. Heidemarie Wieczorec-Zeul and Jürgen Meyer, *op. cit.*, p. 61.
5. The proposal to distinguish a Charter of Rights from an Act specifying the organizational principles differs from other proposals which either grant precedence to the first, or are centered on the second. Cf., for example, the Club of Florence, *op. cit.*

Also from Algora Publishing

CLAUDIU A. SECARA
THE NEW COMMONWEALTH
From Bureaucratic Corporatism to Socialist Capitalism

The notion of an elite-driven worldwide perestroika has gained some credibility lately. The book examines in a historical perspective the most intriguing dialectic in the Soviet Union's "collapse" — from socialism to capitalism and back to socialist capitalism — and speculates on the global implications.

IGNACIO RAMONET
THE GEOPOLITICS OF CHAOS

The author, Director of *Le Monde Diplomatique*, presents an original, discriminating and lucid political matrix for understanding what he calls the "current disorder of the world" in terms of Internationalization, Cyberculture and Political Chaos.

TZVETAN TODOROV
A PASSION FOR DEMOCRACY –
Benjamin Constant

The French Revolution rang the death knell not only for a form of society, but also for a way of feeling and of living; and it is still not clear as yet what did we gain from the changes.

MICHEL PINÇON & MONIQUE PINÇON-CHARLOT
GRAND FORTUNES –
Dynasties of Wealth in France

Going back for generations, the fortunes of great families consist of far more than money— they are also symbols of culture and social interaction. In a nation known for democracy and meritocracy, piercing the secrets of the grand fortunes verges on a crime of lèse-majesté . . . *Grand Fortunes* succeeds at that.

CLAUDIU A. SECARA
TIME & EGO –
Judeo-Christian Egotheism and the Anglo-Saxon Industrial Revolution

The first question of abstract reflection that arouses controversy is the problem of Becoming. Being persists, beings constantly change; they are born and they pass away. How can Being change and yet be eternal? The quest for the logical and experimental answer has just taken off.

JEAN-MARIE ABGRALL
SOUL SNATCHERS: THE MECHANICS OF CULTS

Jean-Marie Abgrall, psychiatrist, criminologist, expert witness to the French Court of Appeals, and member of the Inter-Ministry Committee on Cults, is one of the experts most frequently consulted by the European judicial and legislative processes. The fruit of fifteen years of research, his book delivers the first methodical analysis of the sectarian phenomenon, decoding the mental manipulation on behalf of mystified observers as well as victims.

JEAN-CLAUDE GUILLEBAUD
THE TYRANNY OF PLEASURE

The ambition of the book is to pose clearly and without subterfuge the question of sexual morals -- that is, the place of the forbidden -- in a modern society. For almost a whole generation, we have lived in the illusion that this question had ceased to exist. Today the illusion is faded, but a strange and tumultuous distress replaces it. No longer knowing very clearly where we stand, our societies painfully seek answers between unacceptable alternatives: bold-faced permissiveness or nostalgic moralism.

SOPHIE COIGNARD AND MARIE-THÉRÈSE GUICHARD
FRENCH CONNECTIONS –
The Secret History of Networks of Influence

They were born in the same region, went to the same schools, fought the same fights and made the same mistakes in youth. They share the same morals, the same fantasies of success and the same taste for money. They act behind the scenes to help each other, boosting careers, monopolizing business and information, making money, conspiring and, why not, becoming Presidents!

VLADIMIR PLOUGIN
INTELLIGENCE HAS ALWAYS EXISTED

This collection contains the latest works by historians, investigating the most mysterious episodes from Russia's past. All essays are based on thorough studies of preserved documents. The book discusses the establishment of secret services in Kievan Rus, and describes heroes and systems of intelligence and counterintelligence in the 16th-17th centuries. Semen Maltsev, a diplomat of Ivan the Terrible's times is presented as well as the much publicised story of the abduction of "Princess Tarakanova".

JEAN-JACQUES ROSA
EURO ERROR

The European Superstate makes Jean-Jacques Rosa mad, for two reasons. First, actions taken to relieve unemployment have created inflation, but have not reduced unemployment. His second argument is even more intriguing: the 21st century will see the fragmentation of the U. S., not the unification of Europe.